# RENAISSANCE AND BAROQUE LYRICS

# RENAISSANCE
# AND BAROQUE LYRICS

*An Anthology of Translations*
*from the*
*Italian, French, and Spanish*

HAROLD MARTIN PRIEST

NORTHWESTERN UNIVERSITY PRESS

PN
6100
. P7

TO WILLA

# Contents

INTRODUCTION                                        xvii
   Renaissance, Mannerism, and Baroque         xvii
   On Translating Poetry                        xlvii

## ITALIAN POEMS

FRANCESCO PETRARCA, *Rime*                           3
   In Vita 3                                    4
   In Vita 14                                   5
   In Vita 28                                   6
   In Vita 47                                   6
   In Vita 69                                   7
   Canzone: Chiare, fresche e dolci acque       7
   Canzone: Italia mia                          9
   In Vita 102                                  13
   In Vita 104                                  14
   In Vita 113                                  14
   In Vita 156                                  15
   In Vita 157                                  15
   In Morte 1                                   16
   In Morte 2                                   17
   In Morte 4                                   18
   In Morte 24                                  19
   In Morte 42                                  19
   In Morte 43                                  20
   In Morte 86                                  20
   In Morte 90                                  21

GIOVANNI BOCCACCIO                                   22
   Ballata                                      22

ANGELO POLIZIANO                                     24
   Ballata                                      24

LORENZO DE' MEDICI                              26
    Canzone                                      26

LODOVICO ARIOSTO                                28
    Capitolo VIII                                28

GIOVANNI GUIDICCIONI                            31
    To Italy                                     31

GIOVANNI STROZZI                                32
    On Buonarroti's Statue of Night              32

MICHELANGELO BUONARROTI                         33
    To Night                                     34
    David                                        34
    On the Painting of the Sistine Chapel        35
    To Vittoria Colonna                          35
    The Lover and the Sculptor                   36
    The Artist and His Work                      36
    Out of a Living Stone                        37
    Beauty and the Artist                        37
    You Have a Face                              37
    Madrigal                                     38
    Danger of Loss Eternal                       39
    Love Lifts to God                            39
    Just as a Silkworm                           39
    Just as an Empty Form                        40
    I Know Not If from Uncreated Spheres         40
    Love's Justification                         41
    Love Is a Refiner's Fire                     41
    If My Rough Hammer                           42
    Dante                                        42
    On Rome in the Pontificate of Julius II      43
    When Contracting, the Lash                   43
    Why Should it Come So Seldom                 44
    Light and Darkness                           44
    Simply Because the Sun                       45
    A Prayer for Purification                    45
    Heart-Coldness                               46
    On the Brink of Death                        46

LUIGI ALAMANNI                                    47
   On His Return to Italy                         47

GIOVANNI DELLA CASA                               48
   To Sleep                                       48

LUIGI TANSILLO                                    49
   The Philosophic Flight                         49

FRANCESCO BERNI                                   50
   Pope Clement's Illness                         50
   Portrait                                       51
   The Deuce                                      51

GASPARA STAMPA                                    53
   Ladies, Who of My Lord Would Fain Be Told      53
   Oh Night                                       54
   I am Now So Weary with Waiting                 54
   Deeply Repentant                               55

TORQUATO TASSO                                    56
   Aurora                                         57
   Dawn                                           57
   From the Mantle of Night                       58
   The Rose                                       58
   The Happiness of a Flea                        58
   Of That Same                                   59
   Of a Bee                                       59
   To Lucrezia d'Este                             59
   This Is Not Death                              60
   Love Is the Soul of All Things                 60
   Ancient, Winged God                            61
   The Golden Age                                 61
   To Madame Lucrezia d'Este, Duchess of Urbino   63
   To Her Grace, the Duchess of Ferrara           64
   To Guglielmo Gonzaga, Duca di Mantova          64

GIOVANNI BATTISTA GUARINI                         65
   The Microcosm                                  65
   Madrigal I                                     65

GIOVANNI BATTISTA MARINO                                      67
  The Proem. To Love                                         67
  Broken Faith                                               68
  Sonnet. Unhappy Man                                        68
  Cynthia Sporting                                           69
  Apollo and Daphne                                          69
  Chloris' Eyes and Breasts                                  70
  Ice and Fire                                               71
  While His Lady Combs Her Hair                              71
  During the Bath                                            72
  Conscience                                                 72
  Christo Smarrito                                           73
  And She Washed His Feet with Her Tears, and Wiped
    Them with the Hairs of Her Head                          75
  The Fountain                                               75
  The Book of the World                                      76

GIROLAMO PRETI                                               77
  Describes the Place Where Cynthia Is Sporting Herself      77
  Complains, Being Hind'red the Sight of His Nymph           78
  Love Once, Love Ever                                       78

CLAUDIO ACHILLINI                                            80
  A Sonnet, Written by a Nymph in Her Own Blood              80

TOMASSO CAMPANELLA                                           81
  The People                                                 81

FRANCESCO REDÌ                                               83
  Bacchus in Tuscany                                         83

VINCENZO DA FILICAIA                                         87
  To Italy                                                   87

## FRENCH POEMS

MARGUERITE DE NAVARRE                                        91
  Dizain to Clément Marot                                    91

CLÉMENT MAROT                                                92
  Marot to the Queen of Navarre                              92
  A Love-Lesson                                              93
  Madame d'Albert's Laugh                                    93

CONTENTS

Au Bon Vieulx Temps 93
Song: Since Loving Countenance ... 94
Epitaph on Jean Veau 94

MAURICE SCÈVE, *Délie* 95
In the April of My Age 96
Some Delight in Telling Stories 96
Already the Moon 97
Let Silence or Speech Be Permitted 97
Like Hecate You Will Make Me Wander 97
If It Is Love, Why Then Does He Kill Me 98
Bound to the Caucasus 98
The Indolence of Soft Feathers 98
O Years, O Months 99
The Happiness of Our Happiness 99
If with Her Hand My Fatal Enemy 99
I by Myself, She in Another's Arms 100
All Judgment of this Infinity 100
Longer than a Platonic Century 101
Lady, You Are the Body 101
The White Dawn 101

JEAN PARMENTIER 102
The Wonders of the Deep 102

LOUISE LABÉ 104
Sonnet V 104
Sonnet VII 105
Sonnet IX 105
Sonnet XIII 106
Sonnet XIV 106
Sonnet XVIII 107

PIERRE DE RONSARD 108
And Lightly, Like the Flowers 109
Let Me Decease within Thine Arms 110
To His Young Mistress 110
Marie, Arise 111
"Who," Cried the Elders on the Trojan Wall 111
Deadly Kisses 112
On His Lady's Waking 112

Roses 113
When You Are Very Old 113
His Lady's Death 114
His Lady's Tomb 114
The Paradox of Time 115
Carpe Diem 116
To Remi Belleau 117
To a Fountain 118
Epitaph on Rabelais 119
On the Choice of His Sepulchre 121

JOACHIM DU BELLAY 125
L'Olive, XIV 126
On His Deafness 126
To His Friend in Elysium 127
A Sonnet to Heavenly Beauty 127
Rome 128
Happy Who Like Ulysses 128
Sonnet: I Hate the Money-Lending Avarice 129

ANTOINE DE BAÏF 130
Carpe Diem 130

VAUQUELIN DE LA FRESNAYE 132
O Gentle Breeze 132

PHILLIPPE DESPORTES 133
Villanelle a Rozette 133
Sonnet: Dress Your Gold Locks 134
Invocation 135
Epigramme 135

MATHURIN RÉGNIER 137
A Confession in Brief 137
Epitaph 138

FRANÇOIS MAYNARD 139
Epitaph: Time, Which Does All Creatures 139
Armand! I Lose My Vital Heat 139

JEAN DE SCHÉLANDRE 141
To the Poets of Our Time 141

JEAN DE LA CEPPÈDE, *Théorèmes Spirituels*  142
My Victorious King  142
Love Has Given Him  143
O Kingdom of Christ  143
O Cross  143
Great Sun, Flame of Christ  144
O Phoenix  144

JEAN DE SPONDE  145
Sonnets d'Amour III: Qui seroit dans les cieux  145
Sonnets d'Amour XXVI: Les vents grondoyent en l'air  146
Sonnets de la Mort IV: Pour qui tant de travaux  146
Sonnets de la Mort V: Helas! contez vos jours  147
Sonnets de la Mort: Yet we must die  147
Sonnets de la Mort: Who, who are these  148
Sonnets de la Mort: All swells against me  148

JEAN-BAPTISTE CHASSIGNET  149
His Scorn of Life and Consolation for Death  149

THÉOPHILE DE VIAU  150
Ode  150
To Corinna  151

FRANÇOIS DE MALHERBE  154
Consolation to M. du Périer  154
To Louis XIII  156

HONORÉ D'URFÉ  157
Song of the Inconstant Hylas  157

VINCENT VOITURE  159
Rondeau: In Good Plain French  159
On the Way from Fontenay  160
Evening Beauty  160

TRISTAN L'HERMITE  161
The Bracelet  161

ANTOINE-GIRARD DE SAINT-AMANT  162
The Alpine Winter  162
The Enjoyment  163
The Orgy  165

PIERRE CORNEILLE                                    168
   Stanzas to the Marquise                          168

*Guirlande de Julie*                                170

CHARLES DE SAINTE-MAURE, DUC DE MONTAUSIER          171
   Madrigal                                        171
   Le Narcisse                                     172

JEAN DESMARETS DE SAINT-SORLIN                      173
   La Violette                                     173

CLAUDE DE MALLEVILLE
   La Couronne Impériale                           174

JEAN OGIER DE GOMBAULD                              175
   L'Amarante                                      175

## SPANISH POEMS

ANONYMOUS                                           179
   Galleys of Spain                                180

JUAN DEL ENCINA                                     181
   Chorus                                          181
   Mingo's Discourse                               182

GIL VICENTE                                         184
   Cantiga                                         184
   Song                                            185
   Ballad of Flérida                               185

GARCILASO DE LA VEGA                                188
   Sonnet: Fair Naiads of the River                188
   Sonnet X: On Finding Some Keepsakes of His Dead
      Mistress                                   189
   Song III                                        189

SAINT TERESA OF JESÚS                               191
   God Suffices                                    191
   Let Mine Eyes See Thee                          192
   On the Words "Dilectus Meus Mihi"               193
   Vertiendo Está Sangre                           193
   En Las Internas Entrañas                        194
   Lines Born of the Fire of Love for God          195

FRA MIGUEL DE GUEVARA                             198
  To Christ Crucified                             198

FRAY LUIS PONCE DE LEÓN                           199
  Ode to Felipe Ruiz                              199
  The Life of the Blessed                         202

LUIS VAZ DE CAMOËNS                               204
  On the Death of Catarina de Attayda             204
  On Revisiting Cintra after the Death of Catarina   205

BALTASAR DE ALCÁZAR                               206
  Tres Cosas                                      206

FERNANDO DE HERRERA                               208
  Ideal Beauty                                    208
  To Don Juan de Austria                          209

SAINT JOHN OF THE CROSS                           210
  Dark Night of the Soul                          210
  O Flame of Living Love                          211
  Verses Written upon an Ecstasy of High Contemplation   212
  Spiritual Canticle: Songs between the Soul and the Spouse   214
  Other Verses with a Divine Meaning              218
  Other Stanzas with a Divine Meaning Concerning Christ
    and the Soul                                  219

MIGUEL DE CERVANTES SAAVEDRA                       221
  Ye Trees and Shrubs                             221
  Love's Mariner Am I                             222
  Oh, Could My 'Was' an 'Is' Become               223
  O Thou Above Who in Thy Bed                     224
  Epitaph                                         227
  Epitaph                                         227

LUIS DE GÓNGORA Y ARGOTE                           228
  The Rosemary Spray                              229
  The Rose of Life                                230
  The Country Bachelor's Complaint                230
  Not All Sweet Nightingales                      232
  Romance                                         233
  Let Me Go Warm                                  234

Love in Reason 235
The Nativity of Christ 236
Clear Honor of the Liquid Element 237
Sonnet: Yesterday a Human Deity 238
Sonnet: The Planking of the Vessel 238
Sonnet: Dear Geese 239
When Don Luis Was in Cuenca 239
From *The Solitudes* 241

LOPE DE VEGA 252
Tomorrow 253
If Her Forehead Was Not Snow 253

FRANCISCO GOMEZ DE QUEVEDO Y VILLEGAS 254
The Fly 254
To a Nose 256
Sonnet: Death Warnings 257

PEDRO CALDERON DE LA BARCA 258
Sonnet 258
The Dying Eusebio's Address to the Cross 259

SISTER MARCELA DE CARPIO DE SAN FELIX 260
Amor Mysticus 260

NOTES TO THE POEMS 265

# Introduction

## RENAISSANCE, MANNERISM, AND BAROQUE

And have I not Saint Praxed's ear to pray
Horses for ye, and brown Greek manuscripts,
And mistresses with great smooth marbly limbs?*
ROBERT BROWNING

It is significant that Petrarch's volume of lyrics was called simply *Rime*, and so were the collections of many another poet after him; or perhaps the title given was *Chansons* or *Amours* or *Sonnets* or a similar unpretentious caption. To several generations there appeared no need to flash across the page such a fanciful title as "A Paradise of Dainty Devices." Poetry needed no justification, no salesmanship. The writing of poetry was to the Renaissance an important feature of civilized living, almost like food and wine, music and love. Certainly it was not regarded as an activity reserved for the professional. And as there was much writing of verse, so there was much reading of it. According to Castiglione's model of the versatile Renaissance gentleman, the cultivation of letters was a point of exceptional import.

[To] returne againe unto our Courtier, whom in letters I will have to be more than indifferently well seene, at the least in those studies, which they call Humanitie....

Let him much exercise him selfe in Poets, and no lesse in Oratours and Historiographers, and also in writing both rime and prose, and especially in this our vulgar tongue. For beside the contentation [contentment] that hee shall receive thereby him selfe, hee shall by this meanes never want pleasant intertainements with women which ordinarily love such matters....

For at the least wise hee shall receive so much profit, that by that exercise hee shall be able to give his judgement upon other mens doinges. For it happeneth very seldome, that a man not exercised in

* From "The Bishop Orders His Tomb at St. Praxed's Church."

writing, how learned soever he be, can at any time know perfectly
the labour and toile of writers, or tast of the sweetnesse and excellency
of styles, and those inner observations that often times are founde in
them of olde time.

While the outpourings of many versifiers and a large and enthusiastic
reading public do not necessarily make a great period of poetry, they
are undoubtedly valuable in creating a climate for high poetic achievement. Whatever the causes, this age was one of the most brilliant in the
history of the lyric—and one of the most varied in both theme and
style. It is this matter of variety that prompts the following discussion.

The term Renaissance has the familiarity of a household word to all
college students, but the scholar has trouble defining it, at least to the
satisfaction of other scholars. And the further we delve into questions
of chronological boundaries and subdivisions, the more frightening
the difficulties appear. For purposes of clarification we may speak of the
"greater Renaissance" and the "lesser Renaissance." The greater
Renaissance covers the period from approximately 1340 to 1660: from
Petrarch to the age of Louis XIV in France and the Restoration in
England. However, the major literary production of the age is pretty
well concentrated between 1470 and 1630. This major period, which I
have called the "greater" Renaissance, encompasses the earlier (lesser)
Renaissance and one or more succeeding periods.

The lesser Renaissance, according to this terminology, designates
the first major phase of the greater period, a phase which is sometimes
considered to be *the* Renaissance. It constitutes approximately half of
the greater Renaissance. The question of when the lesser or earlier
development ended and the later development commenced is difficult
to settle because there was no clear-cut break. The spirit of the earlier
Renaissance, the "pure" or classical Renaissance, persisted in many
circles up to the end of the sixteenth century, yet the earliest signs of the
restlessness and revolt against that spirit began to appear as early as the
1530's, particularly in the lyrics of Michelangelo, Scève, and—to a
certain degree—Wyatt. It would only be misleading to try to fix a
date for the break between the two phases of the greater Renaissance,
so great is their overlap. The more important task must be to arrive at
a comprehension of what differentiates the phases, or movements.

A student of literature in the 1920's might never have heard "Baroque" as a term applied to poetry. Actually literary historians on the

Continent were beginning to adopt the term in the first quarter of the century, but its general acceptance, especially for literary studies in English, came considerably later. Except that it seemed to be equated with what had commonly been designated as "late Renaissance," it was difficult to be quite certain of its precise significance. Was Baroque a period or a movement? That is to say, did it include all of the literature within certain years, or did it merely identify certain kinds of writing within a period of history? By mid-century, the term had wide if not entirely uniform currency. Then there sprang up a new school of historians maintaining that what we had been calling Baroque actually represented two quite distinct movements; and they borrowed a second term from the vocabulary of the art historian—Mannerism. A sorting of terms then seems to be in order. However, a clear definition of these three movements—Renaissance, Mannerism, and Baroque— does not end the problem, because within the age there are a good many important schools and "isms" which have to be identified: Petrarchan, Metaphysical, Euphuism, Préciocité, Cultism, Marinismo, and Gongorism. Defining these schools and then relating them to the major phases of the age constitutes one of our prime objectives in this essay.

However, before attempting to settle any issues regarding definition, relation, and subordination of movements, we need to undertake a survey of the age, and to identify particular features of the poetry which, in combination, go into identification of schools and styles.

The progress of poetry over the two centuries of our study is, in the broadest terms, from the simpler forms and concepts to the more highly complex, the tortured, and the elaborately decorative; in other words, from the songs and madrigals of Marot, Vicente, and Wyatt to the verse of Marino, Góngora, Donne, and Crashaw. This is much like the progress in painting from the art of Fra Angelico or the early madonnas of Raphael to the work of Veronese, Rubens, and El Greco.

We can start at one end of the scale with poems of comparatively simple nature. One type of poem common to the age is written in plain, everyday language, its rhyme and stanza pattern is easy, it makes slight use of figurative devices and those of the most familiar sort, and it presents a pattern of thought which involves no strain, no great surprises for the reader. The poem is "available," we say. The poet feels no compulsion to amaze the reader with his ingenuity or impress him with his brilliance. He finds the common objects and timeworn emotions interesting. This familiar world is still a pleasant place to sing about, and his hope is that his audience will savor with him a moment of pleasure or pain. This is an idea of poetry that held a high place in the earlier Renaissance. Even in the later decades of the age, when ingenuity and flamboyant decoration had come into vogue, the simple, graceful song was still cultivated, and indeed it has found practitioners in almost every age from Sappho's to this day. Although critics and professors of literature do not find much opportunity to display their wit and erudition in the discussion of such pieces, the simple lyric still holds an honored position among readers. Simplicity is not a guarantee of greatness; nevertheless hundreds of the lyrics of this stamp which have been preserved for four or five centuries are of exceptional quality.

To illustrate the fashion for simplicity, we may sample a few pieces which were of scattered origin. A "Song" by Gil Vicente (1470?–1536):

> If thou art sleeping, maiden,
>     Awake and open thy door,
> 'Tis the break of day, and we must away
>     O'er meadow, and mount, and moor.
>
> Wait not to find thy slippers,
>     But come with thy naked feet:
> We shall have to pass through the dewy grass
>     And waters wide and fleet.
>
>                     HENRY WADSWORTH LONGFELLOW

It would be difficult to find a poem simpler in its diction and its stanzaic pattern. Moreover, there is no figure of speech, no decoration of any sort; yet by a fusion of the agreeable sound of words with objects and ideas of appealing association it stands as a charming poem.

Another poem which appears comparable to Vicente's in its simplicity of language and its metrical and rhyme forms but which in certain respects proves to be a degree removed in sophistication is "And Lightly Like the Flowers" by Ronsard (1524–1585).

And lightly, like the flowers,
  Your beauties Age will dim,
  Who makes the song a hymn,
And turns the sweets to sour.

Alas, the chubby Hours
  Grow lank and gray and grim,
And lightly, like the flowers,
  Your beauties Age will dim.

Still rosy are the bowers,
  The walks yet green and trim.
  Among them let your whim
Pass sweetly, like the showers,
And lightly, like the flowers.

W. E. HENLEY

The unusual rhyme pattern deserves attention. Also a slight, subtle deviation from the stanzaic form occurs in the repetition of the opening line of the poem as an extra line at the end of the last stanza.

The poem deals with an idea of some solemnity, old and familiar it is true, but still susceptible to fresh utterance. The poet has not held himself to plain statement altogether but has introduced suggestions of allegory, allegory so familiar to all readers of poetry as to pass almost unnoticed as figurative device.

In the "Ballata" of Poliziano (1454–1494), we find a slightly more complex stanza with a simple refrain.

I found myself one day all, all alone,
For pastime in a field with blossoms strewn.

I do not think the world a field could show
  With herbs of perfume so surpassing rare;
But when I passed beyond the green hedge-row,
  A thousand flowers around me flourished fair,
  White, pied and crimson, in the summer air;
Among the which I heard a sweet bird's tone.

I found myself one day all, all alone,
For pastime in a field with blossoms strewn.

Her song it was so tender and so clear
   That all the world listened with love; then I
With stealthy feet a-tiptoe drawing near,
   Her golden head and golden wings could spy,
   Her plumes that flashed like rubies neath the sky,
Her crystal beak and throat and bosom's zone.

. . . . . . . . . . . . . . . . . . . . . . . . . . . . . . . .

Fain would I snare her, smit with mighty love;
   But arrow-like she soared, and through the air

. . . . . . . . . . . . . . . . . . . . . . . . . . . . . .

Yea, I might spread some net or woven wile;
   But since of singing she doth take such pleasure,
Without or other art or other guile
   I seek to win her with a tuneful measure;
   Therefore in singing spend I all my leisure,
To make by singing this sweet bird my own.

I found myself one day all, all alone,
For pastime in a field with blossoms strewn.

           JOHN ADDINGTON SYMONDS

In this poem of thirty-four lines, figurative ornament is at a minimum and what is there is in no way startling. The poet describes the bird as:

    Her golden head and golden wings . . .,
    Her plumes that flashed like rubies neath the sky,
    Her crystal beak . . .

The translator has introduced one further figure which was not in the original:

    But arrow-like she soared, . . .

The simplicity of the poem is belied, or at least qualified in that the whole piece is a metaphor, or allegory. A suspicion enters the reader's mind at some point that there is double meaning here, that, indeed, this is a love poem. We presume that this would occur to the fifteenth century audience even more readily than to us; it must have been instinctive with them to search for such added levels of meaning. In any case, the reading of the poem is a relatively uncomplicated experience, pleasurable but not particularly taxing.

The poems we have examined, three out of many score of this general type, are in no striking feature distinct from the lyrics of the later Middle Ages, nor indeed from many classical Latin lyrics. However, this pattern of simple and relatively unadorned lyric is not the sole, or even the most widely recognized, type of Renaissance poem. A more elaborate scheme of lyricism is that commonly identified as Petrarchan verse. No name enjoyed greater renown among lyric poets throughout Europe in the sixteenth century than that of Petrarch, and no poet exerted a wider influence. His *Rime*, which was recovered after more than a century of neglect, set a fashion of prodigious proportions. Good and bad imitations sprang up everywhere on the Continent and in England, and it is to the serious detriment of the master that a separation of the true quality of Petrarch and that of his more florid imitators is not always sharply defined.

The poetry of Petrarch falls within the range of the earlier or classical Renaissance school, being essentially restrained in tone, ordered and polished, and giving careful attention to the music of its language. In comparison with the poems we have previously discussed, the Petrarchan poem frequently develops a more subtle thought pattern. However, one of its chief distinctions lies in its attention to rhetoric and its fondness for figurative decoration. In the best Petrarchan lyrics the decoration is superbly controlled, inviting comparison with the Florentine school of painters, especially Fra Filippo Lippi and Botticelli. The second-rate imitators, the Petrarchisti, copied and exaggerated the gestures of Petrarch but, lacking his art, produced poems with little matter but much ornamentation; hence the hue and cry against the prettiness of the "Petrarchan" school. It must be recognized that hundreds of fine lyrics were written in the tradition of the school of Petrarch; it could claim in its ranks such poets as Ronsard, Garcilaso de la Vega, Tasso, Wyatt, and Spenser as well as Petrarch himself; and even Shakespeare's sonnets owed a considerable debt to the school. Surely this must be ranked among the best chapters in the history of the lyric.

Inevitably, the classical quality of the pure Renaissance began to pall for some of the writers, and a reaction developed. The earliest signs of this appeared as early as the 1530's, although the peak of the revolt did not come until near the end of the century, at least in the northern countries. When the simpler, plainer forms began to tire, the poet gradually sought for some new way to impress the reader, and this rebellion could take one of several forms: a more involved syntax, a startling novelty in diction and imagery, dramatic utterance, a multiplication of figures, subtlety and complexity of intellection—or any combination of these features. This road led to a poetic system which, in its extreme forms, elevated decoration, subtlety, and ingenuity to the danger point. If the poet could not astonish, stupefy the audience, he was marked a failure. This naturally encouraged modes of expression difficult of comprehension, placing greater and greater demands on the reader, hence limiting the audience to more and more select groups or coteries. However, between the extremes of simplicity and complexity or of bareness and flamboyance, ran a rich variety of poetic achievement.

English readers, who are in the habit of associating with Donne and the Metaphysical poets a whole set of characteristics which have commonly been styled Baroque poetry, will discover in the examination of Continental lyric verse that there existed striking parallels for every trait or concept identified with the English school. Even the intensity of Donne can be matched. Only the special concatenation of elements of Donne remain to set him apart as we like to think of him.

In one way or another, all of the developing features sprang from a restlessness and took the form of reactions against the ease, melody, availability, and conventionality of the established forms. The early Renaissance had been marked by balance, composure; the new age was recognized by its tension, distortion, and imbalance—its straining for novelty and for spectacular effects. The new age with its disturbed outlook can be related to historical events and to attitudes arising from revolutions in the scientific and religious life of Europe—the Copernican astronomy, the Council of Trent, the "new philosophy" which cast all in doubt.

In literature the revolt against old forms and established attitudes can be seen in numerous elements of thought and technique. As a reaction against the cultivation of fluent, melodious language, we may encounter a deliberate use of rough meters, vehement ejaculations, imprecations, and exhortations—staccato phrasing. Normal sentence order is violently wrenched. The patterns of speech are dramatic rather than lyric. Though this type of poetic language is by no means as common among Continental poets as it is in Donne, there are a few notable examples. Jean de Sponde (1557–1595), in the sestet of his sonnet, "All Swells Against Me," uses a dramatic phrasing which is far from melodious.

> For what? Oh God, I often feel the war
>   This rebel angel wages still with Your
>   Own temple, hand, and voice: My flesh, this world.
> But yet Your altar, hand, and voice will be
>   Ship, strength, and ear which break the spell for me
>   And turn each wave, each onslaught that is hurled.*
>
> JOHN E. GALT

Michelangelo (1475–1564), more than any other poet before the seventeenth century, actually cultivates such vehement and staccato effects, as, for example:

> O flesh! O blood! O cross! O pain extreme!
>   By you may those foul sins be purified,
>   wherein my fathers were, and I was born!
> Lo, Thou alone art good: let Thy supreme
>   pity my state of evil cleanse and hide—
>   so near to death, so far from God, forlorn.†
>
> JOHN ADDINGTON SYMONDS

* Et quoi? Mon Dieu, je sens combattre maintesfois
    Encor avec ton temple et ta main et ta voix
    Cet ange révolté, cette chair, et ce monde.
  Mais ton temple pourtant, ta main, ta voix sera
    La nef, l'appui, l'oreille, où ce charme perdra,
    Où mourra cet effort, où se rompra cette onde.

  † O carne, o sangue, o legno, o doglia estrema,
      giusto per vo' si faccia il mio peccato,
      di ch' i' pur nacqui, e tal fu 'l padre mio.
    Tu sol se' buon: la tua pietà suprema
      soccorra al mio predetto iniquo stato;
      sì presso a morte, e sì lontan da Dio.

In other ways we find deviations from the smooth running line of the earlier, more traditional poets, sometimes through abnormal distortions of sentence order, sometimes simply through contorted phrasing of difficult concepts. Maurice Scève (1510?–1564?) is much given to such passages. A demonstration of the degree of eccentricity of his language appears in the following dizain. Not only does the poet employ a number of substitutions of parts of speech—adjective for noun, adverb for noun—but his entire poem reveals a compression of thought into a few lines. This hermetic writing places a heavy demand upon the reader. The poem is translated quite literally in order to reveal its special qualities.

> All judgment of this infinity,
>   Where all conception is found superfluous,
>   And all the keen[ness] of perspicuity
>   Could not attain to the summit of her more.
>     For the first snow sovereign in its white[ness]
>   Is only in appearance superior
>   To the pure of her hands, delicately hale,
>   Would shame the naked[ness] of Bathsheba,
>   And the fragrant of her sweet breath
>   Would putrefy the scented Sheba.*
>                                       HAROLD M. PRIEST

For different linguistic innovations, we can turn to such devices as we commonly associate with Góngora (1561–1627), namely the figures of substitution: synecdoche and metonymy. Avoiding the plain naming of objects, Góngora refers rather to a part for the whole object or

> * Tout jugement de cette infinité,
>     Où tout concept se trouve superflu,
>     Et tout aigu de perspicuité
>     Ne pourraient joindre au sommet de son plus.
>       Car seulement l'apparent du surplus,
>     Première neige en son blanc souveraine,
>     Au pur des mains délicatement saines,
>     Ahontirait le nu de Bethsabée,
>     Et le fragrant de sa suave haleine
>     Apourrirait l'odorante Sabée.

uses an attribute to stand for the thing itself. We are all familiar with the identification of a ship by reference to a sail or even a mast, but Góngora carries this quite beyond standard practice when, in a key passage in *The Solitudes*, he speaks of three fir trees to identify the ships of Columbus.

> Three fir trees late of this all-powerful one
> (Where hitherto no other sailor trod)
> Wrested his trident from the watery god,
> Kissing the turquoise curtains that the West
> Has drawn around the azure couch of rest
> Of the declining sun.
>
> EDWARD MERYON WILSON

Another startling example is found in a passage relating how the youthful hero of *The Solitudes* paused to listen to some music. The *remora* of the passage is a fish that attaches itself to the side of a ship, hence acts as a drag against its speed.

> When remora to his footsteps was his ear
> By sweet canorous instrument constrained,
> Which, fingered by a mountain maiden near
> Above a streamlet from complaining hoarse,
> Silenced the ripples it had near restrained.
>
> EDWARD MERYON WILSON

The opening lines of *The Solitudes*, introducing the season of spring with allusions to the Zodiac, permit an interesting comparison with Chaucer's more direct statement:

> Whan that Aprill with his shoures soote
> The droghte of March hath perced to the roote,
> . . . . . . . . . . . . . . . . . . . . . . . . . . . . . . . .
> . . . and the yonge sonne
> Hath in the Ram his halve cours yronne.
>
> *Canterbury Tales*, ll. 1–8

Góngora's passage reads:

> It was the flowery season of the year
> In which Europa's perjured robber strays
> —Whose brow the arms of the half-moon adorn,
> The sun the shining armour of his hide—
> Through sapphire fields to feast on stellar corn, . . .
>
> EDWARD MERYON WILSON

In a body of lyric poetry, the figurative language serves as much as any feature to identify the style and spirit of the age. For the early seventeenth century, especially for the Metaphysical school, we have come to associate the nature of figures with the striking characteristics assigned to them by Dr. Johnson. "The most heterogeneous ideas are yoked by violence together; nature and art are ransacked for illustrations, comparisons, and allusions; their learning instructs and their subtlety surprises; . . ."

Much of what Johnson says here of the English writers is equally applicable to the poets on the Continent, though we are bound to recognize at least minor variations. One interesting point is that so-called "metaphysical" writing began to appear on the Continent long before the seventeenth century. In fact before the middle of the sixteenth century, Scève and Michelangelo were writing in this vein, and in the latter half of the century numerous other poets display certain of these tendencies, notably Tasso, La Ceppède, and Sponde.

Marino's phrase concerning the code of poetry serves as a key to one prominent current of the movement:

> È del poeta il fin la meraviglia
> (parlo de l' eccellente e non del goffo):
> chi non sa far stupir, vada alla striglia!

> The aim of the poet is the marvellous
> (I speak of the excellent and not the dull one):
> who knows not how to astonish, go back to the
>     curry comb.

Ingenuity, then, becomes a major goal for many of the writers, but the avenues for approaching this goal differ considerably. Two major patterns need to be recognized: one in which the reader is startled because a figure of comparison (simile, metaphor, conceit), though employing elements which have long been recognized as standard equipment for poetry, develops them in relationships that are unexpected; the second which introduces objects previously regarded as outside the pale of poetic convention. Marino and Crashaw are among the most notable practitioners of the first mode of ingenious writing, using traditional poetic elements in novel combinations; though nearly every poet of the school sometimes follows the practice. The second type is best represented by Donne and Herbert, but it is occasionally revealed on the Continent as well—in the poetry of Michelangelo, Tasso, and Góngora.

Marino's "Chloris' Eyes and Breasts" is intended to strike a spark for the jaded reader. The elements of imagery are not in themselves startling, eyes and breast, fire and snow. The piece makes no pretense at high voltage production, and its appeal is entertaining on a purely mental plane.

Chloris! on thine eyes I gaz'd;
When amaz'd
At their brightness,
On thy breasts I cast my look;
No less took
With their whiteness:
Both I justly did admire.
These all snow, and those all fire.

Whilst these wonders I survey'd,
Thus I said
In suspense,
Nature could have done no less
To express
Her providence,
Than that two such fair worlds might
Have two Suns to give them light.

SIR EDWARD SHERBURNE

Tasso, a generation earlier than Marino, was employing much the same ingenuity in some of his minor verse. "The Rose" is a degree more intricate because it involves the Adonis myth:

> Flower, which of Adon's blood
> Sprang, when of that clear flood
> Which Venus wept another white was born,
> The sweet Cynarean youth thou right dost show:
> But this sharp-pointed thorn,
> Which does so proud about thy crimson grow,
> What doth it represent?
> Boars' tusks, perhaps, his snowy flank which rent:
> O show of shows! of unesteemed worth,
> Which both what kill'd and what was kill'd sett'st forth.
>
> WILLIAM DRUMMOND

Góngora, still depending on familiar elements, develops an extravagant conceit in the following sonnet, an admirable example of *agudeza*.

> Clear honor of the liquid element,
>     Sweet rivulet of shining silver sheen!
>     Whose waters steal along the meadows green,
>     With gentle step, and murmur of content!
> When she, for whom I bear each fierce extreme,
>     Beholds herself in thee,—then Love doth trace
>     The snow and crimson of that lovely face
>     In the soft gentle movement of thy stream.
> Then, smoothly flow as now, and set not free
>     The crystal curb and undulating rain
>     Which now thy current's headlong speed restrain;
> Lest broken and confused the image rest
>     Of such rare charms on the deep-heaving breast
>     Of him who holds and sways the trident of the sea.
>
> HENRY WADSWORTH LONGFELLOW

In religious poetry quite as clearly as in amorous verse, the straining for ingenuity appears. There is a serious risk that this sort of cleverness will raise suspicions about the sincerity of the poet's expression and the true depth of his feeling. The reader will, of course, make up his own mind about the merits of a given work. It may not be improper, however, to observe that the experience of wide reading in the period develops a surer basis for passing judgments. In some ways the modern reader, having been brought up with a background of romanticism and realism, is somewhat handicapped in reading the literature of the early seventeenth century. He needs immersion.

I should like to quote three religious pieces involving fantastic imagery, which can serve as a comparative study in the intent of the poets and in the success of their achievement. The first is one of Marino's Magdalene poems, "She Washed His Feet with Her Tears and Wiped Them with the Hairs of Her Head."

> The proud Egyptian queen, her Roman guest,
> (T' express her love in height of state and pleasure)
> With pearl dissolv'd in gold did feast,
> Both food and treasure.
>
> And now (dear Lord!) thy lover, on the fair
> And silver tables of thy feet, behold!
> Pearl, in her tears and in her hair
> Offers thee gold.
>
> SIR EDWARD SHERBURNE

Góngora, treating "The Nativity of Christ," reveals a quite uncommon sensibility.

> Today from the Aurora's bosom
> A pink has fallen—a crimson blossom;
> And oh, how glorious rests the hay
> On which the fallen blossom lay!

When silence gently had unfurled
Her mantle over all below,
And crowned with winter's frost and snow,
Night swayed the sceptre of the world,
Amid the gloom descending slow,
Upon the monarch's frozen bosom
A pink has fallen—a crimson blossom.

The only flower the Virgin bore
(Aurora fair) within her breast,
She gave to earth, yet still possessed
Her virgin blossom as before;
The hay that colored drop caressed—
Received upon its faithful bosom
That single flower—a crimson blossom.

The manger, unto which 'twas given,
Even amid wintry snows and cold,
Within its fostering arms to fold
The blushing flower that fell from heaven,
Was as a canopy of gold—
A downy couch—where on its bosom
That flower had fallen—that crimson blossom.

HENRY WADSWORTH LONGFELLOW

In the following passage by Calderon, the identification of the cross
with the tree of the Garden of Eden is a thoroughly familiar concept,
but the combined effect of the extraordinary variety of images creates
an impression of extreme agitation.

### THE DYING EUSEBIO'S ADDRESS TO THE CROSS

Tree, whereon the pitying skies
Hang the true fruit love doth sweeten,
Antidote of that first eaten,
Flower of man's new paradise,
Rainbow, that to tearful eyes

Sin's receding flood discloses—
Pledge that earth in peace reposes,
Beauteous plant, all fruitful vine.
A newer David's harp divine,
Table of a second Moses;—
. . . . . . . . . . . . . . . . . . . . . . . . .

D. F. MCCARTHY

A practice of the religious mystics was their constant use of the
language of passionate sensuous lovers to express their love for Christ.
This transference, familiar in the works of some English seventeenth
century poets, was much in use among the Spanish and French religious
mystics of the sixteenth century. In the poem of Saint Teresa (1515–
1588) "On the Words 'Dilectus Meus Mihi'" the lover is pierced by
Love's dart. In the entire poem only one word in the final stanza reveals
the religious intent of the poet—"Creator."

I have yielded utterly,
And so changed the heart I give,
That my Love lives but for me
And for Him I live.

When the blessed hunter's wound
Left me fallen and subdued,
In the arms of love I swooned,
And was there imbued
With new life that has renewed
And so changed the heart I give
That my Love lives but for me
And for Him I live.

Lifted high with love His dart
Wounded me, and by its aid
One with the Creator's heart
Was my spirit made,
And by no other love is swayed
Since to God myself I give,
And my Love lives but for me
And for Him I live.

JESSIE READ WENDELL

"The Dark Night of the Soul" by St. John of the Cross (1542–1591), relating the poet's experience in the terms of an amorous nocturnal rendezvous, treats one of the recognized stages in the symbolic progress of the soul toward the perfect love of Christ. The pattern of allegory becomes more readily comprehensible when we remember the traditional interpretation of the *Song of Songs* as symbolic of the wedding of the soul with Christ. In the following poem, the soul of the writer becomes the bride in the mystic union, with the result that the love poem reads as though it had been written by a woman.

> In an obscure night,
> With anxious love inflamed,
> O happy lot!
> Forth unobserved I went,
> My house being now at rest.
> . . . . . . . . . . . . . . . . . . . . . .
> O guiding night!
> O night more lovely than the dawn!
> O night that hast united
> The lover with his beloved
> And charged her with her love.
>
> On my flowery bosom,
> Kept whole for him alone,
> He reposed and slept:
> I kept him, and the waving
> Of the cedars fanned him.
> . . . . . . . . . . . . . . . . . . . . . .

> DAVID LEWIS

The second category of unconventional imagery and no doubt the chief source of Dr. Johnson's strictures is that type which astonishes by introducing objects and concepts not generally regarded as belonging to the territory of the poet. With the Metaphysicals fleas and worms have found a place within the pale of imagery available to the poet, along with the terminology of science, mechanics, and business. Fleas had been encountered in humorous or satirical verse before this, but to introduce them in a love poem was scarcely normal. Tasso has two lyrics about those troublesome creatures. To read these poems requires that we accept their playful spirit, as is the case with Donne's more complex poem, "The Flea." Nevertheless, some readers with whom I have discussed the matter still find these poems offensive.

### THE HAPPINESS OF A FLEA

How happier is that flea
Which in thy breast doth play,
Than that pied butterfly
Which courts the flame, and in the same doth die!
That hath a light delight,
Poor fool! contented only with a sight;
When this doth sport, and swell with dearest food,
And if he die, he, knight-like, dies in blood.

WILLIAM DRUMMOND

To introduce figures from the world of art and music was not new to this age, but the kind of images we find in Michelangelo's verse is sometimes unexpected and most arresting. The homely tools of the sculptor, the struggle with hard stone, the fierceness and color of fire are his frequent themes, not for themselves basically but for their effectiveness in illuminating the mysteries of earthly love and the love of God. Here in a love poem he makes use of the goldsmith's plaster mold which ends in shattered fragments.

Just as an empty form
Awaits its gold or silver liquefied,
And, broken, then, reveals
The perfect work; thus I can only fill
With inner fire of love my void and need
Of the immortal beauty of my lady,
Both mind and heart of these my fragile days.

Through such a narrow space
Her gentleness and love pour into me,
That, to draw forth her perfect image, I
Must agonize and die.

JOSEPH TUSIANI


In his sonnet based on the silkworm conceit, Michelangelo is addressing his beloved friend, Tommaso de' Cavalieri. This is a remarkable example of the daring disregard for Petrarchan conventions which sets Michelangelo apart from his literary contemporaries. The allusion to the snake's cast off skin in this frame of reference is startling but much more so is the image of the hairy skin.


Just as a silkworm with much selfless pain,
    to make man happy, leaves its dear cocoon
    and, dying, gives the hand a silken boon
    and, dead, through such a gift, is born again;
so would that my skin, falling dead and vain,
    could be his living flesh! Oh how I soon
    would change, as does a snake beneath a stone,
    my nature and my fate, through such a gain!
Would that I were—my hairy skin alone—
    the skin that makes with its soft hairs a plate
    (O happy dress!) around his handsome breast
all day! Were I two slippers he could own
    and use as base to his majestic weight!
    I would enjoy two snowy feet at least.

JOSEPH TUSIANI


Of the many poems by Michelangelo relating to sculpture, one of the most complex involves a series of hammer figures. Through the shifting of the hammer symbol, a curious tension develops. At diverse points in the sonnet the hammer refers to the actual implement, the driving force of God the Creator, his beloved who has died, and the inspiration for his life and for his art.

If my rough hammer gives a human face
  to this or that of all hard blocks that wait,
  it is another smith makes me create,
  controlling each my motion, each my pace.
But that high hammer beyond stars and space
  makes self, and others, with each stroke, more great
  and bright; and since the first must generate
  all hammers, *that* gives life to all, always.
And since the most effective is that blow
  which falls from highest in the smithy, mine
  shall fall no more—my hammer having flown.
Now here am I, unskilled, and do not know
  how to go on, unless the smith divine
  teaches me how, who am on earth alone.

JOSEPH TUSIANI

In addition to the eccentricities and extravagances which the poetic images reveal in works such as we have examined, there are numerous other rhetorical devices which contribute to the decorative, the complex, or the hermetic quality of the newer school. I refer to the use of paradox, pun, and dramatic juxtaposition, none of which can be considered as innovations in themselves; but when they are heightened and multiplied and thrown into combination with other figurative devices in quick succession, they can add to the effect of intensity.

However, there are two other features of the later Renaissance poetry deserving particular notice because of their part in the development of those peculiar tensions which mark the spirit of the period. Mr. Lowry Nelson, Jr., who has offered the most comprehensive examination of these devices, discusses them under the designation, "Time as a Means of Structure" and "Drama as a Means of Structure."[*] By the former he refers to an eccentric or distorted treatment of time planes. This can be illustrated in simplified terms by observing the handling of tenses in Milton's "Ode on the Morning of Christ's Nativity." At one point the poet treats in the present tense the time of the writing of the piece and speaks of the birth of Christ in the past tense, which is of course the normal procedure. However, in another

---

[*] Lowry Nelson, Jr., *Baroque Lyric Poetry* (New Haven and London: Yale University Press, 1961).

passage, he speaks of the time of the birth in the historical present; and we recognize that had he elected to follow that rhetorical device from the first, it would have caused no surprise. Even the shift from the one traditional time plane to the other traditional scheme would have passed without exceptional notice. But in the course of the poem, there is a frequent, erratic switching from one to the other of these temporal systems which constitutes an important stylistic feature of the poem. The result is that the poem achieves a subtly impressionistic sense of time values cosmic in character.

Professor Nelson has presented an elaborate analysis of this and two other rather long poems, Góngora's "Polifemo" and Milton's "Lycidas." For obvious reasons this kind of tense development cannot be found commonly among shorter lyric poems. However, one example from a poem by St. Teresa will serve to show the kind of distortion involved and the tension produced by it.

### Vertiendo Está Sangre

See, His blood He's shedding:
*Dominguillo, why?*
*I have no reply.*

Why is it, I ask you,
Why in justice' name?
For the child is guiltless,
Free from sin and shame.
Wherefore does He love me?
I have no reply.
Yet He yearns to save me:
*Dominguillo, why?*

Must His cruel torments
At His earth begin?
Yes, for He is dying
To remove our sin.
What a mighty Shepherd
Have we, by my fay!
*Dominguillo, eh!*

You have not yet seen Him :
Such an innocent?
"No but I've been told by
Brasil and Llorent."
We must surely love Him
From this very day,
*Dominguillo, eh?*

E. ALLISON PEERS

There are four time planes involved here with no pretense of a logical ordering. The present is at different points in the poem used to designate the time of the birth of Christ (For the child is guiltless), the time of the writing of the poem (Wherefore does He love me?), the time of the crucifixion (He is dying/To remove our sin). In the second stanza the future tense occurs, though the translator has used the present.

*O qué gran Zagal*
*Sera por me fe!*

This future depends on the assumption that the present is the time of Christ's infancy.

In the study of "Drama as a Means of Structure," Mr. Nelson remarks that "some of the very best Baroque lyrics derived great strength of structure from the original way in which they exploited the rhetorical situation. Never before had the lyric achieved so conspicuous a degree of complexity and dramaticality." This is a complicated concept involving the analysis of various familiar rhetorical devices which, singly or in combination, contribute to the "dramaticality" of a work. For example: the simple varying of the modes of discourse—statement, question, exclamation, hortatory address—may figure in the cultivation of dramatic effects, as well as the inclusion of dialogue or dramatic monologue. The particularization of time and place can serve as a force for dramaticality. Also the development of variant interpretations through alternate metaphors achieves a dramatic effect. For example, Calderon, in a passage previously quoted, identifies the cross with a tree, flower, rainbow, new harp of David, table of Moses.

Another key to the rhetorical situation is found in the attitude of the speaker, who may be identified as the poet or who may be a real or fictitious character; and in cases where conversation is recorded, may represent one or more persons other than the first voice of the poem. When the poem reveals a clearly defined attitude on the part of the speaker or speakers, a certain dramatic quality is achieved; when the attitude undergoes some evolution in the course of the work, and when the development of attitude relates to other rhetorical devices such as exclamations and questions or alternative propositions or multiple metaphors, then the most mature demonstration of dramaticality is attained.

To illustrate this subject adequately would require far more space than we have available. Lowry Nelson's searching analysis occupies approximately half of his book. His best examples are drawn from the works of Marino, Théophile, Donne, and Milton. We can do little more here than to note that certain passages already quoted in this introduction illustrate specific points in his catalogue: notably the exclamatory outbursts of Michelangelo and Sponde and the alternate metaphors of Góngora and Calderon. The dramatic use of monologue or dialogue occurs with some frequency in the anthology selections, especially in the lyrics of Scève, St. Teresa, St. John of the Cross, Góngora, and Marino. And one of the principal poems analyzed in detail by Mr. Nelson to illustrate the complex development of the rhetorical situation, Théophile's "La Solitude," will be found in our collection in abbreviated form under the title "To Corinna."

One further important characteristic of the body of lyrics under discussion merits special attention, one which concerns the intellectual temper of the poems: namely, their concern for ontological problems. Some of these writers undertook to engage the enigmas of the inescapable dualisms of flesh and spirit, time and eternity, microcosm and macrocosm. This earnest search into the nature of reality, which has been recognized as an essential feature of the English Metaphysical school, appears prominently in the writings of several Continental writers as well. Scève, for example, demonstrates this awareness constantly in his love poems; and yet, whereas the cumulative effect throughout his poems is impressive, a single example can merely hint at the disposition of his mind to turn upon these problems.

Lady, you are the body, and I am your shadow,
  Which in my continual silence
  Makes me move, not like Hecate the shadow,
  By dire and great violence,
  But by the power of your high excellence,
  In moving at the sweet outline
  Of all your deeds, and more suddenly
  Than one sees the shadow follow the body,
  Except that I feel too inhumanly
  Our holy wills grow together in discord.

WALLACE FOWLIE

Other poets who reveal a similar turn of mind and whose works would repay examination in this respect are Sponde, La Ceppède, and Michelangelo, all sixteenth century writers. Among numerous pieces by Michelangelo treating the Platonic concept of the relation of earthly and heavenly beauty, the following madrigal is one of the least complex.

Ravished by all that to the eyes is fair,
  Yet hungry for the joys that truly bless,
  My soul can find no stair
  To mount to heaven, save earth's loveliness.
  For from the stars above
  Descends a glorious light
  That lifts our longing to their highest height
  And bears the name of love.
  Nor is there aught can move
  A gentle heart, or purge or make it wise,
  But beauty and the starlight of her eyes.

GEORGE SANTAYANA

For Michelangelo the dualism of day and night held a peculiar fascination, as appears in numerous of his lyrics. For example:

He who ordained, when first the world began,
    time, that was not before creation's hour,
    divided it, and gave the sun's high power
    to rule the one, the moon the other span:
thence fate and changeful chance and fortune's ban
    did in one moment down on mortals shower:
    to me they portioned darkness for a dower;
    dark hath my lot been since I was a man.
Myself am ever mine own counterfeit;
    and as deep night grows still more dim and dun,
    so still of more misdoing must I rue:
meanwhile this solace to my soul is sweet,
    that my black night doth make more clear the sun
    which at your birth was given to wait on you.

                JOHN ADDINGTON SYMONDS

We may now return to the questions posed at the beginning of this discussion concerning the meaning of terms which are used to designate the various stages of the greater Renaissance and the possible identification of schools with those stages. The various stylistic and intellectual features which have been catalogued in the foregoing discussion—complicated and erratic syntax, vehement outbursts, indirect and hermetic phrasing, far-fetched imagery, illogical tense relations, and the rest—are the elements out of which the formulas must be evolved.

First let us consider the major divisions: Renaissance, Mannerist, and Baroque. In this context, Renaissance is employed in its more limited sense, meaning the early stage of the greater Renaissance. Call it the pure Renaissance. Would that we had a more distinctive term.

The early Renaissance is essentially classical in temper; that is to say its spirit is static, balanced, composed. Inasmuch as a study of the art of the period can throw valuable light on its aesthetic values, we may profitably review some of the major characteristics of the painting of the age. By and large, the majority of the frescoes and canvases of the Renaissance reveal a basic composure, which is found, upon analysis, to be the product of a balanced and skillfully proportioned composition, even lighting, easy color transitions, accurate perspective, a degree of restraint in the use of ornamental effects, decoration being subordinated to the total effect. Human figures are in familiar, comfortable, dignified attitudes; the use of gentle curves produces rhythms that are subtly graceful; and the whole reveals a spirit of calm and dignified adjustment within an ordered universe. Almost all of the Italian Renaissance painters from Giotto to Raphael fall within this tradition.

To translate these features into terms applicable to poetry is not simple, but it is possible to recognize a certain number of aesthetic equivalents. A type of lyric commonly produced in this earlier stage of the Renaissance is one that is gracefully formal and pleasing in its oral effects. The syntax is generally uncomplicated, statement is clear and direct, and the total meaning is readily comprehensible. The amount of figurative decoration can vary considerably but is never excessive, and those similes and metaphors introduced are drawn from such familiar and traditionally recognized themes as birds and flowers, the sun, moon, and stars; love is described as a warfare; a courtship is compared to a quest or voyage. The poet recognizes no compulsion to astonish the reader by strange thoughts or novel stylistic devices. Whether he is happy or sad over his love, is musing upon mutability or celebrating conviviality, there is clarity of vision and a simple, uncomplicated association with nature. This lyric is of an almost universal character, not differing radically from Latin poetry or the vernacular lyrics of the later Middle Ages. The main types of early Renaissance lyrics did not disappear even when reactions developed and new forms appeared; poems of this character continued to be written in considerable numbers throughout the sixteenth and early seventeenth century.

A reaction against the complacency and formalism of that school was inevitable, and with this reaction we move into the first phase of the later Renaissance. A new aesthetic gradually evolved which has long been identified by the art historian as Mannerism. In the paintings of this school several if not all of the following features will be recognized: asymmetric design, contrasting use of light and shade, dissonant color transitions, an untrue system of perspective, crowding of decorative features. Distorted human figures are presented in dramatic attitudes portraying muscular strain or agony of mind or body. The underlying effect produced by such painting is one of agitation, nervous excitement, unresolved tension. Michelangelo's later work in both sculpture and painting was moving in the direction of Mannerism.

Prominent in the movement were Caravaggio, Tintoretto, and El Greco.

In poetry the shift to Mannerism involved various literary devices calculated to transform the lyric from an overall tone of composure and adjustment to one of nervousness, excitement, and unresolved tension. Complexity of syntax and deliberate inconsistency with respect to tense sequences put the reader under strain. In the matter of vocabulary, the use of neologisms, Latinisms, and other foreign terms, and the frequent substitution of one part of speech for another further add to the tension. The breaking of the smooth, regular flow of the poetic line by dramatic exclamations, staccato effects, and jerky lists likewise contribute to the disturbing spirit. Discords and dissonances serve to that end. In place of direct statement, we find more or less obscure allusion, involving considerable use of figures such as metonymy, synecdoche, and oxymoron. We also encounter complicated and unexpected mental and emotional processes. Finally there is a straining for novelty in the figures of comparison. "The most heterogeneous ideas are yoked with violence together; nature and art are ransacked for illustrations, comparisons, and allusions; . . ." Through these signs of strain, imbalance, and distortion we detect a world view which distrusted the concept of fixed order in the universe. This outlook, in some instances, led to a mood of pessimism, certainly of insecurity; but in another direction the denial of the immutable, hierarchal structure of the universe opened the way to a philosphy of progress and offered justification for new aspirations. All of the supposed universal laws were subject to investigation, all limits ascribed to human nature subject to challenge. This new spirit is a salient feature of the Renaissance—the greater Renaissance.

The temper of the Baroque is not altogether distinct from the other styles but rather a new combination of elements revealing certain features of each. In the plastic arts it aims for dramatic effects, which are achieved partially by such Mannerist features as chiaroscuro, angular or fore.hortened poses, and an excessive use of sharp curves and sworls. But like the earlier Renaissance style, it employs balance and ordered structure. If not absolutely static, it will tend in that direction. Striving for grandeur of effect, it is often extremely ornamented; but however ornate, it is not nervous, as is the Mannerist work. It has made its adjustments, has rediscovered a sense of order in the world.

What has here been described as Mannerism has often been designated as Baroque by critics who do not recognize Mannerism as a separate movement. However, according to the present usage, which follows the scheme of the art historians, Baroque points to a movement which, though repeating certain features of the former movements, represents an important shift in temperament. In its effort to be impressive, to achieve effects that are striking, it employs a formidable vocabulary, it strives for sonority, it creates scenes on a grandiose scale, and it indulges in lavish decoration. However, it reflects a reversion to Renaissance classicism in its feeling for balance, polish, and a kind of composure and adjustment which carries implications of an acceptance of the universal plan. Certainly it has lost the Renaissance appreciation of the beauty and the wonder of the simplest acts of creation, replacing this with a devotion to the melodramatic, to plenitude, to magnificence. Because of these latter characteristics, it is not easy to find examples of the style in lyric poetry. They are more readily discovered in the drama or in epic poetry. Tasso's *Jerusalem Delivered* illustrates the movement well, Milton's *Paradise Lost* even better. In the classic French theater the dramas of Corneille and Racine illustrate the type, though in different ways and to varying degrees. Among the lyric poets, the best examples are found in the longer and more ambitious and honorific works of such men as Herrera, Malherbe, and Dryden. Indeed it must be acknowledged that Marino and Góngora fall into this category in certain works or passages. Actually it is not always a simple matter to identify a particular work with a movement because there are shades and degrees in all these matters and great variation occurs in the combinations of stylistic features. As a matter of fact, there is almost no author who adheres consistently to one school throughout his career.

As has been noted previously, there are two principal schools of thought concerning the proper subdividing of the greater Renaissance, one recognizing only two main phases—the classical Renaissance and Baroque; the other observing a three-part division—Renaissance, Mannerism, and Baroque. Those critics who support the former view, and they are numerous, are confronted with no difficulty whatsoever in assigning schools and "isms" to the major phases. The Petrarchan school is obviously to be identified with the earlier Renaissance and all others fall into the second division. But if this later division is to be subdivided further into Mannerism and Baroque, the placing of Metaphysical, Préciocité, Góngorism, and the rest in one or the other of the major divisions proves to be rather complex. Nevertheless, since I have espoused the cause of Mannerism, I must offer some judgments on this question, however briefly.

So far as individual poets are concerned, I feel no hesitation in classifying considerable portions of the work of Scève and Michelangelo as Manneristic, remembering at the same time that each man sometimes wrote in the Petrarchan vein as well. These poets are Mannerist in that their language is at times strained, contorted, and violent; their figures are unexpected and unconventional; and their thought content reflects an effort to resolve conflicting elements and concepts. Since these poets have frequently been identified with the Metaphysical school, it follows that Metaphysical poetry should be equated with Mannerism rather than with Baroque literature. To the Metaphysical category the names of La Ceppède and Sponde should be added.

In the case of Marino, his straining for novelty and surprise, his rich and crowded ornament, and his relative freedom from complex or turbulent ideas place him in the camp of the Baroque artist. Similarly the *précieux* poets conform to the Baroque age, demonstrating a devotion to elegance of diction and refinement of thought but avoidance of any serious conflict of ideas.

Góngora performs in several styles. There is a group of his lyrics, a majority of them actually, which follow the tradition of the early Renaissance. However, those of his poems which establish the pattern for "Góngorism" present a radical contrast, actually an open revolt against the conventional forms. In his striving for novelty, he employs a new and strange vocabulary, he practices various forms of substitution and indirection, his figures are crowded, and he shows a special fondness for paradox. In that this style is purposely obscure and of high density, it shows a kinship to Metaphysical poetry; but the emphasis on crowded decoration, the fondness for the spectacular, and the absence of serious intellectual conflict or unresolved tensions identifies it as Baroque.

The principal issue raised here by the triple division of the greater Renaissance centers around the question of whether Metaphysical poetry should be treated as a Mannerist or a Baroque phenomenon. I support the position that it is Mannerist, basically on the grounds that both Mannerism and the Metaphysical school reflect a disturbed world view and that their tensions are unresolved, whereas the Baroque spirit moves within a balanced, ordered scheme.

## ON TRANSLATING POETRY

A poem is a subtle fusion of sense, form, and tone. A perfect translation, then, should faithfully reproduce the original in all of these respects. It can't be done. There are only near-perfect translations, and fairly good ones, and so on down the scale to the violently distorted ones, the out-and-out betrayals.

The reader has often been warned that "something has been lost in the translation," that "it is much finer in the original"; and yet there is a peculiar psychology that operates to lull the reader into a happy acceptance of what he finds in print. In spite of his telling himself occasionally that this is not the real thing, he soon falls into the frame of mind of believing in the fidelity of the translation unless some reminder of the authentic work is constantly present to keep before him the possibility for error. This confidence in the translation may at times lead the reader to the point where he is making bold pronouncements about the poetry, even about some matters of style concerning which he is not qualified to speak without a knowledge of the original.

One of the first difficulties of translating, one which is universally recognized, is that of attempting to reproduce the sound quality and the rhythm of a poem when turning it into another language. By substituting words in which the vowel patterns are changed, we inevitably get an altered musical effect. We may note, for example, how the superb musical and emotional quality of Petrarch's original poetry is manifested in such lines as: "*Zefiro torna, e 'l bel tempo rimena,*" or "*Vago augelletto che cantando vai.*" But when lines like these are turned into English verse, though the sense may be faithfully rendered and the new line may be poetic in its own right, nevertheless it will inevitably create a different music. For Dante's well-known *In sua voluntade è nostra pace*, we get the English equivalent: "In his will is our peace." The translation reproduces the meaning of the eleven syllable line in six, but it is flat compared with the beautifully orchestrated line in Italian.

It is instructive to study the effects of translation in connection with the opening phrase of almost any operatic aria. For instance:

| | |
|---|---|
| *Ai nostri monti* | (To our mountains) |
| *Si può? Si può? Signore, signori!* | (If you please! Ladies, gentlemen) |
| *Libiamo, libiamo* | (Let's drink, let's drink) |

*L'amour est un oiseau rebelle*       (Love is a rebel bird)
*Einsam in trüben Tagen*              (Lonely in troubled days).

Some extravagant distortions emerge when an aria is translated for singing, a situation in which the primary requirement is to meet the demands of the musical cadences. A few examples will demonstrate why some opera lovers are so horrified at the idea of translating operatic texts. Sometimes the sound as well as the meaning is given rather rough treatment for the sake of the rhythm. Note this passage from *La Traviata*:

> *Piangi, piangi, piangi, o misera!*
> *corraggio, e il nobile cor vincerà.*

Literally this is:

> Thou weep'st, thou weep'st, thou weep'st, oh
>     miserable one!
> Courage and the noble heart will conquer.

In an English libretto of the opera the passage is given as follows:

> Heaven, heaven, heaven grant you strength
> to bear your burden of sorrow and pain.

In the same opera we find this passage:

> *A quell' amor, quell' amor ch'è palpito*
> *dell' universo, dell' universo intero,*

which literally means:

> Ah, that love, that love which is the heartbeat
> of the universe, of the entire universe.

It comes out this way in the singing version:

> Here is a love that could fill my life for me,
> love that would banish the world and all its madness, ...

Probably the greatest difficulty confronting any translator, and the one which causes him to stray farthest from the true path, is the difficulty caused by attempting to find suitable rhymes. This can become such a trial that many translators have settled for prose, and with some reason. If the prose version sacrifices something of the form and tone of the original poem, the rhyming version may well sacrifice a good deal of the sense of the original. Assuredly the most extravagant distortions of both meaning and spirit in these works must be charged to the necessity for finding rhymes, as will be demonstrated in the comparisons of translations to be presented later in our discussion.

A special kind of difficulty for the translator, the treatment of a pun, is brought out by the following line from one of Petrarch's sonnets:

> *Rotta è l'alta colonna e'l verde lauro*
> (Broken is the tall column and the green laurel).

This passage refers figuratively to the recent deaths of Laura and Cardinal Giovanni Colonna. The wordplay, which is so essential to the reading of the poem, is almost impossible to transmit in another language. Not many readers will perceive the reference to Laura in the word *laurel*. Nobody reading *column* would recognize an allusion to a man named Colonna. Other puns on Laura's name, of which there are a good many, are impossible to convey in English—plays, for example, on *l'aura*, "the air," and *aurea*, "golden."

> *Erano i capei d'oro a l'aura sparsi,*
> (The hair of gold was tossed by the air).

In one passage we find three Laura puns crowded into a single line:

> *L'aura, che 'l verde lauro e l'aureo crine*
> (The air, which the green laurel and the golden tresses . . .)

The pun, good or bad, is clearly an incidental feature of Petrarch's poetic system which is hopelessly beyond us in translation. And this practice of punning on the name of the beloved is not limited to Petrarch. Tasso plays on the names of two young ladies, one Laura, the other Leonora. In the love poems of Herrera, "light" symbolizes his Doña Luz; and Du Bellay entitled a volume of his poems *L'Olive*, an anagram of Mlle de Viole.

The best method I have discovered for coming to an understanding of the problems and niceties of translation is through a detailed examination of a variety of English versions of a given poem. As a basis for examination, I should like to present several sets of comparisons, giving the poem in the original language and then several renditions of it in English prose and verse. A careful scrutiny of these variant interpretations will throw much light on what difficulties are encountered by the translator as well as what erroneous impressions are sometimes foisted upon the unsuspecting reader. Further, one may come to discover some of the various advantages and disadvantages of both prose and verse translations; he may gain some cognizance of what crimes are perpetrated for the sake of rhymes; and he will discover how often the English version may improvise original poetic flights, which might, in rare instances, improve upon the original but which, in any case, do not belong in a translation. Moreover, if the reader has even a slight familiarity with the original language, he will recognize some of the strange transformations that occur in the transmission of that elusive quality—tone.

Our first example is a short lyric by Marino in which the problems facing the translator do not appear to be in any way difficult.

MARINO    FEDE ROTTA

> Sovra l'umida arena
> de le latine sponde
> di propria man Tirrena
> queste parole un dì scriver vid'io:
> Mirzio è sol l'amor mio.
>
> Ahi fu ben degna di sì fral parola,
> crudel, l'arena sola; onde poi l'onde
> e del Tebro in un punto e de l'oblio
> Mirzio, ch'era il tu'amore,
> radessero dal lido e dal tuo core.

*Prose Translation*

BROKEN VOWS

> On the damp sands
> of the Italian shore,
> I saw Tirrena with her own hand
> writing these words one day:
> Mirtius is my only love.
> Ah, cruel fair, the sand alone was fit
> for words so frail; since the waves of the Tiber
> and forgetfulness at the one instant erased
> Mirtius, who was your love,
> from the beach and from your heart.

*Penguin Book of Italian Verse*

*Verse Translation—Observing Original Form*

## BROKEN FAITH

On the soft wet sand
Of the Latian shore
I watched Tirrena's hand
Inscribe her pledge of love in this sweet line:
"Mirtius, I am thine."
  Alas! nought was befitting those frail words
Save only sand; 'twas but a moment ere
The Tiber's tide and thy inconstant mind
Mirtius, that name once loved,
From out her heart as from the sand removed.

HAROLD M. PRIEST

*Verse Translation—Freely Adapted*

## THE BROKEN FAITH

Lately by clear Thames's side,
Fair Lycoris I espi'd
With the pen of her white hand
These words printing on the sand:
"None Lycoris doth approve
But Mirtillo for her love."
Ah false nymph! those words were fit
In sand only to be writ:
For the quickly rising streams
Of oblivion, and the Thames,
In a little moment's stay
From the shore wash'd clean away
What thy hand had there impress'd,
And Mirtillo from thy breast.

SIR EDWARD SHERBURNE

*French Translation—Freely Adapted*

Philis auprès de cet ormeau
Où paissait son petit troupeau
Etant toute triste et pensive,
De son doigt écrivait un jour
Sur le sablon de cette rive:
'Alcidon est mon seul amour.'

Je ne devais pas m'assurer
De voir sa promesse durer,
Parce qu'en chose plus légère,
Ni plus ressemblante à sa foi,
L'ingrate et parjure bergère
Ne pouvait se promettre à moi.

Un petit vent qui s'élevait
En même instant qu'elle écrivait
Cette preuve si peu durable,
Effaça sans plus de longueur
Sa promesse dessus le sable
Et son amour dedans son cœur.

JEAN DE LINGENDES

Sherburne's version as well as de Lingendes' have not only taken such innocent liberties as changing names and locale, but they have changed the "shape" of the poem. The madrigal form of the original with its varied pattern of short and long lines and the irregular rhyme scheme have been ignored by both. The ten lines of Marino's poem have been presented in fourteen in Sherburne's version, eighteen in the French treatment.

On the other hand, the verse translation attempting to conform to the original pattern has been forced into such liberties as "Mirtius, I am thine" for "Mirzio alone is my love."

In the treatment of the following sonnet of Petrarch, some more extraordinary features are illustrated.

PETRARCA, *Rime*, In Vita 14

Movesi il vecchierel canuto e bianco
  del dolce loco ov'ha sua età fornita,
  e da la famigliuola sbigottita
  che vede il caro padre venir manco;
indi, traendo poi l'antiquo fianco
  per l'estreme giornate di sua vita,
  quanto più può col buon voler s'aita,
  rotto da gli anni e dal cammino stanco;
e viene a Roma, seguendo 'l desìo,
  per mirar la sembianza di Colui
  ch'ancor lassù nel ciel vedere spera.
Così, lasso! tal or vo cercand'io,
  Donna, quanto è possibile, in altrui
  la disïata vostra forma vera.

*Prose Translation*

  The poor old man, white and hoary, departs
from the sweet spot where he has passed his years,
and from his frightened family,
who watch him take his leave;
hence, dragging his ancient limbs
through the last days of his life,
as much as possible his will carries him on,
though broken by years and the weary road;
  and comes to Rome, pursuing his desire
to behold the semblance of Him
whom he hopes to see again in heaven.
So, alas, my lady, wherever possible,
I now go searching in others
the semblance of your loved form.

                                    HAROLD M. PRIEST

*Verse Translations*

The palmer bent, with locks of silver grey,
    Quits the sweet spot where he has pass'd his years,
    Quits his poor family, whose anxious fears
    Paint the loved father fainting on his way;
And trembling, on his aged limbs slow borne,
    In these last days that close his earthly course,
    He, in his soul's strong purpose, finds new force,
    Though weak with age, though by long travel worn:
Thus reaching Rome, led on by pious love,
    He seeks the image of that Saviour Lord
    Whom soon he hopes to meet in bliss above:
So, oft in other forms I seek to trace
    Some charm, that to my heart may yet afford
    A faint resemblance of thy matchless grace.

                                LADY DACRE


The pilgrim, pallid and with hair grown gray,
    Takes leave of the sweet spot where life was dear,
    And of his little family whose great fear
    Paints the loved parent fainting on his way;
Then trembling in his body's broken clay,
    Upon the verge of his last vigil here,
    Sustained by his soul's purpose burning clear,
    He steps, though years and leagues by night and day
Oppress him. But his pious love finds Rome
    Somehow at length; he seeks the Face Divine
    Which soon he hopes to see in Kingdom Come:
So Lady, so I go to seek the shrine—
    Your face—in others, hoping for one crumb
    To give my heart a taste of Palestine!

                          JOSEPH AUSLANDER


A detailed examination of the English versions shows us the tendency of translators to embellish the essentially plain diction of the original. The most extreme demonstration of reaching for flights of

eloquence not supplied by the original is found in the last translation
quoted, especially in the closing lines:

> ... he seeks the Face Divine
> Which soon he hopes to see in Kingdom Come:
> So Lady, so I go to seek the shrine—
> Your face—in others, hoping for one crumb
> To give my heart a taste of Palestine!

This kind of improvisation upon Petrarch's language would never
have been permitted, I feel sure, had it not been for the difficulties
imposed upon the translator to force what he wants to say into lines
that rhyme. This was done out of pure desperation.

The question of the borderline between a true translation and a
work which should more properly be called an adaptation or an
imitation is difficult but ever-present in a study such as this. Two
treatments of the Marino poem previously discussed are examples of
free adaptations. In the set of poems to follow, the version by Wyatt
is a clear case in point.


PETRARCA, *Rime*, In Vita 157

> Una candida cerva sopra l'erba
>     verde m'apparve, con duo corna d'oro,
>     fra due riviere, a l'ombra d'un alloro,
>     levando 'l sole, a la stagione acerba.
> Era sua vista sì dolce superba,
>     ch'i'lasciai per seguirla ogni lavoro;
>     come l'avaro che 'n cercar tesoro
>     con diletto l'affanno disacerba.
> "Nessun mi tocchi," al bel collo d'intorno
>     scritto avea di diamanti e di topazi;
>     "libera farmi al mio Cesare parve."
> Ed era 'l sol già vòlto al mezzo giorno;
>     gli occhi miei stanchi di mirar, non sazi;
>     quand'io caddi ne l'acqua, ed ella sparve.

A fair white hind with golden horns
appeared to me in a green field
between two rivers, in the shade of a laurel,
at sunrise, in the bitter season.
Her bearing was so sweetly proud
that I left my labors to pursue her,
like a miser who in his search for treasure
undergoes hardship with pleasure.
"Let no one touch me," about her fair neck
was inscribed with diamonds and topaz;
"By my Caesar's order I go free."
By now the sun had climbed to midday;
my eyes were weary with watching yet unsated;
whereon, I fell into the water, and she vanished.

HAROLD M. PRIEST

Whoso list to hunt, I know where is an hind,
But as for me—alas, I may no more.
The vain travail hath wearied me so sore,
I am of them that farthest cometh behind.
Yet may I, by no means, my wearied mind
Draw from the deer; but as she fleeth afore
Fainting I follow. I leave off therefore,
Since in a net I seek to hold the wind.
Who list her hunt, I put him out of doubt,
As well as I, may spend his time in vain.
And graven with diamonds in letters plain
There is written, her fair neck round about:
Noli me tangere, for Caesar's I am,
And wild for to hold, though I seem tame.

SIR THOMAS WYATT

Wyatt's poem, even though it contains unmistakable echoes of the Italian sonnet, has a number of original details; but, most important, it has an entirely new direction and was obviously written with reference to personal circumstances quite different from anything Petrarch had in mind. The Italian poem presents a kind of mystic vision in which the poet follows a white hind through the forest, fascinated until he learns that she is marked for Caesar. Still enamored, he weeps at her vanishing. Commentators agree that Petrarch meant Caesar to stand for Christ, who has marked Laura for early death. Wyatt announces that he has given up the hunt of the beautiful hind, having learned that Caesar has ordered hands off. The identification of the hind in Wyatt's poem with Ann Boleyn and Caesar with Henry VIII produces an interesting variant on the original. Obviously Wyatt's intention is something quite different from that of a standard translation.

To show that similar deviations occur when other languages are involved, we need to present a few examples from French and Spanish. Let us take first this simple, graceful, and traditional sonnet from the Spanish.

LUIS DE GÓNGORA

VANA ROSA

Ayer naciste, y morirás mañana.
¿Para tan breve ser, quién te dió vida?
¿Para vivir tan poco estás lucida,
y para no ser nada estás lozana?
    Si te engañó tu hermosura vana,
bien presto la verás desvanecida
porque en tu hermosura está escondida
la ocasión de morir muerte temprana.
    Cuando te corte la robusta mano,
ley de la agricultura permitida,
grosero aliento acabará tu suerte.
    No salgas, que te aguarda algún tirano;
dilata tu nacer para tu vida,
que anticipas tu ser para tu muerte.

## VAIN ROSE

You were born yesterday, and will die tomorrow.
For such brief being, who gave you life?
To live so little are you so shining,
And to be nothing are you so sprightly?
If you were misled by your vain beauty,
Too soon you'll see it vanished
Because in your beauty is concealed
The fate to die an early death.
When the stout hand plucks you,
A law by agriculture permitted,
A coarse breath will end your lot.
Don't shout, for a tyrant lies in wait for you,
Postpone your birth in order to have life
For anticipating life you hasten death.

ARTHUR CAMPA

## A ROSE

Blown in the morning, thou shalt fade ere noon:
What boots a life which in such haste forsakes thee?
Th'art wondrous frolick being to die so soon;
And passing proud a little color makes thee.
If thee thy brittle beauty so deceives,
Know then the thing that swells thee is thy bane;
For the same beauty doth in bloody leaves
The sentence of thy early death contain.
Some clown's coarse lungs will poison thy sweet flower
If by the careless plow thou shalt be torn;
And many Herods lie in wait each hour
To murther thee as soon as thou art born,
Nay, force thy bud to blow; their tyrant breath,
Anticipating life, to hasten death.

SIR RICHARD FANSHAWE

## TO A ROSE

Born yesternight, to die to-morrow's morn!
  Who gave thee being for so brief a day?
  For such a span of life, thy air is gay;
For such mock state, thy hues are proudly worn!
Let not thy beauty tempt to idle scorn:
  Soon will it vanish, like thin dreams, away,
  For in that beauty lurks the worm, decay,
Born in that hour when first thy bloom was born.
When some strong hand hath pluck'd thee,—such must be
  Thy fate by field or grove,—all after-strife
Will cease beneath the wind's first ruffling breath:
Keep close, poor Flower: some tyrant waits for thee.
  Put off thy budding birth to save thy life;
For e'en thy being is forestall'd by death.

EDWARD CHURTON

The Fanshawe version indulges in more flourishes than either the original or the translation by Churton. Curiously enough Fanshawe's reference to Herod strikes the reader as being highly characteristic of Gongorism, but a check shows it to be original with the translator. Here again we find an instance of the substitution of a specific reference for a general one.

A second Góngora sonnet, though not so simple as the preceding one, still shows the same problems, the same reaching for a recapturing of the spirit of the work, and much the same extraordinary variations as we pass from one poetic translation to another.

### GÓNGORA  OH CLARO HONOR

¡Oh claro honor del líquido elemento
dulce arroyuelo de corriente plata
cuya agua entre la hierba se dilata
con regalado son, con paso lento!

Pues la por quien helar y arder me siento,
mientras en ti se mira, Amor retrata
de su rostro la nieve y la escarlata
en tu tranquilo y blando movimiento,

véte como te vas; no dejes floja
la undosa rienda al cristalino freno
con que gobiernas tu veloz corriente;

que no es bien que confusamente acoja
tanta belleza en su profondo seno
el gran señor del húmido tridente.


O lucent honour of the liquid element,
sweet brook of running silver,
whose water stretches through the grass
with an exquisite sound, at a slow pace!
Since Love portrays in your quiet and smooth stream
the snow and scarlet of her face,
for whom I feel myself freeze and burn
whilst she gazes at herself in you,
    go as you do; do not slacken
the wavy rein on the crystal bit
with which you guide your swift current;
for it is not right for the great lord
of the watery trident to catch so much beauty
in confusion in his deep breast.

*Penguin Book of Spanish Verse*


GÓNGORA  THE MIRROR IN THE BROOK

Clearest of waters, bright and beauteous rill,
    Whose silvery stream steals calmly on, outspread
    O'er the green herbs that line thy summer-bed,
Scarce heard to flow with gushing soft and still:

While she, whose frown hath power my heart to chill,
  Whose smile lights up its fires, in thee would trace
  The mirror'd image of that roseate face,
And brow, whose snow defines all limner's skill,—
While on thy bank she lingers, stay, oh stay,
  With gentlest pause, nor loose the wavy rein,
Whose curb holds back thy crystal's hurrying flow;
It is not well, her shape to bear away
  Too soon to that Grand Seignior of the main,
Whose mermaid-harem no such form can shew.

EDWARD CHURTON

## CLEAR HONOR OF THE LIQUID ELEMENT

Clear honor of the liquid element,
  Sweet rivulet of shining silver sheen!
  Whose waters steal along the meadows green,
  With gentle step and murmur of content!
When she for whom I bear each fierce extreme,
  Beholds herself in thee,—then Love doth trace
  The snow and crimson of that lovely face
  In the soft gentle movement of thy stream.
Then, smoothly flow as now, and set not free
  The crystal curb and undulating rain
  Which now thy current's headlong speed restrain;
Lest broken and confused the image rest
  Of such rare charms on the deep-heaving breast
  Of him who holds and sways the trident of the seas.

HENRY WADSWORTH LONGFELLOW

In Longfellow's version he has introduced a disturbing element by representing as "broken and confused" the image to be carried to Neptune on the surface of the stream. Churton, in his version, has executed an unauthorized and unworthy flourish in the last lines, especially in the reference to the "mermaid-harem."

A study of the following renditions of Ronsard's most celebrated sonnet reveals the tremendous amount of variation which can evolve from the attempt to recreate the poem in rhymed verse.

Incidentally, it should be noted that only one version has followed Ronsard in the use of Alexandines, the translation by George Wyndham.

RONSARD

Quand vous serez bien vieille, au soir, à la chandelle,
    Assise auprès du feu, dévidant et filant,
    Direz, chantant mes vers, en vous émerveillant:
    "Ronsard me célébrait du temps que j'étais belle."
Lors vous n'aurez servante oyant telle nouvelle,
    Déjà sous le labeur à demi sommeillant,
    Qui au bruit de mon nom ne s'aille réveillant,
    Bénissant votre nom de louange immortelle.
Je serai sous la terre et, fantôme sans os,
    Par les ombres myrteux je prendrai mon repos;
    Vous serez au foyer une vieille accroupie,
Regrettant mon amour et votre fier dédain.
    Vivez, si m'en croyez, n'attendez à demain:
    Cueillez dès aujourd'hui les roses de la vie.

When you are very old, at evening
    You'll sit and spin beside the fire, and say,
    Humming my songs, "Ah well, ah well-a-day.
    When I was young, of me did Ronsard sing."
None of your maidens that doth hear the thing,
    Albeit with her weary task foredone,
    But wakens at my name, and calls you one
    Blest, to be held in long remembering.
I shall be low beneath the earth, and laid
    On sleep, a phantom in the myrtle shade,
    While you beside the fire, a grandame gray,
My love, your pride, remember and regret;
    Ah, love me, love, we may be happy yet,
    And gather roses, while 'tis called today.

                    ANDREW LANG

When you are old, at evening candle-lit
   beside the fire bending to your wool,
      read out my verses and murmur, "Ronsard writ
      this praise for me when I was beautiful."
And not a maid but, at the sound of it,
      though nodding at the stitch on broidered stool,
   will start awake, and bless love's benefit
   whose long fidelities bring Time to school.
I shall be thin and ghost beneath the earth
   by myrtle shade in quiet after pain,
      but you, a crone, will crouch beside the hearth
mourning my love and all your proud disdain.
     And since what comes tomorrow who can say?
     Live, pluck the roses of the world today.

HUMBERT WOLFE

When you are very old, at dusk by candle-light,
   Talking beside the fire the while you spin your wool,
   Singing my verse, you'll say, as something wonderful,
   Thus Ronsard, long ago, for love of me did write.
Then not a serving maid, grown drowsy with the night
   And slumbering o'er the task she plies beneath your rule,
   But startled at my name will quit her spinning-stool,
   To bless your name with praise the years shall never blight.
I shall be in my grave, a disembodied ghost,
   Resting where myrtles bloom along the shadowy coast:
   You crouching o'er the hearth will be an aged crone,
Regretting all the love you proudly put away.
   Wait for no morrow. Ah! believe me, snatch to-day
   The roses of your life, that shall so soon be gone.

GEORGE WYNDHAM

In the foregoing discussion I have emphasized the hazards and failures of translations in order to establish reservations in the reader's mind and to forestall unwarranted verdicts concerning the style. The comparisons of translations are calculated to serve both as a warning and also as encouragement for giving the problems involved some earnest study. On the positive side, however, it must be recognized that there has been much fine work done in translation, that a good many distinguished writers have engaged in this literary pursuit, as the list of translators represented in the volume shows, and that there are many pieces which have surmounted the multiple difficulties involved to produce highly successful, even brilliant, works. A justification for this claim will be found in the best poems of the collection which follows.

# ITALIAN POEMS

# Francesco Petrarca

## (1304–1374)

Styled the "Father of the Renaissance," he did more than any other man to point the new direction and to set men's minds on fire. In his lifetime he won extraordinary honors because of his achievements as a humanist, notably through his research in ancient manuscripts and interpretation of Roman texts, his lectures, and his many Latin writings.

For pleasure and idle pastime he wrote lyric verses in the vernacular, which were regarded as trifles by his contemporaries but which later came to impress and influence posterity. Throughout the sixteenth century the name of Petrarch was unequaled in renown. The "school of Petrarch" dominated lyric poetry through all of western Europe.

His *Rime*, or *Canzoniere*, is a volume containing 365 lyrics, including *canzoni* and *ballate*, madrigals and *sestine*, but chiefly sonnets. With a few exceptions the poems were written to his blond-haired Laura, a lady whom the poet seems not to have been very close to but who nevertheless served as inspiration for his idealized poems through twenty-one years of her life and a number of years after her death; hence the two main divisions of the book, "In Vita" and "In Morte."

The matter of this Petrarchan vein, which became a convention to so many generations of poets, may be briefly summarized as follows: the poet is a humble worshiper of a lady whose beauty and virtue inspire his wonder and devotion; her eyes dart arrows that cause him to bleed and weep; and Love brings him the torments of fire and ice. The spirit of the work is a compound of the troubadour tradition, the *dolce stil nuovo*, and Platonism. One important contribution Petrarch made to Western Literature is that he taught men the infinite number of features, reflections, and occurrences that can be distilled by the poet in love. One further shining quality has been described in the following terms:

"The undying fame of Petrarch's Italian lyrics rests upon their blending of an inner with an outer beauty—the inner beauty of a sensitive, imaginative and reflective response to finely discriminated shadings of emotion, the outer beauty of a verbal and rhythmic artistry that has never been surpassed. The success of the blending results not only from the perfectness of Petrarch's natural sense of euphony, but also from his persistent endeavours to find the very words that will express most faithfully what he desires to express, and to combine and order them in lines that will linger and be dear in memory." (Ernest Hatch Wilkins, *A History of Italian Literature.*)

It is regrettable that Petrarch has been too often associated with the faults of his inferior imitators. He has been as much maligned through the pejorative use of the term "Petrarchan" as has Machiavelli through the connotations of "Machiavellian villain."

## IN VITA 3

*Era il giorno ch' al sol si scoloraro*

It was the day that the sun's rays
were dimmed for pity of his Maker,
when I was taken, not being on guard,
and your fair eyes, Lady, bound me.
It did not seem to me a time to take
precautions against Love's darts; wherefore
I went secure, without suspicion: whence my griefs
had their beginnings in man's common sorrow.
    Love found me all unarmed
and open wide the way through eyes to heart,
which are made the outlet and passage of tears.
Hence, to my thinking, it was little honor to him
to strike me with his arrow in that state,
while to you, well armed, he did not show his bow.[1]*

HAROLD M. PRIEST

* A number at the end of a poem indicates that there is a note on the poem. Cf. p. 265 ff.

It was the morning of that blessèd day
  Whereon the Sun in pity veiled his glare
  For the Lord's agony, that, unaware,
  I fell a captive, Lady, to the sway
Of your swift eyes: that seemed no time to stay
  The strokes of Love: I stepped into the snare
  Secure, with no suspicion: then and there
  I found my cue in man's most tragic play.
Love caught me naked to his shaft, his sheaf,
  The entrance for his ambush and surprise
  Against the heart wide open through the eyes,
The constant gate and fountain of my grief:
  How craven so to strike me stricken so,
  Yet from you fully armed conceal his bow!

JOSEPH AUSLANDER

## IN VITA 14

*Movesi il vecchierel canuto e bianco*

The palmer bent, with locks of silver grey,
  Quits the sweet spot where he has pass'd his years,
  Quits his poor family, whose anxious fears
  Paint the loved father fainting on his way;
And trembling, on his aged limbs slow borne,
  In these last days that close his earthly course,
  He, in his soul's strong purpose, finds new force,
  Though weak with age, though by long travel worn:
Thus reaching Rome, led on by pious love,
  He seeks the image of that Saviour Lord
  Whom soon he hopes to meet in bliss above:
So, oft in other forms I seek to trace
  Some charm, that to my heart may yet afford
  A faint resemblance of thy matchless grace.[2]

LADY DACRE

## IN VITA 28

*Solo e pensoso i più deserti campi*

Alone and ever weary with dark care
   I seek the solitude of desert ways,
   Casting about the while a timid gaze
   Lest alien steps my refuge seek to share.
No other shield I find against the stare
   Of curious folk; too clear my face displays
   In ashen cheerlessness how cruel the blaze
   That burns within, and lays my secret bare.
'Tis only hills, I think, and silent streams
   And meadows and deep thickets that can know
   The tenor of my life, from men concealed.
Yet not so wide I wander with my dreams
   But Love comes with me, following where I go,
   And long we parley on the lonely weald.

T. G. BERGIN

## IN VITA 47

*Benedetto sia 'l giorno e 'l mese e l'anno*

Blest be the year, the month, the hour, the day,
   The season and the time, and point of space,
   And blest the beauteous country and the place
   Where first of two bright eyes I felt the sway:
Blest the sweet pain of which I was the prey,
   When newly doomed Love's sovereign law to embrace
   And blest the bow and shaft to which I trace
   The wound that to my inmost heart found way:
Blest be the ceaseless accents of my tongue,
   Unwearied breathing my loved lady's name:
   Blest my fond wishes, sighs, and tears, and pains:
Blest be the lays in which her praise I sung,
   That on all sides acquired to her fair fame,
   And blest my thoughts! for o'er them all she reigns.

LADY DACRE

## IN VITA 69

*Erano i capei d'oro a l'aura sparsi,*

Loose to the breeze her golden tresses flow'd
  Wildly in thousand mazy ringlets blown,
  And from her eyes unconquer'd glances shone,
  Those glances now so sparingly bestow'd;
And true or false, meseem'd some signs she show'd
  As o'er her cheek soft pity's hue was thrown.
  I, whose whole breast with love's soft food was sown,
  What wonder if at once my bosom glow'd?
Graceful she moved, with more than mortal mien,
  In form an angel; and her accents won
  Upon the ear with more than human sound.
A spirit heavenly pure, a living sun,
  Was what I saw; and if no more 'twere seen,
  T'unbend the bow will never heal the wound.[3]

ANON., Oxford, 1795

## CANZONE

*Chiare, fresche e dolci acque*

Clear, fresh, and dulcet streams,
Which the fair shape, who seems
To me sole woman, haunted at noon-tide;
Fair bough, so gently fit,
(I sigh to think of it)
Which lent a pillar to her lovely side;
And turf, and flowers bright-eyed,
O'er which her folded gown
Flowed like an angel's down;
And you, O holy air and hushed,
Where first my heart at her sweet glances gushed:
Give ear, give ear, with one consenting,
To my last words, my last and my lamenting.

If 'tis my fate below,
And Heaven will have it so,
That Love must close these dying eyes in tears,
May my poor dust be laid
In middle of your shade,
While my soul, naked, mounts to its own spheres.
The thought would calm my fears,
When taking, out of breath,
The doubtful step of death;
For never could my spirit find
A stiller port after the stormy wind;
Nor in more calm, abstracted bourne,
Slip from my travailed flesh, and from my bones outworn.


Perhaps, some future hour,
To her accustomed bower
Might come the untamed, and yet the gentle she;
And where she saw me first,
Might turn with eyes athirst
And kinder joy to look again for me;
Then, oh! the charity!
Seeing amidst the stones
The earth that held my bones,
A sigh for very love at last
Might ask of Heaven to pardon me the past:
And Heaven itself could not say nay,
As with her gentle veil she wiped the tears away.


How well I call to mind,
When from those boughs the wind
Shook down upon her bosom flower on flower;
And there she sat, meek-eyed,
In midst of all that pride,
Sprinkled and blushing through an amorous shower:
Some to her hair paid dower,
And seemed to dress the curls,
Queenlike, with gold and pearls;

Some, snowing on her drapery stopped,
Some on the earth, some on the water dropped;
While others, fluttering from above,
Seemed wheeling round in pomp, and saying, "Here
    reigns Love."

How often then I said,
Inward, and filled with dread,
"Doubtless this creature came from Paradise!"
For at her look the while,
Her voice, and her sweet smile,
And heavenly air, truth parted from mine eyes;
So that, with long-drawn sighs,
I said, as far from men,
"How came I here, and when?"
I had forgotten; and alas!
Fancied myself in heaven, not where I was;
And from that time till this, I bear
Such love for the green bower, I cannot rest elsewhere.[4]

LEIGH HUNT

## CANZONE

### *Italia mia*

O my own Italy! though words are vain
The mortal wounds to close,
Unnumbered, that thy beauteous bosom stain,
Yet may it soothe my pain
To sigh for Tyber's woes,
And Arno's wrongs, as on Po's saddened shore
Sorrowing I wander, and my numbers pour.
Ruler of heaven! By the all-pitying love
That could thy Godhead move
To dwell a lowly sojourner on earth,
Turn, Lord! on this thy chosen land thine eye:

See, God of Charity!
From what light cause this cruel war has birth;
And the hard hearts by savage discord steeled,
Thou, Father, from on high,
Touch by my humble voice, that stubborn wrath may
 yield!


Ye, to whose sovereign hands the fates confide
Of this fair land the reins—
(This land for which no pity wrings your breast)—
Why does the stranger's sword her plains invest?
That her green fields be dyed,
Hope ye, with blood from the barbarians' veins?
Beguiled by error weak,
Ye see not, though to pierce so deep ye boast,
Who love, or faith, in venal bosoms seek:
When thronged your standards most,
Ye are encompassed most by hostile bands.
O hideous deluge gathered in strange lands,
That rushing down amain
O'erwhelms our every native lovely plain!
Alas, if our own hands
Have thus our weal betrayed, who shall our cause
 sustain?


Well did kind Nature, guardian of our state,
Rear her rude Alpine heights,
A lofty rampart against German hate;
But blind ambition, seeking his own ill,
With ever restless will,
To the pure gales contagion foul invites:
Within the same strait fold
The gentle flocks and wolves relentless throng,
Where still meek innocence must suffer wrong:
And these—oh, shame avowed!—
Are of the lawless hordes no tie can hold:

Fame tells how Marius' sword
Erewhile their bosoms gored—
Nor has Time's hand aught blurred the record proud!
When they who, thirsting, stooped to quaff the flood,
With the cool waters mixed, drank of a comrade's blood!

Great Caesar's name I pass, who o'er our plains
Poured forth the ensanguined tide,
Drawn by our own good swords from out their veins;
But now—nor know I what ill stars preside—
Heaven holds this land in hate,
To you the thanks—whose hands control her helm—
You, whose rash feuds despoil
Of all the beauteous earth the fairest realm.
Are ye impelled by judgment, crime, or fate,
To oppress the desolate?
From broken fortunes and from humble toil
The hard-earned dole to wring,
While from afar ye bring
Dealers in blood, bartering their souls for hire?
In truth's great cause I sing,
Nor hatred nor disdain my earnest lay inspire.

Nor mark ye yet, confirmed by proof on proof,
Bavaria's perfidy,
Who strikes in mockery, keeping death aloof?
(Shame, worse than aught of loss, in honor's eye!)
While ye, with honest rage, devoted pour
Your inmost bosom's gore!
Yet give one hour to thought,
And ye shall own how little he can hold
Another's glory dear who sets his own at nought.
O Latin blood of old,
Arise and wrest from obloquy thy fame,
Nor bow before a name
Of hollow sound, whose power no laws enforce.
For if barbarians rude
Have higher minds subdued,
Ours, ours the crime—not such wise Nature's course.

Ah, is not this the soil my foot first pressed?
And here, in cradled rest,
Was I not softly hushed? here fondly reared?
Ah, is this not my country? so endeared
By every filial tie.
In whose lap shrouded both my parents lie.
Oh, by this tender thought,
Your torpid bosoms to compassion wrought,
Look on the people's grief,
Who, after God, of you expect relief;
And if ye but relent,
Virtue shall rouse her in embattled might,
Against blind fury bent,
Nor long shall doubtful hang the unequal fight;
For no—the ancient flame
Is not extinguished yet, that raised the Italian name.


Mark, soverign Lords, how Time, with pinion strong
Swift hurries life along.
Even now, behold, Death presses on the rear.
We sojourn here a day—the next, are gone.
The soul disrobed—alone,
Must shuddering seek the doubtful pass we fear.
Oh, at the dreaded bourne,
Abase the lofty brow of wrath and scorn,
(Storms adverse to the eternal calm on high!)
And ye, whose cruelty
Has sought another's harm, by fairer deed
Of heart, or hand, or intellect, aspire
To win the honest meed
Of just renown—the noble mind's desire.
Thus sweet on earth the stay,
Thus to the spirit pure unbarred is Heaven's way.


My song, with courtesy and numbers sooth,
Thy daring reasons grace,
For thou the mighty in their pride of place
Must woo to gentle ruth,

Whose haughty will long evil customs nurse,
Ever to truth averse.
Thee better fortunes wait,
Among the virtuous few—the truly great.
Tell them—but who shall bid my terrors cease?
Peace, peace, on thee I call, return, O heaven-born
    peace! [5]

LADY DACRE

## IN VITA 102

*S'amor non è, che dunque è quel ch'io sento?*

If no love is, O God, what fele I so?
   And if love is, what thing and which is he?
   If love be good, from whennes cometh my woo?
   If it be wikke, a wonder thynketh me,
   When every torment and adversite
   That cometh of hym, may to me savory thinke,
   For ay thurst I, the more that ich it drynke.
And if that at myn owen lust I brenne,
   From whennes cometh my waillynge and my pleynte?
   If harm agree me, wherto pleyne I thenne?
   I noot, ne whi unwery that I feynte.
   O quike deth, O swete harm so queynte,
   How may of the in me swich quantite,
   But if that I consente that it be?
And if that I consente, I wrongfully
   Compleyne, iwis. Thus possed to and fro,
   Al sterelees withinne a boot am I
   Amydde the see, bitwixen wyndes two,
   That in contrarie stonden evere mo.
   Allas! what is this wondre maladie?
   For hete of cold, for cold of hete, I dye. [6]

GEOFFREY CHAUCER

## IN VITA 104

*Pace non trovo e non ho da far guerra;*

I find no peace, and all my war is done;
    I fear and hope, I burn and freeze like ice;
    I fly above the wind, yet can I not arise;
    And nought I have, and all the world I season.
That looseth nor locketh holdeth me in prison,
    And holdeth me not, yet can I 'scape no wise;
    Nor letteth me live, nor die, at my devise,
    And yet of death it giveth none occasion.
Without eyen, I see; and without tongue, I plain;
    I desire to perish, and yet I askë health;
    I love another, and thus I hate myself;
I feed me in sorrow, and laugh in all my pain.
    Likewise displeaseth me both death and life,
    And my delight is causer of this strife.

SIR THOMAS WYATT


## IN VITA 113

*Pommi ove'l sole occide i fiori e l'erba*

Set me whereas the sun doth parch the green,
    Or where his beams do not dissolve the ice,
    In temperate heat where he is felt and seen;
    In the presence prest of people, mad or wise;
Set me in high or yet in low degree,
    In longest night or in the shortest day,
    In clearest sky or where clouds thickest be,
    In lusty youth or when my hairs are gray.
Set me in heaven, in earth, or else in hell;
    In hill, or dale, or in the foaming flood;
    Thrall or at large, alive whereso I dwell,
Sick or in health, in evil fame or good:
    Hers will I be, and only with this thought
    Content myself although my chance be nought.

HENRY HOWARD, EARL OF SURREY

## IN VITA 156

*Passa la nave mia colma d'oblio*

My galley chargéd with forgetfulness
    Thorrough sharp seas, in winter nights, doth pass
    'Tween rock and rock; and eke mine enemy, alas,
    That is my lord, steereth with cruelness;
And every oar a thought in readiness,
    As though that death were light in such a case.
    An endless wind doth tear the sail apace,
    Of forcéd sighs and trusty fearfulness;
A rain of tears, a cloud of dark disdain,
    Have done the wearied cords great hinderance;
    Wreathéd with error and eke with ignorance,
The stars be hid that led me to this pain;
    Drownéd is reason, that should me consort,
    And I remain despairing of the port.

                      SIR THOMAS WYATT

## IN VITA 157

*Una candida cerva sopra l'erba*

    A fair white hind with golden horns
appeared to me in a green field
between two rivers, in the shade of a laurel,
at sunrise, in the bitter season.
Her bearing was so sweetly proud
that I left my labors to pursue her,
like a miser who in his search for treasure
undergoes hardship with pleasure.
    "Let no one touch me," about her fair neck
was inscribed with diamonds and topaz;
"By my Caesar's order I go free."
By now the sun had climbed to midday;
my eyes were weary with watching yet unsated;
whereon, I fell into the water, and she vanished.[7]

                      HAROLD M. PRIEST

Whoso list to hunt, I know where is an hind,
  But as for me—alas, I may no more.
  The vain travail hath wearied me so sore,
  I am of them that farthest cometh behind.
Yet may I, by no means, my wearied mind
  Draw from the deer; but as she fleeth afore
  Fainting I follow. I leave off therefore,
  Since in a net I seek to hold the wind.
Who list her hunt, I put him out of doubt,
  As well as I, may spend his time in vain.
  And graven with diamonds in letters plain
There is written, her fair neck round about:
  *Noli me tangere*, for Caesar's I am,
  And wild for to hold, though I seem tame.

SIR THOMAS WYATT

## IN MORTE 1

### *Oimè il bel viso, oimè il soave sguardo*

Alas! that liquid look, that lovely face!
  Alas! the poised grace of that golden head!
  Alas! the sweetness of the words she said
  That soothed the savage breast, raised up the base!
Alas! the smile—that dart which I embrace,
  Whose hope is death now that all hope is dead;
  O hadst thou not so late inhabited
  This earth, how queenly would have been thy place!
In thee I burn, in thee still draw my breath,
  Being all thine. Death now has disciplined
  All lesser pain to nothing; no sharp teeth
Can gnaw the constant grief-bright music dinned
  By thy last words, snatched up by jealous Death
  To vanish with their hope upon the wind.[8]

JOSEPH AUSLANDER

Alas! the lovely face, the eyes that save,
    Alas! the charming countenance and proud!
    And the speech that could tame each fierce and loud
    Intellect, and make cowardly men brave!
And alas! the sweet laugh whence came the dire
    Arrow of Death, which is now all my hope:
    Royal soul, more than worthy of empire,
    Only looming too late within our scope!
To you I must aspire, in you suspire;
    For I was yours; and now, bereft of you,
    I suffer less for all my other pains.
You filled me once with hope and with desire,
    When I departed from a joy most true;
    But the wind spread our words across the plains.

ANNA MARIA ARMI

## IN MORTE 2

*Rotta è l'alta colonna e 'l verde lauro*

Broken is the tall column and the green laurel
which furnished shelter for my weary thoughts;
I have lost what I can never hope to find
from Boreas to Auster, from Morocco to the Indian sea.
Thou hast snatched from me, oh Death, my double
    treasure
that made me live happy and walk proud;
neither can earth restore it, nor empire,
nor orient gem, nor heaps of gold.
    But if it be that destiny has so conspired,
how could I but bear a spirit sad,
eyes moist and head bowed low?
Oh life that is so fair to view,
how easily in one morning can it lose
what in many years at great pain was acquired.[9]

HAROLD M. PRIEST

Broken the column and the green bay tree
    That lent a shade to my exhausted thought;
    And I have lost what can nowhere be sought
    In any distant wind or distant sea.
You took away from me my double treasure,
    Death, which had made my life proud and secure;
    What neither earth nor kingdom can allure,
    Nor oriental gem, nor golden measure.
But if to accept this is destiny,
    What can I do but wear eyes wet with tears,
    A sad soul and a face shut to all views?
O life that are so beautiful to see,
    How quickly in one morning do we lose
    What we gained with great pain in many years!

ANNA MARIA ARMI

# IN MORTE 4

*La vita fugge, e non s'arresta un' ora*

Life hurries on, a frantic refugee,
    And Death, with great forced marches, follows fast;
    And all the present leagues with all the past
    And all the future to make war on me.
Anticipation joins to memory
    To search my soul with daggers; and at last,
    Did not damnation set me so aghast,
    I'd put an end to thinking, and be free.
The few glad moments that my heart has known
    Return to me; then I foresee in dread
    The winds upgathering against my ways,
Storm in the harbor, and the pilot prone,
    The mast and rigging down; and dark and dead
    The lovely lights whereon I used to gaze.

MORRIS BISHOP

## IN MORTE 24

*Gli occhi di ch' io parlai sì caldamente*

The eyes, the face, the limbs of heavenly mould
　So long the theme of my impassion'd lay,
　Charms which so stole me from myself away,
　That strange to other men the course I hold;
The crisped locks of pure and lucid gold,
　The lightning of the angelic smile, whose ray
　To earth could all of paradise convey,
　A little dust are now!—to feeling cold!
And yet I live!—but that I live bewail,
　Sunk the loved light that through the tempest led
　My shatter'd bark, bereft of mast and sail:
Hush'd be for aye the song that breathed love's fire!
　Lost is the theme on which my fancy fed,
　And turn'd to mourning my once tuneful lyre.

LADY DACRE

## IN MORTE 42

*Zefiro torna, e 'l bel tempo rimena,*

Zephyr returns, and scatters everywhere
　New flowers and grass, and company does bring,
　Procne and Philomel, in sweet despair,
　And all the tender colors of the Spring.
Never were fields so glad, nor skies so fair;
　And Jove exults in Venus' prospering.
　Love is in all the water, earth, and air,
　And love possesses every living thing.
But to me only heavy sighs return
　For her who carried in her little hand
　My heart's key to her heavenly sojourn.
The birds sing loud above the flowering land;
　Ladies are gracious now.—Where deserts burn
　The beasts still prowl on the ungreening sand.[10]

MORRIS BISHOP

## IN MORTE 43

*Quel rosignuol, che sì soave piagne*

The nightingale that so forlornly weeps
    Perchance his little ones or his dear mate,
    Whose fiery, tender song insatiate
    With sweetness fills the air, his vigil keeps
All night with me, and never tires nor sleeps,
    Reminding me of my unhappy fate.
    For I, oh foolish, know it now too late,
    Death the divinest blooms most quickly reaps.
How blind is he who thinks to stand secure!
    Meseemed those fair lamps, than the sun more bright,
    Could ne'er be quenched, and leave us plunged in night.
Now do I know my cruel destiny
    Would have me learn in tears and agony,
    Nought that delighteth may on earth endure.

ROMILDA RENDEL

## IN MORTE 86

*I' vo piangendo i miei passati tempi*

I mourn unhappy days that are no more,
    Days I have spent in loving mortal thing,
    Cleaving to earth, I who had spirit's wing
    Above the shimmer of our dust to soar.
O Thou who seest my plight, whom I adore,
    Deathless, invisible, heaven's mighty king,
    Unto my frail and weary spirit bring
    Succour and grace, that the eternal shore
After long wandering I may attain,
    And if the passage of my life was vain,
    Oh grant that true at least may be its end.
Unto my death Thy strong assistance lend,
    And to the days that are yet left to me.
    Thou knowest all my hope is fixed in Thee.[11]

ROMILDA RENDEL

## IN MORTE 90

*Vago augelletto che cantando vai*

O lovely little bird, I watch you fly,
  And grieving for the past I hear you sing,
  Seeing the night and winter hastening,
  Seeing the day and happy summer die.
If you could hear my heart in answer cry
  Its pain to your sad tune, you'd swiftly wing
  Into my bosom, comfort you would bring,
  And we would weep together, you and I.
'Tis no equality of woe, I fear;
  Perhaps she lives whom you bewail; from me
  Have greedy death and heaven snatched my dear.
But the dark autumn evening hour sets free
  The memory of many a banished year;
  So let us talk of the past then, tenderly.

MORRIS BISHOP

# Giovanni Boccaccio
## (1313–1375)

Standing next to his friend Petrarch as a humanist and promoter of the Renaissance, Boccaccio was an innovator extraordinary, who set numerous patterns for the writers of the high Renaissance. His *Decameron*, of course, established a prolific form of prose fiction, his *Ameto* served as prototype for the pastoral romance, and his *Filostrato* and *Teseide* established the romance-epic genre for narrative poetry, which was to be developed by Boiardo, Ariosto, and Tasso. His *Life of Dante* was an important pioneering work in literary biography. And his encyclopedic Latin works found many imitators.

His lyrics, often fresh and sometimes delicately sensitive, convey a pagan *joie de vivre* which is his special trademark.

## BALLATA

I am young and fain to sing
In this happy tide of spring
Of love and many a gentle thing.
    I wander through green meadows dight
With blossoms gold and red and white;
Rose by the thorn and lily fair,
Both one and all do I compare
With him who, worshipping my charms,
For aye would fold me in his arms
As one unto his service sworn.
    Then, when I find a flower that seems
Like to the object of my dreams,
I gather it and kiss it there,
I flatter it in accents fair,
My heart outpour, my soul stoop down,
Then weave it in a fragrant crown
Among my flaxen locks to wear.

The rapture nature's floweret gay
Awakes in me doth last alway,
As if I tarried face to face
With him whose true love is my grace;
Thoughts which its fragrancy inspires
I cannot frame to my desires,
My sighs their pilgrimage do trace.

My sighs are neither harsh nor sad
As other women's are, but glad
And tender; in so fond a wise
They seek my love that he replies
By coming hither, and so gives
Delight to her who in him lives
Yet almost wept: "Come, for hope dies."[12]

LORNA DE' LUCCHI

# Angelo Poliziano
## (1454–1494)

Tutor to the sons of Lorenzo de' Medici, he is remembered as one of the great humanist scholar-poets of the Renaissance. He was professor of Greek and Latin at Florence and, with Lorenzo and Ficino, founder of the Platonic Academy, which did much to develop the neo-Platonic doctrines so important to the Renaissance. In addition to a considerable body of lyrics, his works include *Orfeo*, the earliest known example of a masque, and *Stanze per la Giostra*, a long, richly colorful poem about a tournament in which Giuliano de' Medici was victor. The latter work was left unfinished because of the death of the lady symbolized by its heroine and, shortly afterward, the murder of Giuliano.

## BALLATA

I found myself one day all, all alone,
For pastime in a field with blossoms strewn.

I do not think the world a field could show
   With herbs of perfume so surpassing rare;
But when I passed beyond the green hedge-row,
   A thousand flowers around me flourished fair,
   White, pied and crimson, in the summer air;
Among the which I heard a sweet bird's tone.

I found myself one day all, all alone,
For pastime in a field with blossoms strewn.

Her song it was so tender and so clear
   That all the world listened with love; then I

With stealthy feet a-tiptoe drawing near,
  Her golden head and golden wings could spy,
  Her plumes that flashed like rubies neath the sky,
Her crystal beak and throat and bosom's zone.

I found myself one day all, all alone,
For pastime in a field with blossoms strewn.

Fain would I snare her, smit with mighty love;
  But arrow-like she soared, and through the air
Fled to her nest upon the boughs above;
  Wherefore to follow her is all my care,
  For haply I might lure her by some snare
Forth from the woodland wild where she is flown.

I found myself one day all, all alone,
For pastime in a field with blossoms strewn.

Yea, I might spread some net or woven wile;
  But since of singing she doth take such pleasure,
Without or other art or other guile
  I seek to win her with a tuneful measure;
  Therefore in singing spend I all my leisure,
To make by singing this sweet bird my own.

I found myself one day all, all alone,
For pastime in a field with blossoms strewn.

                    JOHN ADDINGTON SYMONDS

# Lorenzo de' Medici
## (1449–1492)

"Lorenzo the Magnificent" was the most brilliant member of the Medici line and one of the most remarkable examples of the versatility so prized during the Renaissance. A "strong man" of the age of tyrants, he was an astute statesman and an enlightened leader, who contributed greatly to the development of Florence in her finest era. In his patronage of the arts he has few peers, and he played a significant role in the famous Platonic Academy. In the best tradition of the Renaissance courtier, he not only exhibited a devotion to letters and a cultivated taste but also wrote a considerable body of lyric poetry and is accounted one of the best lyrists of the Quattrocento. He frequently treats classical themes, but he also handles the Tuscan scene and life engagingly, the country in spring or the city in high carnival. In addition he contributed a volume of spiritual lauds.

## CANZONE

Into a little close of mine I went
    One morning, when the sun with his fresh light
    Was rising all refulgent and unshent.
Rose-trees are planted there in order bright,
    Whereto I turned charmed eyes, and long did stay,
    Taking my fill of that new-found delight.
Red and white roses bloomed upon the spray;
    One opened, leaf by leaf, to greet the morn,
    Shyly at first, then in sweet disarray;
Another, yet a youngling, newly born,
    Scarce struggled from the bud, and there were some
    Whose petals closed them from the air forlorn;
Another fell, and showered the grass with bloom;
    Thus I behold the roses dawn and die,
    And one short hour their loveliness consume.

But while I watched those languid petals lie
  Colorless on cold earth, I could but think
  How vain a thing is youthful bravery.
Trees have their time to bloom on winter's brink;
  Then the rathe blossoms wither in an hour,
  When the brief days of spring towards summer sink
The fruit, as yet unformed, is tart and sour;
  Little by little it grows large, and weighs
  The strong boughs down with slow persistent power;
Nor without peril can the branches raise
  Their burden; now they stagger 'neath the weight
  Still growing, and are bent above the ways;
Soon autumn comes, and the ripe, ruddy freight
  Is gathered: the glad season will not stay;
  Flowers, fruit, and leaves are now all desolate.
Pluck the rose, therefore, maiden, while 'tis May.

                    JOHN ADDINGTON SYMONDS

# Lodovico Ariosto
## (1474–1533)

The two greatest names in Italian Renaissance poetry were Ariosto and Tasso, but their fame came from their long poems rather than from their lyrics. Ariosto was a court poet at Ferrara under the patronage of the ruling house of Este, as was Tasso a generation later. Ariosto's major work, *Orlando Furioso*, was basically a tale of Medieval adventure, romance, and wizardry around the French hero Roland, his uncle Charlemagne, and the peers of France in their war against the Saracens. However, Ariosto was steeped in classical studies and he added to his poem not only episodes adapted from Homer, Virgil, and Ovid but also a quality of style which is distinctly Virgilian. He has a fertility of imagination, a fluent narrative, brilliant irony, and rich humor. Spenser's *Faerie Queene* was greatly indebted to the *Orlando Furioso*, both in the general matter of style and for numerous episodes.

## CAPITOLO VIII

O night, more shining and clear, sweeter, gladder,
more fortunate than the day to me, so much the
dearer as I little expected you.

Stars learned in helping love's own thefts that
dimmed your light, not by you were the friendly
shades broken.

Timely sleep, that leaving two wide-awake lovers
alone, had so overcome everyone else, that I was invisible.

Kindly door, that were opened with so subdued and
low a sound, that he who was close to you hardly heard.

O mind still uncertain if it dreamed or not, when I
saw myself clasped by my goddess, and my mouth was
enclosed in hers.

O blessed hand, that next lead me; o quiet steps
that proceed me, o room, that then so secure me.

O repeated embraces, that bind hips, breast, neck,
with so many twinings that ivy or acanthus have fewer.

Mouth, whence I sup ambrosia, nor ever come away
satiate; o soft tongue, o dewiness, in which I bathe
and soften my burnt heart again.

Breath, that inhale far more pleasant fragrance than
the phoenix on his pyre, on which he flames and dies,
yields among Indians or Sabaeans.

O bed, witness to my pleasures; bed, cause of my
tasting a sweetness such that I do not envy the gods
their nectar.

O bed, giver of just rewards, bed, which was often
moved, ruffled, and shaken by the loving tussle.

All of you, one by one, shall I keep in everlasting
memory as ministers of my high pleasure, and I praise
you as much as in my power.

Nor should I keep more silent about you, lantern,
that, staying awake with us, desire that my eyes
should perceive the good I know.

My happiness was doubled through you; nor can
love enjoyed by extinguished light be truly said
to be perfect.

How much more it adds, to such sweet consequence, to
feed the gaze upon the divine eyes, her forehead, her
ivory bosom;

look upon her eyelids and hair of curling gold, look
on the roses shed upon her lips, put your mouth there,
and fear no thorns;

look upon her limbs, which no other whiteness can equal
and think as you look that heaven's graces were never
wanting there,

and now indulge one sense, and now another and in such a
style that all have play, and not even one stays banished!

O why are the fruits of love so rare? o why the time for
enjoying them so short? why so long and endless are our griefs?

Why, envious Dawn, ah me! did you leave your ancient
Tithonus so promptly, and speed my time of parting?

If only I could hurt you like that, for I am your enemy!
If your old man bores you, why not find a younger lover?
and live, and let live in joy!

*Penguin Book of Italian Verse*

# Giovanni Guidiccioni
## (1500–1541)

A humanist cleric, he held numerous important ecclesiastical and civil offices: canon of Lucca Cathedral, Governor of Rome, Bishop of Fossombrone, Papal Nuncio to Spain, and Governor of Romagna. His poetry shows an allegiance to Petrarch. The following selection is obviously reminiscent of the canzone "Italia Mia."

## TO ITALY

Thou who didst nurture mighty men of old
  Who ere these darkened days the world did sway,
  Once happy home of gods secure and gay,
  Now 'neath the bitter rule of strangers cold,
Oh how may I thy sovereign power behold
  Trampled and crushed, thy greatness passed away
  And all thy splendour, without sore dismay,
  Or hear unmoved thy mournful story told?
If in thy fall such majesty dost bear,
  And echoes in my heart thy name so loud
  Thy vestiges I cannot but adore,
What were't to see thee throned 'mid honours proud,
  A queen, and on thy worshipful bright hair
  A jewelled diadem, thy crown of yore?

ROMILDA RENDEL

# Giovanni Strozzi

## (1517–1570)

A member of a powerful Florentine family which was traditionally in opposition to the Medici, Giovanni was a minor versifier and held the office of consul in the famous Academy of the Umidi. His quatrain on Michelangelo's statue is his chief, if not his only, claim to literary recognition.

### ON BUONARROTI'S STATUE OF NIGHT

Night, that thou seest in so sweet attitude
  sleeping, by an Angel was sculptured
  in this stone; and as she is sleeping, she has life.
  Wake her, if thou believest not, and she will speak to
    thee.[13]

HAROLD M. PRIEST

# Michelangelo Buonarroti

## (1475–1564)

Michelangelo's standing as a poet has been recognized only tardily, primarily because of the impression made by the first (posthumous) edition, which was "corrected," polished, and emasculated by the artist's well-meaning grand-nephew. Joseph Tusiani gives Michelangelo the unqualified rank of "greatest lyric poet of the Renaissance," and George Kay, editor of the *Penguin Book of Italian Verse*, has represented him with more poems than any other poet in the entire anthology.

The volume of his verses had to be made up by adding to the group of poems which he intended for publication a strange assortment of pieces written on pages filled with anatomical sketches or on the backs of letters that he saved, some of them complete poems, some fragments or *abbozzi*.

Though he sometimes attempted to follow the Petrarchan manner, his best poems strike a different note, radically contrasting with the polite tradition of the period. The poet is engaged in a struggle over hard thoughts whose working into language is like the treatment of granite or marble. In this he shows a kinship to Dante, whom he greatly admired. The torment of emotions is powerfully revealed through his rude words and eccentric grammar. It is curious to note how often he reminds the English reader of Donne, both with respect to his involved thought patterns and his rasping and vehement tone.

Those of his poems touching on the nature of art—of sculpture and painting—or referring to well known pieces like "Night" in the Medici Chapel or the Sistine ceiling rouse a ready interest in many readers. But his range of themes includes a few pieces of rough humor, many devoutly religious poems, reflections on old age, and poems of love and beauty—all of them interwoven and related so that we see how a study of beauty leads to a love of God or how the inspiration of his beloved clears his soul of the shell of flesh as a sculptor chips away marble to release the statue in the rock.

His love poems were written to several different persons, the most important being Vittoria Colonna and Tommaso de' Cavalieri. His friendship for Vittoria, a celebrated poetess, began in his sixty-third year, and accounted for a considerable body of his best love poems, some of them written after her death. Another very considerable group of poems was written to Tommaso de' Cavalieri, whose face and form excited his sculptor's eye and whose indifferent response to proffered friendship evoked poems whose language is often similar to that of the poems to Vittoria. This feature of his poetry provides an instructive parallel to those sonnets of Shakespeare which were addressed to a man.

## TO NIGHT

*(Buonarroti's Reply)*

Caro m'è il sonno e più l'esser di sasso,
    mentre che 'l danno e la vergogna dura.
    Non veder, non sentir m'è gran ventura;
    però non mi destar, deh! parla basso.

Dear is sleep; better to be stone now,
    while envy and corruption vile endure.
    Neither to see nor hear is blessing sure;
    therefore disturb me not; pray speak low.[14]

HAROLD M. PRIEST

## DAVID

*(Verses Written on a Sketch of David)*

David with the sling
    And I with the bow,
    Michelangelo.

Broken is the tall column and the green [laurel.][15]

HAROLD M. PRIEST

*To Giovanni da Pistoia*

# ON THE PAINTING OF THE SISTINE CHAPEL

I've grown a goitre by dwelling in this den—
  as cats from stagnant streams in Lombardy,
  or in what other land they hap to be—
  which drives the belly close beneath the chin:
my beard turns up to heaven; my nape falls in,
  fixed on my spine: my breast-bone visibly
  grows like a harp: a rich embroidery
  bedews my face from brush-drops thick and thin.
My loins into my paunch like levers grind:
  my buttock like a crupper bears my weight;
  my feet unguided wander to and fro;
in front my skin grows loose and long; behind,
  by bending it becomes more taut and strait;
  crosswise I strain me like a Syrian bow:
    whence false and quaint, I know,
  must be the fruit of squinting brain and eye;
  for ill can aim the gun that bends awry.
    Come then, Giovanni, try
  to succour my dead pictures and my fame;
  since foul I fare and painting is my shame.[16]

JOHN ADDINGTON SYMONDS

# TO VITTORIA COLONNA

As when one sets himself, Lady, to raise
  a living figure and unfold
  in alpine stone and cold,
  as stone is chipped away, he form imparts;
so any acts that merit praise
  from soul that trembling starts,
  are hidden 'neath the covering of flesh
  within a hard and crusty unworked shell.
Thou only from my outward parts
  canst raise deeds fair and fresh,
    for in me neither strength nor will doth dwell.

HAROLD M. PRIEST

## THE LOVER AND THE SCULPTOR

The best of artists hath no thought to show
  which the rough stone in its superfluous shell
  doth not include; to break the marble spell
  is all the hand that serves the brain can do.
The ill I shun, the good I seek, even so
  in thee, fair lady, proud, ineffable,
  lies hidden: but the art I wield so well
  works adverse to my wish, and lays me low.
Therefore not love, nor thy transcendent face,
  nor cruelty, nor fortune, nor disdain,
  cause my mischance, nor fate, nor destiny;
since in thy heart thou carriest death and grace
  enclosed together, and my worthless brain
  can draw forth only death to feed on me.[17]

JOHN ADDINGTON SYMONDS

## THE ARTIST AND HIS WORK

How can that be, lady, which all men learn
  by long experience? Shapes that seem alive,
  wrought in hard mountain marble, will survive
  their maker, whom the years to dust return!
Thus to effect cause yields. Art hath her turn,
  and triumphs over Nature. I, who strive
  with Sculpture, know this well; her wonders live
  in spite of time and death, those tyrants stern.
So I can give long life to both of us
  in either way, by colour or by stone,
  making the semblance of thy face and mine.
Centuries hence when both are buried, thus
  thy beauty and my sadness shall be shown,
  and men shall say, 'For her 'twas wise to pine.'[18]

JOHN ADDINGTON SYMONDS

Out of a living stone
Art wants on earth my lady's face to live
All years. What should God say,
If I can claim but this, and He made *her*,
Divine, not mortal, for all eyes to see?
And yet it fades—forever cannot be.
Oh, luck is lame, if stone
Can live, and she must die!
Who will avenge her, then? Nature alone,
If the work of its children can survive,
While its own work is soon erased by time.

JOSEPH TUSIANI

## BEAUTY AND THE ARTIST

A heart of flaming sulphur, flesh of tow,
  bones of dry wood, a soul without a guide
  to curb the fiery will, the ruffling pride
  of fierce desires that from the passions flow;
a sightless mind that weak and lame doth go
  mid snares and pitfalls scattered far and wide;—
  what wonder if the first chance brand applied
  to fuel massed like this should make it glow?
Add beauteous art, which, brought with us from heaven,
  will conquer nature;—so divine a power
  belongs to him who strives with every nerve.
If I was made for art, from childhood given
  a prey for burning beauty to devour,
  I blame the mistress I was born to serve.[19]

JOHN ADDINGTON SYMONDS

You have a face that's sweeter than grape mash,
that shines as though 'twere tracked o'er by a snail,
more beauteous than a turnip; teeth that flash
as white, I swear, as is a parsnip pale;

you might entice the pope to conduct rash;
your eyes a treacle color, clear and hale;
your hairs more blond, or white, than any leek:
before I die, oh grant the boon I seek.

Your beauty strikes me as more beautiful
than a man's face depicted in a shrine;
to me your mouth is like a wallet full
of beans; that's much the same as mine;
your brows, like sooty fryingpan, are dull,
more bent than Syrian bow their arching line;
when sifting meal, your cheeks are white and red,
resembling poppies by fresh cheese or bread.

And when I gaze upon your breasts, the pair
resembles two nice melons in a sack,
whence I am kindled, quick as tow to flare,
even though I'm fagged or have been cudgeled black.
I think: if you still had that goblet fair,
I'd follow only you, like hound on track:
wherefore, if I could have a monstrous block,
a wonder I'd create from the bare rock.[20]

HAROLD M. PRIEST


## MADGRIGAL

Ravished by all that to the eyes is fair,
Yet hungry for the joys that truly bless,
My soul can find no stair
To mount to heaven, save earth's loveliness.
For from the stars above
Descends a glorious light
That lifts our longing to their highest height
And bears the name of love.
Nor is there aught can move
A gentle heart, or purge or make it wise,
But beauty and the starlight of her eyes.[21]

GEORGE SANTAYANA

Danger of loss eternal
Comes from your youthful breath
To one who is, like me, so close to death;
Therefore, I arm, intending
To save myself from it, before I die.
But oh, your love can tie
So sweetly, that, despite
My death, I am not free;
And loss eternal does not scare at all:
One moment cannot make two decades fall.[22]

JOSEPH TUSIANI

## LOVE LIFTS TO GOD

*(To Tommaso de' Cavalieri)*

From thy fair face I learn, O my loved lord,
    that which no mortal tongue can rightly say;
    the soul, imprisoned in her house of clay,
    holpen by thee to God hath often soared:
and though the vulgar, vain, malignant horde
    attribute what their grosser wills obey,
    yet shall this fervent homage that I pay,
    this love, this faith, pure joys for us afford.
Lo, all the lovely things we find on earth,
    resemble for the soul that rightly sees
    that source of bliss divine which gave us birth:
nor have we first-fruits or remembrances
    of heaven elsewhere. Thus, loving loyally,
    I rise to God, and make death sweet by thee.[23]

JOHN ADDINGTON SYMONDS

Just as a silkworm with much selfless pain,
    to make man happy, leaves its dear cocoon
    and, dying, gives the hand a silken boon
    and, dead, through such a gift, is born again;

so would that my skin, falling dead and vain,
 could be his living flesh! Oh how I soon
 would change, as does a snake beneath a stone,
 my nature and my fate, through such a gain!
Would that I were—my hairy skin alone—
 the skin that makes with its soft hairs a plate
 (O happy dress!) around his handsome breast
all day! Were I two slippers he could own
 and use as base to his majestic weight!
 I would enjoy two snowy feet at least.[24]

JOSEPH TUSIANI

Just as an empty form
Awaits its gold or silver liquefied,
And, broken, then, reveals
The perfect work; thus I can only fill
With inner fire of love my void and need
Of the immortal beauty of my lady,
Both mind and heart of these my fragile days.
Through such a narrow space
Her gentleness and love pour into me,
That, to draw forth her perfect image, I
Must agonize and die.[25]

JOSEPH TUSIANI

I know not if from uncreated spheres
 some longed-for ray it be that warms my breast,
 or lesser light, in memory expressed,
 of some once lovely face, that reappears,
or passing rumor ringing in my ears,
 or dreamy vision, once my bosom's guest,
 that left behind I know not what unrest,
 haply the reason of these wayward tears.
But what I feel and seek, what leads me on,
 comes not of me; nor can I tell aright
 where shines the hidden star that sheds this light.

Since I beheld thee, sweet and bitter fight
within me. Resolution have I none.
Can this be, Master, what thine eyes have done?

GEORGE SANTAYANA

## LOVE'S JUSTIFICATION

It must be right sometimes to entertain
  chaste love with hope not over-credulous;
  since if all human loves were impious,
  unto what end did God the world ordain?
If I love thee and bend beneath thy reign,
  'tis for the sake of beauty glorious
  which in thine eyes divine is stored for us,
  and drives all evil thought from its domain.
That is not love whose tyranny we own
  in loveliness that every moment dies;
  which, like the face it worships, fades away:
true love is that which the pure heart hath known,
  which alters not with time or death's decay,
  yielding on earth earnest of Paradise.

JOHN ADDINGTON SYMONDS

## LOVE IS A REFINER'S FIRE

It is with fire that blacksmiths iron subdue
  unto fair form, the image of their thought:
  nor without fire hath any artist wrought
  gold to its utmost purity of hue.
Nay, nor the unmatched phoenix lives anew,
  unless she burn: if then I am distraught
  by fire, I may to better life be brought
  like those whom death restores nor years undo.

The fire whereof I speak, is my great cheer;
    such power it hath to renovate and raise
    me who was almost numbered with the dead;
and since by nature fire doth find its sphere
    soaring aloft, and I am all ablaze,
    heavenward with it my flight must needs be sped.[26]

JOHN ADDINGTON SYMONDS

If my rough hammer gives a human face
    to this or that of all hard blocks that wait,
    it is another smith makes me create,
    controlling each my motion, each my pace.
But that high hammer beyond stars and space
    makes self, and others, with each stroke, more great
    and bright; and since the first must generate
    all hammers, *that* gives life to all, always.
And since the most effective is that blow
    which falls from highest in the smithy, mine
    shall fall no more—my hammer having flown.
Now here am I, unskilled, and do not know
    how to go on, unless the smith divine
    teaches me how, who am on earth alone.[27]

JOSEPH TUSIANI

## DANTE

What should be said of him cannot be said;
    by too great splendor is his name attended;
    to blame is easier those who him offended,
    than reach the faintest glory round him shed.
This man descended to the doomed and dead
    for our instruction; then to God ascended;
    Heaven opened wide to him its portals splendid,
    who from his country's, closed against him, fled.
Ungrateful land! To its own prejudice
    nurse of his fortunes; and this showeth well
    that the most perfect most of grief shall see.

Among a thousand proofs let one suffice,
    that as his exile hath no parallel,
    Ne'er walked the earth a greater man than he.[28]

HENRY WADSWORTH LONGFELLOW

## ON ROME IN THE PONTIFICATE OF JULIUS II

Here helms and swords are made of chalices:
    the blood of Christ is sold so much the quart:
    his cross and thorns are spears and shields; and short
    must be the time ere even his patience cease.
Nay let him come no more to raise the fees
    of this foul sacrilege beyond report!
    For Rome still flays and sells him at the court,
    where paths are closed to virtue's fair increase.
Now were fit time for me to scrape a treasure!
    Seeing that work and gain are gone; while he
    who wears the robe, is my Medusa still.
God welcomes poverty perchance with pleasure:
    but of that better life what hope have we,
    when the blessed banner leads to nought but ill?[29]

JOHN ADDINGTON SYMONDS

When contracting, the lash seems not to cause
    Suffering with its shadow: with no pain
    To both extremities the eye still goes.
Beneath, the eye, revolving with no strain,
    Shows but a little part of its own ball,
    And the span of its clearness is in vain,
For, covered by the lash, it does not fall
    Or climb, making the lid, which, used, gives room
    To less wrinkles, appear both short and small.
The white, true white; the black is black as tomb
    (If that can be); the yellow, leonine,
    Which makes one fibril to the other come.
Though touched above and under its own confine,
    The eye allows no yellow, black, or white
. . . . . . . . . . . . . . . . . . . . . . . . . . . . . . . . . . . .[30]

JOSEPH TUSIANI

Why should it come so seldom, why so late,
That inner flame which, held by burning trust,
Lifts suddenly my heart from this vile dust
To heaven, where it fails through its own fate?
Perhaps, such a long time I had to wait
For this new ardent wonder, for one must
Realize what is rare is more august,
And beauty long-desired is far more great.

Night is the interval, and day is light:
One freezes all my heart, the other warms it
With love and faith and with immortal fire.
. . . . . . . . . . . . . . . . . . . . . . . . . . . . . . . . . . . .
. . . . . . . . . . . . . . . . . . . . . . . . . . . . . . . . . . . .
. . . . . . . . . . . . . . . . . . . . . . . . . . . . . . . .[31]

JOSEPH TUSIANI

## LIGHT AND DARKNESS

He who ordained, when first the world began,
    time, that was not before creation's hour,
    divided it, and gave the sun's high power
    to rule the one, the moon the other span:
thence fate and changeful chance and fortune's ban
    did in one moment down on mortals shower:
    to me they portioned darkness for a dower;
    dark hath my lot been since I was a man.
Myself am ever mine own counterfeit;
    and as deep night grows still more dim and dun,
    so still of more misdoing must I rue:
meanwhile this solace to my soul is sweet,
    that my black night doth make more clear the sun
    which at your birth was given to wait on you.[32]

JOHN ADDINGTON SYMONDS

Simply because the sun does not embrace
   with lucent arms this cold and humid globe,
   they thought of calling 'night' his other face,
   that second sun they fail to know and prove.
Oh, but so frail is night, that one quick blaze
   of torch can rend her life, and can disrobe her;
   and so foolish is she, that the swift trace
   of a gunshot can make her bleed and throb.
If something she must be, she doubtless is
   the daughter of the sun and of the earth:
   one gives her life, the other holds her here.
Wrong are all those who praise her qualities:
   she is so dark, lost, lonely, that the birth
   of one small firefly can make war on her.

JOSEPH TUSIANI

## A PRAYER FOR PURIFICATION

Perchance that I might learn what pity is,
   that I might laugh at erring men no more,
   secure in my own strength as heretofore,
   my soul hath fallen from her state of bliss:
nor know I under any flag but this
   how fighting I may 'scape those perils sore,
   or how survive the rout and horrid roar
   of adverse hosts, if I Thy succour miss.
O flesh! O blood! O cross! O pain extreme!
   By you may those foul sins be purified,
   wherein my fathers were, and I was born!
Lo, Thou alone art good: let Thy supreme
   pity my state of evil cleanse and hide—
   so near to death, so far from God, forlorn.[33]

JOHN ADDINGTON SYMONDS

## HEART-COLDNESS

Fain would I wish what my heart cannot will:
    between it and the fire a veil of ice
    deadens the fire, so that I deal in lies;
    my words and actions are discordant still.
I love Thee with my tongue, then mourn my fill;
    for love warms not my heart, nor can I rise,
    or ope the doors of Grace, who from the skies
    might flood my soul, and pride and passion kill.
Rend Thou the veil, dear Lord! Break Thou that wall
    which with its stubbornness retards the rays
    of that bright sun this earth hath dulled for me!
Send down Thy promised light to cheer and fall
    on Thy fair spouse, that I with love may blaze,
    and, free from doubt, my heart feel only Thee!

JOHN ADDINGTON SYMONDS

## ON THE BRINK OF DEATH

Now hath my life across a stormy sea
    like a frail bark reached that wide port where all
    are bidden, ere the final reckoning fall
    of good and evil for eternity.
Now know I well how that fond phantasy
    which made my soul the worshiper and thrall
    of earthly art, is vain; how criminal
    is that which all men seek unwillingly.
Those amorous thoughts which were so lightly dressed,
    what are they when the double death is nigh?
    The one I know for sure, the other dread.
Painting nor sculpture now can lull to rest
    my soul that turns to His great love on high,
    whose arms to clasp us on the cross were spread.[34]

JOHN ADDINGTON SYMONDS

# Luigi Alamanni
## (1495–1556)

A native of Florence, he "took the wrong side," conspiring against Giulio de' Medici, who became Pope Clement VII. Escaping to France, he prospered under the patronage of Francis I, and served as major-domo to Catherine de' Medici. His lyric poems, which have a refinement and dignity, attracted the attention of English poets, notably Sir Thomas Wyatt.

## ON HIS RETURN TO ITALY

Therefore, proud Italy, I, by God's grace,
    After six years come back to gaze on thee,
    This only, for barbarians fill the place
    Where I once lay upon thy breast, ah me!
With tearful eyes and drooping head I greet
    The country of my birth, to her I yearn
    With pain and fear and anger, stripped of sweet
Delight and every hope. Then I return
Again beyond the Alps, all wreathed with snow,
    To honest Gallic earth, a better friend
    To strangers than thou art unto thine own!
There, in a sheltered haven till the end
    I will abide, mid those cool valleys lone,
    Since Heaven agrees and thou hast willed it so.

LORNA DE' LUCCHI

# Giovanni della Casa
## (1503–1556)

He was born in Florence, studied at Bologna, and lived much of his adult life in Venice and Rome. Besides holding important church offices—Archbishop of Benivento, Papal Nuncio to Venice—he was a member of two learned societies, the Accademia Vignaiuoli in Rome and the Accademia Fiorentina in Florence. His principal literary work was the discourse on manners, *Il Galateo*, one of the best books of its kind to come out of the Renaissance.


## TO SLEEP

O Sleep, O tranquil son of noiseless Night,
    Of humid, shadowy Night; O dear repose
    For wearied men, forgetfulness of woes
    Grievous enough the bloom of life to blight!
Succor this heart that hath outworn delight,
    And knows no rest; these tired limbs compose;
    Fly to me, Sleep; thy dusky vans disclose
    Over my languid eyes, then cease thy flight.
Where, where is Silence, that avoids the day?
    Where the light dreams, that with a wavering tread
    And unsubstantial footing follow thee?
Alas! in vain I call thee; and these gray,
    These frigid shades flatter in vain. O bed,
    How rough with thorns! O nights, how harsh to me![35]

JOHN ADDINGTON SYMONDS

# Luigi Tansillo
## (1510–1568)

He spent many years at the Court of Naples, held the office of Captain of Justice at Gaeta. He seems to be remembered in literary circles chiefly for a poem called *Il Vendemmiatore*, which Pope Paul IV placed on the index because he found it shocking.

## THE PHILOSOPHIC FLIGHT

Now that these wings to speed my wish ascend,
    The more I feel vast air beneath my feet,
    The more toward boundless air on pinions fleet,
    Spurning the earth, soaring to heaven, I tend:
Nor makes them stoop their flight the direful end
    Of Daedal's son; but upward still they beat.
    What life the while with this death could compete,
    If dead to earth at last I must descend?
My own heart's voice in the void air I hear.
    Where wilt thou bear me, O rash man! Recall
    Thy daring will! This boldness waits on fear!
Dread not, I answer, that tremendous fall:
    Strike through the clouds, and smile when death is near,
    If death so glorious be our doom at all![36]

JOHN ADDINGTON SYMONDS

# Francesco Berni
## (1497–1535)

Though born in Lamporecchio, he grew up in Florence. From 1517 to 1532 he lived in Rome where he served under several ecclesiastical officials, notably Cardinal Bibbiena and Bishop Giberti. Later another patron, Cardinal Ippolito de' Medici secured him an appointment as canon in Florence. According to report, he was poisoned by Cardinal Cibo for refusing to administer poison to Cardinal Salvati.

His shorter poems, sonnets and *capitoli*, are full of coarse humor, burlesque, and parody. His satires on the life of the papal court are caustic and highly diverting. He inveighs against the tergiversations and weaknesses of Clement VII, and he ironically represents the indignation of ecclesiastical circles upon the election of the austere Pope Adrian VI because he tried to interfere with the gaiety of Roman life. His one long poem of distinction is entitled *Orlando Innamorato*, a *rifacimento* or retelling of Boiardo's famous poem of the same title. This treatment of the fanciful tale of chivalry is enriched by witty, satiric, and iconoclastic passages.

## POPE CLEMENT'S ILLNESS

The good old pope does nothing now but eat;
    The good old pope does nought but sleep or doze:
    Such is the answer you must give to those
    Who are solicitous about the holy seat.
He has good voice, good color, and good vision,
    A healthy tongue, clean spital, hearty cough.
    Now these are signs he is not shuffling off;
    But doctors give an alternate decision.
It would not be reflecting to their credit
    If he escaped alive their tender care:

"He's going to die," they'd said, and having said it,
They note signs horrible and symptoms rare;
   He had a paroxism; now we dread it
   Will come anon his aged frame to tear;
     A dog it would not spare,
Much less the pope. They'll take such pains to save
   Their patient that they'll send him to his grave.

HAROLD M. PRIEST

## PORTRAIT

Her hair of silver fine, bristling doth part
   All artlessly about a gilded face:
   Her forehead curled, whence timidly I trace
   Where Love and Death discharge a dart.
Those lovely pearly eyes, whose glances start
   At every object that less flashing shows;
   Brows snowy, and—what's rarest—those
   Fingers and hands so sweetly thick and short.
Lips soft as milk, her mouth an ample mine,
   With wandering teeth of ebony so rare,
   Whence harmonies exquisite unheard swell;
Her raiment proud and weighty. You my fine
   Devoted lovers, I to you declare
   The charms of this my wondrous demoiselle.[37]

HAROLD M. PRIEST

The deuce, a roast of scraggy quails, a bit
   Of salted pork to cram down a dry throat;
   To be dead tired and find nowhere to sit;
   To have the fire near by, the wine remote;
To pay cash down but to be paid at leisure;
   To be compelled to grant a profitless boon;
   Not to see aught when you've gone out on pleasure;
   To stew in January as you did in June:

To have a pebble lurking in your boot;
　　To feel a flea a-running round about
　　Your stirrup-leg, inside your sock; to know
One hand is clean and one is black as soot,
　　One foot is with a shoe and one without;
　　To be kept waiting when you're wild to go;
　　　　Add to all this what tries you most in life,
Vexation, care, grief, every sort of strife,
　　You'll find that far away the worst's a wife.

　　　　　　　　　　　　LORNA DE' LUCCHI

# Gaspara Stampa
## (1523?–1554)

Born in Padua, she spent most of her life in Venice, where she was recognized for her talents in music and poetry. Her fame as a poet, now revived after long neglect, depends on a volume containing three hundred lyrics, most of which report the course of her unhappy love affair with a handsome nobleman, Il Conte Collaltino di Collalto. The gentleman apparently did not long respond with a fervor equal to hers; and after a brief interlude he departed from Venice, first going to his estate in the country and later to France where he fought in the army of François I.

Subsequently, it is reported, Gaspara became involved in another love affair, but this was productive of no such poetry as the first amour. Finally she found in religion an object for her impassioned verses.

It would, in any case, be somewhat refreshing for us to hear a woman speak of her love, considering the scarcity of poetesses; but the appeal of these verses goes well beyond that of novelty. Though little distinguished for polish or style, she nevertheless records her joy and anguish with a striking candor and feverish passion, setting a mark for genuine feeling not often equaled in this period.

Ladies, who of my lord would fain be told,
   Picture a gentle knight, full sweet to see,
   Though young in years, in wisdom passing old,
   Model of glory and of valiancy;
Fair-haired, bright colour glowing in his face,
   Tall and well-set, broad-shouldered, finally,
   In all his parts a paragon of grace
   Except in loving wantonly, ah me!

Who'd know myself, picture a woman wrought
  In passion and in presence after pain's
  And death's own bitter images, a port
Of safety where untroubled rest remains;
  One who with neither tears, nor sighs, nor zest
Wakes pity in her cruel lover's breast.

                                    LORNA DE' LUCCHI


## OH NIGHT

O night, to me brighter and more blest
than the brightest and most blessed day,
night worthy of praise, not by me alone,
but by the first and rarest geniuses;
thou only hast been the faithful minister
to all my joys; thou all my bitterness
of my life hast made sweet and dear,
restoring to my arms him who has bound me.
  All that I needed then was to become
the fortunate Alcmene, for whom the dawn
stayed its return more than was its wont.
Thus I could never speak so much
in thy praise, pale night, but the word
would still be conquered by the matter.[38]

                                    HAROLD M. PRIEST


I am now so weary with waiting,
so overcome with grief and with desire,
for the faithlessness and great forgetfulness
of him for whose return, alas, I long,
that her who with her scythe causes the world
to pale and brings the final penalty,—
her do I call upon for my relief,
so greatly wells the sorrow in my breast.

And she turns deaf to my pleading,
mocking my foolish, erring thoughts,
as he remains deaf to his returning.
So with plaints, whence my eyes are moist,
I make piteous these waves, this sea;
and he lives happily up in his hills.

HAROLD M. PRIEST


Deeply repentant of my sinful ways
    And of my trivial, manifold desires,
    Of squandering, alas, these few brief days
    Of fugitive life in tending love's vain fires,
To Thee, Lord, Who dost move hard hearts again,
    And render warmth unto the frozen snow,
    And lighten every bitter load of pain
    For those who with Thy sacred ardours glow,
To Thee I turn, O stretch forth Thy right hand
    And from this whirlpool rescue me, for I
    Without Thine aid could never reach the land;
O willingly for us didst suffer loss,
    And to redeem mankind hung on the Cross,
    O gentle Saviour, leave me not to die.[39]

LORNA DE' LUCCHI

# Torquato Tasso
## (1544–1595)

Tasso was regarded by his contemporaries as the finest poet of his age, perhaps the greatest since Virgil. His father, Bernardo, was a poet of considerable repute. The young Torquato was educated at various Italian courts and finally at the universities of Padua and Bologna. His publication, at the age of eighteen, of *Rinaldo* won him an invitation to the court of Ferrara under the patronage of the d'Este family, and his career is mainly associated with that city and that house.

At the height of his career he suffered a mental breakdown (possibly the result of a blow on the head), and for his last twenty years he was afflicted intermittently with attacks of insanity and periods of depression, as a result of which he was held in confinement much of that time, mainly in the asylum of Santa Anna at Ferrara.

While his love poems were written to a number of ladies, his most publicized attachment was for the Princess Leonora d'Este. Though the affair was extravagantly over-romanticized by early biographers, it undoubtedly accounts for some of his best love lyrics.

His reputation rests primarily on his epic of the first Crusade, *Jerusalem Delivered*. Nevertheless, he distinguished himself in several other fields: notably, pastoral drama (*Aminta*) and literary criticism (Discourses on the Heroic Poem). His lyrics number about 2000. The grace and melody of his verses, the delicacy of his sentiment, and his rich enjoyment of the sensuous world characterize both his lyrics and his epic as well. Although the exceptional beauty of his language is, naturally, difficult to capture in a translation, still those personal lyrics written in anguish from his asylum possess a poignancy that will not escape the reader who understands the circumstances.

## AURORA

*(To Laura Peperara)*

Ecco mormorar l'onde
   e tremolar le fronde
   a l'aura mattutina e gli arboscelli,
   e sovra i verdi rami i vaghi augelli
   cantar soavemente
   e rider l'orïente:
   ecco già l'alba appare
   e si specchia nel mare,
   e rasserena il cielo
   e le campagne imperla il dolce gelo,
   e gli alti monti indora.
O bella e vaga Aurora.
   L'aura è tua messaggera, e tu de l'aura
   ch'ogni arso cor ristaura.

## DAWN

The waves are murmuring
   and the leaves are trembling,
   the morning breeze in the branches is heard,
   and soaring high above the trees a bird
   chants his song beguiling,
   the orient sky is smiling;
   the dawn is gloriously
   mirrored in the sea,
   heaven's dome serenely bright,
   the fields with dewy pearls are all alight,
   and the mountains tipped with gold.
Aurora, lovely to behold!
   The breeze becomes thy messenger, as hers thou art,
   That soothes each burning heart.[40]

HAROLD M. PRIEST

From the mantle of night,
From the pale, star-strewn sky,
What tears in my sight,
What dews gather nigh?
White moon, why dost sow
Crystal stars in a ring?
Where the green grasses grow,
Why dolefully sing
Wandering breezes alway
From the dusk to the day?
Is it presage of death,
O breath of my breath?

LORNA DE' LUCCHI

## THE ROSE

Flower, which of Adon's blood
Sprang, when of that clear flood
Which Venus wept another white was born,
The sweet Cynarean youth thou right dost show:
But this sharp-pointed thorn,
Which does so proud about thy crimson grow,
What doth it represent?
Boars' tusks, perhaps, his snowy flank which rent:
O show of shows! of unesteemed worth,
Which both what kill'd and what was kill'd sett'st forth.

WILLIAM DRUMMOND

## THE HAPPINESS OF A FLEA

How happier is that flea
Which in thy breast doth play,
Than that pied butterfly
Which courts the flame, and in the same doth die!
That hath a light delight,
Poor fool! contented only with a sight;
When this doth sport, and swell with dearest food,
And if he die, he, knight-like, dies in blood.[41]

WILLIAM DRUMMOND

## OF THAT SAME

Poor flea! then thou didst die;
Yet by so fair a hand,
That thus to die was Destine to command:
Thou die didst, yet didst try
A lover's last delight,
To vault on virgin plains, her kiss and bite:
Thou diedst, yet hast thy tomb
Between those paps, O dear and stately room!
Flea, happier far, more blest
Than Phoenix burning in his spicy nest!

WILLIAM DRUMMOND

## OF A BEE

As an audacious knight,
Come with some foe to fight,
His sword doth brandish, makes his armour ring;
So this proud bee, at home perhaps a king,
Did buzzing fly about,
And, tyrant, after thy fair lip did sting:
O champion strange as stout!
Who hast by nature found
Sharp arms, and trumpet shrill, to sound and wound.

WILLIAM DRUMMOND

## TO LUCREZIA D'ESTE

In tender youth a red, red rose didst seem
  Who in the tepor of the early light
  Veileth her breast and, virgin still, doth dream
  Shyly in her green drapery out of sight;
Or, since no mortal thing resembleth thee,
  Thou wast more kin to the celestial dawn,
  Dewy and bright in Heaven's serenity,
  Crowning the hills with gold, pearling the lawn;

But riper age no charm from thee withholds,
 And thou to-day art sweeter, though forlorn,
 Than in the bloom of girlhood, or as sweet;
Thus lovelier is the blossom who unfolds
 Her fragrant petals, greater light and heat
 Flow from the sun at noonday than at morn.[42]

LORNA DE' LUCCHI

This is not death, immortal Margaret,
But early passing to another day,
Nor pain nor sorrow doth in thee beget
This pilgrimage along an unknown way,
But only pity for the last farewell;
Now taking leave of earth, O spirit pure,
With us thy thoughts compassionately dwell,
But thou thyself art happy and secure.

LORNA DE' LUCCHI

Love is the soul of all things, the desire
 That guides the sun in his unerring ways,
 And moves the stars, as in a golden maze
 They dance and swing to the celestial lyre.
A mystic stream to nourish and inspire,
 He fills the earth, the winds and waters sways,
 And maketh man to hunger all his days,
 Sorrow, and hope, and joy, and be afire.
 Yet though he ruleth all things and create,
 Illumine all things, and through all things shine,
 In us Love showeth most his power divine:
And, as in heaven spheres on spheres arise,
 Hath set his highest throne in thy fair eyes,
 And in my heart his temple consecrate.

ROMILDA RENDEL

Ancient, winged god, thou who didst first draw breath
　　With sun and stars together at one birth,
　　Thou who to all things givest life and death,
　　Flying by devious pathways through the earth,
My heart which languisheth in bitter pain,
　　Seeking for thorny and malignant grief
　　A thousand remedies, but all in vain,
　　In thee, O Time, alone findeth relief.
Thought thou uprootest, with forgetfulness
　　　Healest our wounds, and lastly dost dispel
　　The mists which have these royal cloisters sealed;
Truth in her pure, unveilèd loveliness
　　Thou hast uplifted even from the well
　　Where she lay hid, and to all eyes revealed.

LORNA DE' LUCCHI

## THE GOLDEN AGE

　　O lovely age of gold!
　　Not that the rivers rolled
　　With milk, or that the woods dropped honeydew;
　　Not that the ready ground
　　Produced without a wound,
　　Or the mild serpent had no tooth that slew;
　　Not that a cloudless blue
　　For ever was in sight,
　　Or that the heaven, which burns
　　And now is cold by turns,
　　Looked out in glad and everlasting light;
　　No, nor that even the insolent ships from far
　　Brought war to no new lands nor riches worse than war:

　　But solely that that vain
　　And breath-invented pain,
　　That idol of mistake, that worshiped cheat,
　　That Honour,—since so called
　　By vulgar minds appalled,
　　Played not the tyrant with our nature yet.

It had not come to fret
The sweet and happy fold
Of gentle human-kind;
Nor did its hard law bind
Souls nursed in freedom; but that law of gold,
That glad and golden law, all free, all fitted,
Which Nature's own hand wrote—What pleases is
  permitted.


Then among streams and flowers,
The little winged Powers
Went singing carols without torch or bow;
The nymphs and shepherds sat
Mingling with innocent chat
Sports and low whispers; and with whispers low,
Kisses that would not go.
The maiden, budding o'er,
Kept not her bloom uneyed,
Which now a veil must hide,
Nor the crisp apples which her bosom bore;
And oftentimes, in river or in lake,
The lover and his love their merry bath would take.


'Twas thou, thou, Honour, first
That didst deny our thirst
Its drink, and on the fount thy covering set;
Thou bad'st kind eyes withdraw
Into constrained awe,
And keep the secret for their tears to wet;
Thou gather'dst in a net
The tresses from the air,
And mad'st the sports and plays
Turn all to sullen ways,
And putt'st on speech a rein, in steps a care.
Thy work it is,—thou shade that wilt not move,—
That what was once the gift, is now the theft of Love.

Our sorrows and our pains,
These are thy noble gains.
But O, thou Love's and Nature's masterer,
Thou conqueror of the crowned,
What dost thou on this ground,
Too small a circle for thy mighty sphere?
Go, and make slumber dear
To the renowned and high;
We here, a lowly race,
Can live without thy grace,
After the use of mild antiquity.
Go, let us love; since years
No truce allow, and life soon disappears.
Go, let us love; the daylight dies, is born;
But unto us the light
Dies once for all; and sleep brings on eternal night.[43]

LEIGH HUNT

## TO MADAME LUCREZIA D'ESTE, DUCHESS OF URBINO

When the storm-tossed mariner Ulysses lay
    forlorn and naked on the sandy coast,
    who not long hence upon the surge was tossed,
    where long he dwelt, to pain and hunger prey;
then as the fates decreed, lo, it befell,
    a royal lady came to end his woes:
    "Come to my father's garden, where there grows
    fruit everlasting, there in joy to dwell."
But me, now stricken by an unjust blow,
    upon a lone shore, famished and supine,—
    who will lead me to the gardens fair,
if not your grace, to whom I make my prayer?
    What should I call thee, mortal or divine?
    O *dea certe!* By the signs I know.[44]

HAROLD M. PRIEST

## TO HER GRACE THE DUCHESS OF FERRARA

Now, royal bride, begins that season keen,
    inviting lovers forth to mask and ball,
    when dance and laughter mark the carnival,
    when revel fills the nights chill and serene.
The maiden longs to hear her love declare
    his secret sufferings in her chaste ear,
    and yet she holds the lad in doubt and fear,
    'twixt death and life, waging a sweet warfare.
The noble palace and the stately hall
    ring loud with song; I in my cell, alone,
    lament my state. Is this your promised aid?
And is it thus my pleadings you recall?
    Is this your pity then, this cell of stone?
    And with a coffin is your mercy paid?

                                    HAROLD M. PRIEST


## TO GUGLIELMO GONZAGA, DUCA DI MANTOVA

Sir, down the precipice by Fortune flung,
    Ever more toward the abyss I fall
    No one till now has heard my pleading tongue,
    None turns in pity at my urgent call.
Indeed I see the sun as when a veil
    In Shadowy eclipse subdues his color;
    I see the fixed and wandering stars grow pale:
    What hand has stained them with such gloomy pallor?
To you now from the black depths of my night
    I turn and cry: You who well can, give me
    Your right hand in my undeserved plight;
Raise me up; from its crushing burden free
    The wing of swift invention vilely bowed,
    And you will see me fly far from the crowd.

                                    IDA FASEL

# Giovanni Battista Guarini

## (1538–1612)

Born at Ferrara, he returned there after studying at the University of Padua to join the court of Duke Alfonso II of the Este family. He served as professor of rhetoric and was employed in numerous important missions and one ambassadorial post. He was a contemporary of Tasso at Ferrara, a friend and admirer, though they ultimately had a quarrel. Later he was in court service in Florence and Urbino, and he finally went to Rome.

His *Pastor Fido* was a pastoral drama rivalling Tasso's *Aminta*, with which it automatically invites comparison. Together these plays established a genre which was popular for more than a century. The poetry of his drama is like that of his lyrics: limpid, graceful, and full of musical sweetness.

## THE MICROCOSM

Man of himself's a little world, but join'd
With woman, woman for that end design'd,
(Hear cruel fair one whilst I this rehearse!)
He makes up then a complete universe.
Man, like this sublunary world, is born
The sport of two cross planets, love, and scorn:
Woman the other world resembles well,
In whose looks Heav'n is, in whose breast is Hell.[45]

SIR EDWARD SHERBURNE

## MADRIGAL I

This life, which seems so fair,
Is like a bubble blown up in the air
By sporting children's breath,

Who chase it everywhere,
And strive who can most motion it bequeath:
And though it sometime seem of its own might,
Like to an eye of gold, to be fix'd there,
And firm to hover in that empty height,
That only is because it is so light.
But in that pomp it doth not long appear;
    For even when most admir'd, it in a thought,
    As swell'd from nothing, doth dissolve in nought.

              WILLIAM DRUMMOND

# Giovanni Battista Marino
## (1569–1625)

Born at Naples, he studied law but despised it and turned to the cultivation of poetry. Forced to leave Naples because of a scandal, he spent some time in Rome and then settled for a considerable period at Turin under the patronage of Carlo Emanuele. In 1615 he went to Paris where, in the regency of Marie de Medicis, he enjoyed a tremendous success. After the publication of his epic poem *L'Adone* in 1623, he returned to Naples where he was accorded a triumphant reception, hailed as the wonder of the world of letters.

In his poetry, both lyric and epic, he developed a mannered style which had a considerable following and was known simply as "Marinismo." He aimed for a polished, highly ornamental style. Priding himself above all for his ingenuity, he impresses the reader by his straining after novelty. His advice to poets, "Who knows not how to astonish, go back to the curry comb," conveys his attitude nicely. It is not surprising that he was well received in Paris by the *précieux* at the Hôtel de Rambouillet, whose first rule was never to say anything that would be comprehended by the multitude. His practice is in certain respects analogous to that of two great contemporaries, Góngora in Spain and John Donne in England; and though he is a lesser poet, his best work is of extraordinary beauty and flair.

In an age when most epic poets were choosing Biblical subjects (Du Bartas, Tasso), Marino produced one of the most sensuous of all pagan love stories. *L'Adone* is a new version of the Ovidian tale of Venus and Adonis which runs to 45,000 lines.

## THE PROEM. TO LOVE

Let others sing of Mars, and of his train,
  Of great exploits, and honourable scars,
  The many dire effects of Civil Wars,
Death's triumphs, and encomiums of the slain.

I sing the conflicts I myself sustain,
　With her (Great Love) the cause of all my cares,
　Who wounds with looks, and fetters with her hairs.
This mournful tale requires a tragic strain.

Eyes were the Arms, did first my Peace control,
　Wounded by them, a source of Tears there sprung,
Running like blood from my afflicted soul;
　Thou *Love* to whom this conquest does belong,
Leave me at least the comfort to condole,
　And as thou wound'st my Heart, inspire my Song.

PHILIP AYRES

## BROKEN FAITH

### *Sovra l'umida arena*

On the soft wet sand
Of the Latian shore
I watched Tirrena's hand
Inscribe her pledge of love in this sweet line:
"Mirtius, I am thine."
　Alas! nought was befitting those frail words
Save only sand; 'twas but a moment ere
The Tiber's tide and thy inconstant mind
Mirtius, that name once loved,
From out her heart as from the sand removed.

HAROLD M. PRIEST

## SONNET

Unhappy man, as soon as he is born
　Into this sorry world, openeth his eyes
To tears before he looks upon the morn,
　And within swaddling bands imprisoned lies;
Then later, when grown old enough to wean,
　A rigid lash his actions doth restrain,
　And come unto more steadfast years serene,
　'Twixt fate and love he lives, dies, lives again.

O many a death and weariness untold
 Doth he sustain when poor, aged, stricken with grief
 His worn bones lean upon a fragile stave;
Lastly, a narrow stone his spoils doth fold
 So swiftly that I sigh and say: "How brief
 A step between the cradle and the grave!"

LORNA DE' LUCCHI

## CYNTHIA SPORTING

Along the river's side did Cynthia stray,
More like a Goddess, than a Nymph, at play;
The flood stopt to behold her; pleas'd to see't,
She to its kisses yields her naked feet.

Brisk air saluted her, ne'er stay'd to woo;
The very boughs reach'd to be toying too;
The little birds came thronging to admire,
And for her entertainment made a choir:

The meadows smile, and joy surrounds the place,
As if all things were infl'enc'd by her face;
The grass and leaves take freshness from her eyes,
And as of lesser force, Sol's beams despise.

No herb press'd by her foot but blossoms straight,
Flowers, for her touch to ripen them, do wait;
They, from her hand, new fragrancy do yield,
Her presence fills with perfumes all the field.

PHILIP AYRES

## APOLLO AND DAPHNE

Panting for breath, towards her parent brook
 Like the tir'd deer before an eager chase,
Fair Daphne ran, nor durst behind her look:
 With wingèd feet, and with a blubb'red face.

The beardless God, who, taken with her charms,
  Had long pursu'd, by his hot passion led,
Straight saw her stop, and upward stretch her arms
  On Peneus' banks, where she for aid had fled.

He saw her nimble feet take root and grow,
  And a rough bark her tender limbs enclose;
Her hair, which once like curls of gold did show,
  Chang'd green, and in a shade of boughs arose.

To the resistless tree he courtship makes,
  And with vain kisses his fond love deceives;
Then of her bays by force a chaplet takes:
  So 'stead of fruit, he only gathers leaves.[46]

PHILIP AYRES


CHLORIS' EYES AND BREASTS

Chloris! on thine eyes I gaz'd;
        When amaz'd
      At their brightness,
On thy breasts I cast my look;
      No less took
      With their whiteness:
Both I justly did admire,
These all snow, and those all fire.

Whilst these wonders I survey'd,
        Thus I said
      In suspense,
Nature could have done no less
        To express
      Her providence,
Than that two such fair worlds might
Have two Suns to give them light.

SIR EDWARD SHERBURNE

## ICE AND FIRE

Naked Love did to thine eye,
Chloris, once to warm him, fly;
But its subtle flame, and light,
Scorch'd his wings, and spoil'd his sight.

Forc'd from thence he went to rest
In the soft couch of thy breast:
But there met a frost so great,
As his torch extinguish'd straight.

When poor Cupid, thus (constrain'd
His cold bed to leave) complain'd;
"'Las! What lodging's here for me,
If all ice and fire she be?"

SIR EDWARD SHERBURNE

## WHILE HIS LADY COMBS HER HAIR

Through waves of gold, the waves which were her hair,
    A little ship of ivory sailed one day,
    A hand of ivory steered it on its way
    Through precious undulations here and there.
And while along the tremulous surge of beauty
    She drove a straight and never-ending furrow,
    From the rows of tumbled gold Love sought to borrow
    Chains to reduce a rebel to his duty.
My shipwrecked heart veers down to death so fast
    In this stormy, blond and gilded sea that I
    Am caught forever in its waves at last.
In golden gulfs, at least, I come to my
    Tempestuous end, on rocks of diamond pressed,
    —O rich disaster in which submerged I die.

FRANK J. WARNKE

## DURING THE BATH

On a silver base, within a shell of gold,
  I saw two alabaster pillars rise,
  While perfumed crystal floods revealed the prize
  Of purest pearl, a treasure manifold.
I said, "O destined solace of my pain,
  Divine repast of nature and of love,
  From the ocean of your sweetness do not move
  But in this final hiding place remain.
Were I a new Alcides I should show
  Erect my standard where until this morrow
  No man's desire has reached; or could I borrow
The strength of Samson, I should overthrow
  Those columns, which in falling would bestow
  A fragrant tomb to death, death to my sorrow.

FRANK J. WARNKE

## CONSCIENCE

Internal Cerberus! whose griping fangs,
  That gnaw the soul, are the mind's secret pangs:
  Thou greedy vulture! that dost gorging tire
  On hearts corrupted by impure desire:
Subtle and buzzing hornet! that dost ring
  A peal of horrour, ere thou giv'st the sting:
  The soul's rough file, that smoothness does impart!
  The hammer, that does break a stony heart!
The worm that never dies! the thorn within,
  That pricks and pains: the whip and scourge of sin!
  The voice of God in man! which, without rest,
  Doth softly cry within a troubled breast:
"To all temptations is that soul left free,
  That makes not to itself a curb of me."

SIR EDWARD SHERBURNE

## CHRISTO SMARRITO

Sighing, her sad heart fraught with fears,
Whilst from her eyes gush streams of tears,
Seeking again how to retrieve
Her little wand'ring fugitive,
Each where with weary steps doth rove,
The virgin Mother of lost Love.
Like a sad turtle, up and down
She mourning runs through all the town:
With searching eyes she pries about
In every creek; within, without.
Sticks at each place, looks o'er and o'er;
Searches, where she had search'd before:
Old Joseph following with sad face,
A heavy heart, and halting pace.

Thrice had the day been born i' th' East,
As oft been buried in the West,
Since the dear comfort of her eyes
She miss'd; yet still her search she plies.
Each where she seeks, with anxious care,
To find him out, yet knows not where.
When the third morn she saw arose,
And yet no beam of hope disclose:
Looking to Heaven, in these sad words
She vent to her full grief affords:
"O my dear God! Son of my womb!
My joy, my love, my life, for whom
These tears I shed, on thee I call,
But, oh! thou answer'st not at all.
For thee I search, but cannot find thee:
Say (dear!) what new embraces bind thee?
What heart, enamour'd on thy eyes,
Enjoys what Heaven to me denies?

"Daughters of Sion! you which stray
With nimble feet upon the way,
I beg of you, (if you can tell)
To show me where my Love doth dwell:
Whose beauty with celestial rays

The light of Paradise displays.
Perhaps to you he is unknown;
Ah! if you wish to hear him shown,
I'll tell y' him: Snow her whiteness seeks,
Vermilion blushes from his cheeks:
His eye a light more chaste discloses
Than amorous doves, his lips than roses.
Amber and gold shine in his hair,
(If gold or amber may compare
With that) a beauty so divine,
No tongue, pen, phant'sy, can design.
   "Why break'st thou not (my soul) this chain
Of flesh? why lett'st thou that restrain
Thy nimble flight into his arms,
Whose only look with gladness charms?
But (alas!) in vain I speak to thee,
Poor soul! already fled from me;
To seek out him, in whose lov'd breast
Thy life, as mine in thee, doth rest."
   Blest Virgin! who, in tears half-drown'd,
Griev'st that thy son cannot be found,
The time will come when men shall hear thee
Complain that he is too, too near thee.
When in the midst of hostile bands,
With pierced feet and nailed hands,
Advanc'd upon a cursed tree
His naked body thou shalt see,
As void of coverture as friends,
But what kind Heaven in pity lends,
Thy soul will then abhor the light,
And think no grief worse than his sight.
   But, lo! as thus she search'd and wept,
By chance she to the temple stept,
Where her dear son, with joyful eyes,
Set 'mongst the Rabbins she espies.
And as the light of some kind star
To a distressed mariner,
So his dear sight to her appears,
Toss'd in this tempest of her fears.

But O! what tongue can now impart
The joy of her revived heart?
The welcome, spoke in mutual blisses
Of sweet embraces, sweeter kisses!
Muse, since too high for thy weak wing
It is, contemplate what thou canst not sing.[47]

SIR EDWARD SHERBURNE

## AND SHE WASHED HIS FEET WITH HER TEARS, AND WIPED THEM WITH THE HAIRS OF HER HEAD

The proud Egyptian queen, her Roman guest,
(T' express her love in height of state and pleasure)
   With pearl dissolv'd in gold did feast,
      Both food and treasure.

And now (dear Lord!) thy lover, on the fair
And silver tables of thy feet, behold!
   Pearl, in her tears and in her hair
      Offers thee gold.[48]

SIR EDWARD SHERBURNE

## THE FOUNTAIN

Stranger, whoe'er thou art, that stoop'st to taste
These sweeter streams, let me arrest thy haste;
      Nor of their fall
   The murmurs (though the lyre
   Less sweet be) stand t'admire:
      But as you shall
   See from this marble tun
   The liquid christal run,
      And mark withal
   How fixt the one abides,
   How fast the other glides;
Instructed thus, the difference learn to see
'Twixt mortal life and immortality.

SIR EDWARD SHERBURNE

## THE BOOK OF THE WORLD

Of this fair volume which we world do name,
If we the sheets and leaves could turn with care,
Of him who it corrects, and did it frame,
We clear might read the art and wisdom rare;
Find out his power which wildest pow'rs doth tame,
His providence extending everywhere,
His justice which proud rebels doth not spare,
In every page, no, period of the same:
But silly we, like foolish children, rest
Well pleas'd with colour'd vellum, leaves of gold,
Fair dangling ribbons, leaving what is best,
On the great writer's sense ne'er taking hold;
   Or if by chance our minds do muse on aught,
   It is some picture on the margin wrought.

WILLIAM DRUMMOND

# Girolamo Preti

## (1582–1626)

Though his birthplace is uncertain, it is thought to have been Bologna. He abandoned the study of law to enter upon a career as a poet as his master Marino had done. Most of his life was spent in courts in the service of various noblemen. In his youth he served under Alfonso II d'Este at Ferrara, then later under Cardinal Barberini, nephew of Pope Urban VIII.

Among the host of followers of Marino, Preti was probably the most important. It is indicative of his contemporary reputation that his works were extensively translated and adapted in France and England.

## DESCRIBES THE PLACE WHERE CYNTHIA IS SPORTING HERSELF

Behold yon' hill, how it is swell'd with pride,
And that aspiring oak upon its side,
With how much scorn they overlook the plain,
Proud of the lovely guest they entertain.

See with what haste those crystal springs do flow,
T'incorporate with the silver brook below;
There does my wanton Cynthia sporting stand,
Printing her footsteps on the yielding sand.

Look, Thyrsis, how she fills with joy the place,
She bathes her feet, and views her angel's face;
Sure I've a rival of that amorous hill,
And those are streams of tears which thence distil.

PHILIP AYRES

## COMPLAINS, BEING HIND'RED THE
## SIGHT OF HIS NYMPH

To view these walls each night I come alone,
And pay my adoration to the stone,
Whence Joy and Peace are influenc'd on me,
For 'tis the temple of my Deity.

As nights and days an anxious wretch by stealth
Creeps out to view the place which hoards his wealth,
So to this house that keeps from me my heart,
I come, look, traverse, weep, and then depart.

She's fenc'd so strongly in on ev'ry side,
Thought enters, but my footsteps are deny'd.
Then sighs in vain I breathe, and tears let fall:
Kiss a cold stone sometimes, or hug the wall.

For like a merchant that rough seas has crost,
Near home is shipwrack'd, and his treasure lost;
So, toss'd in storms of sorrow, on firm ground,
I in a sea of mine own tears am drown'd.

PHILIP AYRES

## LOVE ONCE, LOVE EVER

Shall I hopeless then pursue
   A fair shadow that still flies me?
Shall I still adore, and woo
   A proud heart, that does despise me?
I a constant love may so,
But, alas! a fruitless show.

Shall I by the erring light
   Of two crossed stars still sail?
That do shine, but shine in spite,
   Not to guide, but make me fail?
I a wand'ring course may steer,
But the harbour ne'er come near.

Whilst these thoughts my soul possess,
    Reason, passion would o'er sway;
Bidding me my flames suppress,
    Or divert some other way:
But what reason would pursue,
That my heart runs counter to.

So a pilot, bent to make
    Search for some unfound out land,
Does with him the magnet take,
    Sailing to the unknown strand;
But that (steer which way he will)
To the loved north points still.

SIR EDWARD SHERBURNE

# Claudio Achillini
## (1574–1640)

A native of Bologna, he taught civil law at the university there and later held chairs at Ferrara and Parma. He was secretary to various prelates including Monsignor Ludovisi, who became pope in 1621, assuming the name Gregory XV. Achillini, one of the better known Marinisti, gained extraordinary celebrity both in France and throughout Italy for a sonnet written in praise of the French victory at La Rochelle which he dedicated to Louis XIII.

## A SONNET, WRITTEN BY A NYMPH IN HER OWN BLOOD

Since, cruel Thyrsis, you my torments slight,
   And take no notice of my amorous flame,
In these vermilion letters thus I write
   My bloody reasons to confirm the same.

These of my passion are the lively marks,
   Which from my veins you here in blood see writ,
Touch them, your breast will kindle with the sparks,
   The ardent characters are reeking yet.

Nor can my pen alone my heart explain,
My very soul o'ercharg'd with grief, I fain
   Would send enclos'd herein, the truth to prove.
And if I've been too sparing of my blood,
This is the reason why I stopp'd the flood,
   I would not spoil the face I'd have you love.

PHILIP AYRES

# Tomasso Campanella
## (1568–1639)

Here is a figure in the tradition of Giordano Bruno. As a youth he entered the Dominican order but was soon in trouble with the ecclesiastical authorities because of the advanced views he espoused both in science and theology. After several years of persecution he was brought to trial for heresy; and though he saved his life by pretending insanity, he was sentenced to life imprisonment. From 1599 to 1626 he remained a prisoner, during which time he read widely and wrote an astonishing number of works on philosophy, chiefly in Latin. When he was released from prison, he fled to Paris where he was well received and where several of his works were published.

One of the few works published during his imprisonment was *Apologia pro Galileo*. His most widely read work today is his *City of the Sun*, one of the most important works of utopian literature of all times. His poetry, vastly different from the main fashions of the period, is concerned with the human condition, with metaphysics, and with the cosmos.

## THE PEOPLE

The people is a beast of muddy brain
    That knows not its own force, and therefore stands
    Loaded with wood and stone; the powerless hands
    Of a mere child guide it with bit and rein:
One kick would be enough to break the chain;
    But the beast fears, and what the child demands,
    It does; nor its own terror understands,
    Confused and stupefied by bugbears vain.

Most wonderful! with its own hand it ties
  And gags itself—gives itself death and war
  For pence doled out by kings from its own store.
Its own are all things between earth and heaven;
  But this it knows not; and if one arise
  To tell this truth, it kills him unforgiven.[49]

                    JOHN ADDINGTON SYMONDS

# Francesco Redi
## (1626–1697)

A native of Arezzo, student of medicine and philosophy, he was also a linguist extraordinary, having a knowledge of Greek, Latin, and five modern European languages plus Arabic. He was a member of the Accademia della Crusca and the Cimento and taught rhetoric at the Colonna Palace in Rome. He became physician to Ferdinand II and to Cosimo III of Tuscany. Most of his writing was in scientific fields.

In poetry one of the anti-Marinisti, he is best known for his *Bacchus in Tuscany*, a work of some 1000 lines celebrating the glories of Italian wines. It is composed in a racy style, with short, uneven lines and a slap-dash system of rhyming. The English reader will be reminded at times of Skelton, at times of Samuel Butler or even Ogden Nash.

## BACCHUS IN TUSCANY

If the grape's kindly juice
Could not stir life again,
This were too frail a thing,
Too brief and fraught with pain.
Such juice is the bright ray
Of suns in heaven ashine,
Caught and held captive by
The bunches of the vine.
Up, up, let us therein
Muscles and veins renew,
Preparing vigour for
The old and weary too.
In gay festivities,
In laughter and in jest,
Let us pass by, pass by
Him whose consuming zest
In sum and number lies,

Him known as Time below,
And drinking, drinking, send
Care unto Jericho!
. . . . . . . . . . . . . . . . . . . . . . .
    Who water drinks
But vainly thinks
To win my grace.
Be water fresh and clear to see,
Or dim in deep abyss,
Her love will not entangle me,
The tiresome little Miss.
This silly one who often flaunts
Capricious, saucy ways,
Doth with her proud and noisy vaunts
And with her insolence and lies
Turn upside down both earth and skies.
And banks and bridges she doth break,
And stormy showers she doth down-shake,
Green, flowery fields are in her wake
Forlorn, and tenderest blossoms quake.
About each steadfast wall
Her ruthless downpours rage,
And of their fatal fall
To ruin is presage.
The Mamelukes may praise
The waters of the Nile,
And Spaniards boast the while
Of Tagus constantly:
These have no charms for me!
But, if one of my band
Should dare to quaff a drop,
At strangling I'd not stop,
I'd do it with this hand!
Let certain skinny quacks
Seek herbs and chicories,
Since water they aver
Will cure each fell disease.
But merry crew
Of mine eschew

Each single vat
With water flat,
Filled to the brim.
And water, soured
By lemons, be
Forbidden in
Our hostelry.
Sweet jessamine
I do not care
To drink, but twine
About my hair.
Eggs beaten up in sugared milk
I neither fancy nor desire,
Nor unto syrups golden-hued
Nor scented waters do aspire;
These for a weakling's sips
Or woman's puling lips.
Wine, wine alone for him be named
Who would forget his grief and fear:
Within my cups I'm not ashamed
To drown my wits six times a year!

LORNA DE' LUCCHI


Talk of Chocolate!
Talk of Tea!
Medicines, made—ye gods!—as they are,
Are no medicines made for me.
I would sooner take to poison
Than a single cup set eyes on
Of that bitter and guilty stuff ye
Talk of by the name of Coffee.
Let the Arabs and the Turks
Count it 'mongst their cruel works:
Foe of mankind, black and turbid,
Let the throats of slaves absorb it.
Down in Tartarus,
Down in Erebus,
'Twas the detestable Fifty invented it;

The Furies then took it
To grind and to cook it,
And to Proserpina all three presented it.
If the Mussulman in Asia
Doats on a beverage so unseemly,
I differ with the man extremely.
. . . . . . . . . . . . . . . . . . . . . . . .
There's a squalid thing, called Beer:
The man whose lips that thing comes near
Swiftly dies; or falling foolish,
Grows, at forty, old and owlish.
She that in the ground would hide her,
Let her take to English Cider:
He who'd have his death come quicker,
Any other Northern liquor.
Those Norwegians and those Laps
Have extraordinary taps:
Those Laps especially have strange fancies;
To see them drink,
I verily think,
Would make me lose my senses.
But a truce to such vile subjects,
With their impious, shocking objects.
Let me purify my mouth
In a holy cup o' th' South;
In a golden pitcher let me
Head and ears for comfort get me,
And drink of the wine of the vine benign
That sparkles warm in Sansovine.[50]

LEIGH HUNT

# Vincenzo da Filicaia
## (1642–1707)

He was born at Florence, studied at the University of Pisa. Queen Christina of Sweden was for a time his patron. He was a senator under Cosimo III of Tuscany and Governor of Volterra and Pisa. Classified as an Arcadian poet, he wrote political sonnets and odes conveying genuine feeling.

## TO ITALY

Italy, O thou to whom belong
    Th' unhappy gift of loveliness, a dower
    Of woe; upon whose head the gods did shower
    Beauty, with its bloody trail of wrong;
Would that thou wert less fair, or wert more strong,
    That they who, worshipping the fatal flower
    Of beauty in thee, yet defy thy power,
    Might love thee less, or fear thee more. The throng
Of armèd men now would I not behold
    Pouring from alpine snows, and gallic horde
    Drinking the crimson stream where thou hast bled,
Nor see thee girt with foreign steel, and sold
    To strangers, fighting with an alien sword,—
    A slave—or conquering or vanquishèd.

                      ROMILDA RENDEL

# FRENCH POEMS

# Marguerite de Navarre
## (1492–1549)

The sister of François I, Marguerite de Navarre was the wife first of the duc d'Alençon and then of the King of Navarre. Undoubtedly one of the most cultivated women of the French Renaissance, she acted as patroness and inspiration to many writers and other intellectuals who frequented her court. A woman gifted in literature, she is most famous as the author of the *Heptaméron*, a collection which rivals Boccaccio's *Decameron* and which consists of more than seventy prose stories interspersed with occasional verse. As a poet, she was a minor talent, her light verse displaying a certain elegance and charm, typical of the poetic style developed by Clément Marot, with whom she was closely associated.

## DIZAIN TO CLÉMENT MAROT

If but your creditors, the which you chyde,
    Did knowe as I the worth of your rare wit,
    Of all your dettes you might full soon be quit
Or great or smalle, whatever still maye byde;
    If each did holde a dizain duly writ,
    What sum soever the full worth of it
Would then be his by thousands multiplied.
The worth of money maye by weight be tolde,
    But none maye knowe what guerdon doth befit
Such skill as yours beyond all worth of gold.

                    WILFRID THORLEY

# Clément Marot
## (1496–1544)

Born at Cahors, Marot was at an early age brought into contact with the French court and spent much of his life in various posts in several noble households, including that of Marguerite de Navarre, who was for a long while his patroness. As a young man, Marot became interested in the Protestant evangelical movement in France, was imprisoned briefly for heresy, ostensibly on the charge of failing to observe a Lenten fast, and finally was exiled in Switzerland and later in Italy, where he died. His early poetic work was published in 1532, under the title of *Adolescence Clémentine*, a collected edition of his verse appeared in 1538, and finally, in 1543, he brought forth his translation of the first fifty *Psalms*, a work he had undertaken chiefly to please Marguerite. Marot's poetry illustrates his mastery of the ingenious, traditional, late medieval forms of French poetry. His style is neat, smooth, and elegant, and especially in his occasional verse, it suggests a personality marked by consummate tact and civilized wit. However, in his more serious poetry, his deeper feelings and often his religious earnestness become apparent.

## MAROT TO THE QUEEN OF NAVARRE

My creditors, whose hearts no poem stirs,
    Chanced to read yours. On which I simply said:
"Michel! and Bonaventure! honoured sirs,
    For me these lines the King's own sister made."
    When they this proof of mighty favour weighed,
They dub me "Sir," and high in credit hold;
Your verses proved to me as good as gold.
    For they not only promised me to wait,
But vowed to lend me money as of old;
    I vowed in turn to borrow, as of late.

HENRY CARRINGTON

## A LOVE-LESSON

A sweet "No, no,"—with a sweet smile beneath,
   Becomes an honest girl: I'd have you learn it:—
As for plain "Yes," it may be said, i'faith,
   Too plainly and too oft:—pray, well discern it.

Not that I'd have my pleasure incomplete,
   Or lose the kiss for which my lips beset you;
But that in suffering me to take it, sweet,
   I'd have you say, "No, no, I will not let you."

LEIGH HUNT

## MADAME D'ALBERT'S LAUGH

Yes, that fair neck, too beautiful by half,
   Those eyes, that voice, that bloom, all do her honour:
Yet after all, that little giddy laugh
   Is what, in my mind, sits the best upon her.

Good God! 'twould make the very streets and ways
   Through which she passes, burst into a pleasure!
   Did melancholy come to mar my days,
   And kill me in the lap of too much leisure,
No spell were wanting, from the dead to raise me,
But only that sweet laugh, wherewith she slays me.

LEIGH HUNT

## AU BON VIEULX TEMPS

In old good days a mode of loving reigned
With no great art nor offerings sustained,
So that a nosegay given of love sincere,
Was an endowment with the whole earth's sphere,
For save the heart all else was then disdained.

And if by chance the joys of love were gained,
Know you how such good hap was entertained?
It lasted on and on, from year to year
      In good old days.

Now all is lost that love of old ordained.
We have but changes and tears falsely feigned.
If then ye will that love I should revere,
You first must furnish love with other gear
And use the manner of it men maintained
      In good old days.

GEORGE WYNDHAM

## SONG: SINCE LOVING COUNTENANCE...

### I

Since loving countenance you still refuse,
  I to some desert shall, a hermit, fly,
And pray that if another lover sues,
  He may as true and faithful prove as I.

### II

Then, Love, farewell! farewell to beauty's queen!
  Farewell to charms and never-ending store!
To me they little recompense have been.
  May one who loves you less be cherished more.

HENRY CARRINGTON

## EPITAPH ON JEAN VEAU

Beneath this stone lies young John Calf,
  Who would have been an Ox or Bull
Had he but lived to feed and quaff;
  But death in childhood chose to call,
  And life, while still a Calf, annul.
His death, the hopes of many, mocks:
  For he had grown so fat and full,
He must have made a famous ox.[1]

HENRY CARRINGTON

# Maurice Scève
## (1510?–1564?)

In the sixteenth century, Lyons was a city marked by an exceptionally active, intellectual and literary life. With the Petrarchism of Italy exerting a powerful influence upon them, a group of poets known as the *poètes Lyonnaises* attempted to inject a new note of emotional intensity into French poetry. Of these poets, Maurice Scève is the most remarkable. From a rich bourgeois family, Scève received a humanist education and became a painter and musician as well as a poet. His original genius, however, is displayed best in his poetic work, even though he was influenced by the Italian master, Petrarch. The best known of Scève's works, *Délie, object de plus haulte vertu* (1544), is a sequence of 450 dizains, ten line stanzas of decasyllabic verse using an elaborate rhyme pattern. In the sequence, the poet records the progress of a man in love with a distant woman and finally shows the unsuccessful lover painfully achieving a victory over his emotions. These dizains are extremely subtle, intellectually complex, often obscure, and generally on a high, spiritual plane. *Délie* is thought to be an anagram of *l'Idée*, but probably the dizain sequence was inspired by a real woman, Pernette du Guillet, a poet in her own right and a disciple of Scève. In most respects a poet out of his time, Scève has frequently been classified as metaphysical. The style of his poetry is also reminiscent in some ways of that of modern symbolism, of which, indeed, the poet is sometimes called a precursor. Certainly his manner of condensing his ideas and emotions into a few ingeniously chosen words has a power of suggestion similar to that of the better symbolists of the modern period.

## DÉLIE

Libre vivais en l'avril de mon âge,
    De cure exempt sous cette adolescence,
    Où l'œil, encor non expert de dommage,
    Se voit surpris de la douce présence,
    Qui par sa haute et divine excellence
    M'étonna l'âme et le sens tellement,
    Que de ses yeux l'archer tout bellement
    Ma liberté lui a toute asservie:
    Et dès ce jour continuellement
    En sa beauté gît ma mort et ma vie.

In the April of my age I was living free,
    My years of youth as yet unclaimed by care,
    When my eye, still heedless of injury,
    Was suddenly and sweetly made aware
    Of one who stood proud and divinely fair.
    So startled were my soul and sense, I saw
    The archer from her eyes quite gently draw,
    Enslaving me completely with her gaze.
    And since then, in her face without a flaw
    Lies all my death, and all my living days.[2]

                                        IDA FASEL

Some delight in telling stories,
    Perpetuating the deeds of great princes,
    Some triumph in noble victories,
    Some grow bitter over painful satire,
    Some sing their loves clearly.
    Or are happy in amiably describing
    Farces and games provoking people to laugh,
        But I have no other care
    Save writing of you, and yet I know not what to say
    But cry pity, pity, pity.[3]

                                    WALLACE FOWLIE

Already the moon has shown me two crescents,
  That same number of times the full moon has waned,
  And two suns, which met me here,
  Have increased my memory of you as much
  As my strength has grown in waiting
  Through the long time which separates us,
  So that life and I cannot be together.
    For dying in this long absence
  (Yet not without living in you) seems to me
  A service equal to suffering in your presence.

                        WALLACE FOWLIE


Let silence or speech be permitted each one
  Who binds freedom to his will.
  But if it happens that one in a large company
  Should say to you: Lady, either your lover forgets
    himself,
  Or feigns this name Delia for the moon
  To show you as changeable as it is:
  May such a guilty name be far from you,
  And come to him who secures for us such harm.
    For I conceal you in that praiseworthy name
  Since you light up in me the dark night.[4]

                        WALLACE FOWLIE


Like Hecate you will make me wander
  Alive and dead a hundred years among the shades;
  Like Diana, will shut me up in heaven,
  Whence you came down among these mortal pitfalls;
  As queen of the infernal shades,
  Will lessen or increase my torments.
    But as Moon infused in my veins
  This you were, are, and will be Delia—
  Whom love has joined to my fruitless thoughts
  So closely that death can never separate her from them.[5]

          *Penguin Book of French Verse, II*

If it is Love, why then does he kill me
   Who have loved so much and never hated?
I am infinitely bewildered by this,
Especially since I never offended him.
But still suffer, without any complaint,
That he consume me, as wax is consumed in the fire.
And killing me, he wants me to live,
So that in loving another, I shall cease loving myself.
   What need is there to continue slaying me,
Since he knows death who loves in vain?[6]

WALLACE FOWLIE

Bound to the Caucasus of my suffering
   Within the hell of my eternal pain,
   This great desire of my forgotten good,
   Like the vulture of my immortal death,
   Gnaws my spirit in such fury
That consumed by this ardent pursuit,
Hope makes it, not for my good, live again,
And ceaselessly be reborn in evil,
So that in me my wretched life
Prometheus torments in innocence.[7]

WALLACE FOWLIE

The indolence of soft feathers,
   Familiar bed, not of my sleep,
   But of labor when you kindle my ardor
      Often, beyond time and sense,
Holds me restless between its sheets,
So weak an enemy does it esteem me.
   There my spirit leaves my sleeping body
Transformed into the image of death,
In order to show you that then half-man,
In you I am alive, and in me I am dead.

WALLACE FOWLIE

O years, O months, weeks, days and hours,
  O intervals, O minute, O moment,
  Which consume the realest pains
  Without one seeing how,
  Don't you feel that this sweet torment of mine
  Wears you out in me and deceives your strength?
    If then the heart to the pleasure it receives
  Comes to give itself over to martyrdom,
  We must believe that death is sweet
  Which can free the soul from anguish.

                    WALLACE FOWLIE

The happiness of our happiness enflaming desire
  Unites a double soul in the same power;
  One, dying, lives on the sweet anguish
  Which makes the other, alive, receive death.
    Blinded God, you made us have,
  Without our mutual consent,
  And possess, without our repenting,
  The good of that desirable suffering.
  Allow us to feel for a long time
  Such a sweet dying in our breathing life.[8]

                    WALLACE FOWLIE

If with her hand my fatal enemy,
  And still the joy of my soul,
  Should touch me slightly, my sleeping thought,
  More than the dead man under his heavy stone,
  Trembles in me, as if with burning flame,
  One touched me in deep sleep.
    Then my spirit rising up strongly
  Wishes to flee from her and from me, its nearest kin,
  And at this point (to speak bluntly)
  Fleeing my death, I hasten my end.[9]

                    WALLACE FOWLIE

I by myself, she in another's arms,
I in my sorrow, she in her soft bed:
On thorns I toss, under grief that scarcely warms,
And she lies naked with the one she wed.
　　He holds her in embrace not merited:
She yields to him, and, as the weaker one,
And so defiles love by that wrongful union
Which human law, and not divine, decreed.
　　O holy law, unjust to me alone,
You punish me because of her misdeed.[10]

IDA FASEL

Tout jugement de cette infinité,
　　Où tout concept se trouve superflu,
　　Et tout aigu de perspicuité
　　Ne pourraient joindre au sommet de son plus.
　　　Car seulement l'apparent du surplus,
　　Première neige en son blanc souveraine,
　　Au pur des mains délicatement saines,
　　Ahontirait le nu de Bethsabée,
　　Et le fragrant de sa suave haleine
　　Apourrirait l'odorante Sabée.

All judgment of this infinity,
　　Where all conception is found superfluous,
　　And all the keen[ness] of perspicuity
　　Could not attain to the summit of her more.
　　　For the first snow sovereign in its white[ness]
　　Is only in appearance superior
　　To the pure of her hands, delicately hale,
　　Would shame the naked[ness] of Bathsheba,
　　And the fragrant of her sweet breath
　　Would putrefy the scented Sheba.[11]

HAROLD M. PRIEST

Longer than a Platonic century,
  Was the month I lived without you,
  But when I saw once again your peaceful face,
  High sojourn of all grace,
  Where the empire of council is made,
  My dreams then I believed prophetic.
    For you returned into my body and soul,
  And I felt her hands, hands heavenly white,
  With their arms mortally divine,
  One around my neck, the other around my thighs.[12]

WALLACE FOWLIE


Lady, you are the body, and I am your shadow
  Which in my continual silence
  Makes me move, not like Hecate the shadow,
  By dire and great violence,
  But by the power of your high excellence,
  In moving at the sweet outline
  Of all your deeds, and more suddenly
  Than one sees the shadow follow the body,
  Except that I feel too inhumanly
  Our holy wills grow together in discord.[13]

WALLACE FOWLIE


The white dawn had hardly finished
Embellishing its head shining with gold and roses,
When my spirit, which was perishing
In the confused depths of so many diverse things,
Returned to me under the closed bed curtains
To make me more invincible toward death.
    But you, who have (you alone) the power
To give happiness to my fatality,
You will be for me the incorruptible myrrh
Against the worms of my mortality.[14]

WALLACE FOWLIE

# Jean Parmentier

## (1494–1530)

A famous voyager from Dieppe, Parmentier had the distinction of being the first Frenchman to land in Brazil. Also one of the earliest explorers of Sumatra, he died in that exotic land, but not before he had composed a long poem in twelve line stanzas, *Description nouvelle des merveilles de ce monde et de la dignité de l'homme*, a work which clearly shows his religious and heroic inspiration.

## THE WONDERS OF THE DEEP

Who shall discern the marvels of the sea—
   Its horrible sounds that full of peril be,
Its billows without measure heaved and tossed;
   Who see them foam when the fierce winds awake,
Swell, seethe, in mountains rise, or depths be tossed,
   Then suddenly be calm without a break—
Who shall discern their nature and their law?
But who shall say such incidents I saw,
Save he who on the ocean wont to rove:
   By him alone this may of right be said,
   "O marvellous creation, vast and dread,
Of the most marvellous who dwells above!"

O ye poor mariners, the sailors stout,
   Who well have learnt the nature and the waves
   Of the great sea, whence danger profit craves,
Lift up your eyes, possessing hearts devout,
To heaven, so will I make one of you—
Glory to give to whom is glory due.
Consider well the grandeur and the size
Of that vast sea stretched out before your eyes,

Half of which would suffice the earth to drown;
   Yet, spite its force and raging violent,
   The hand of God, strong and omnipotent,
Does by its power arrest and hold it down;
Does by its providence affix its bounds,
   Its movements, course, and preordained extent;
And when, like dreadful thunder, it resounds,
And works to many a wandering vessel ill,
   His mercy soothes, and silent makes, and still.

Consider too the marvellous vast flocks
   You see across the waste of waters range,
   The mighty fishes, monsters dread and strange,
Of various shapes, and huge as towering rocks;
So, as though false, man's power of thought it shocks
When first such creatures to exist are said—
Numberless are they, and yet all are fed.
He only perfect who in heaven reigns;
Gives all their pasture, and with food sustains,
Which they pursue among the billows dread,
When forth they issue from their dark abyss,
As instinct of their several nature is.

                    HENRY CARRINGTON

# Louise Labé
## (1526?–1566)

Another of the poets of Lyons, Louise Labé circulated with the intellectuals of the city, calling attention to herself by her beauty and her non-conformity in her tastes and loves. In her youth she took a keen interest in fencing and horsemanship, and at one time she is said to have gone off to war in male attire. Upon her return she married a rich rope-maker and thus earned the title *la belle cordière*, under which she was celebrated by several poets. Her poetic works, published in 1555, strike a note of intense, passionate feeling. With penetrating intuition and effusive expression, she has described the troubles and tortures of unrequited love, possibly inspired by her own unsuccessful love for Olivier de Magny. Almost completely devoid of the stamp of schools and mannerism, she presents a striking contrast to her fellow Lyonese, Maurice Scève. Her contemporary Italian poetess, Gaspara Stampa, is at least her match in emotional intensity and candor but not in final artistry.

### SONNET V

Venus, who wander clear among the skies,
   Hear what I say, O listen! For as long
   As you still hang and glitter there, my song
   Of vain and secret withering shall arise.
While still they see you shining through the night
   My eyes lie somehow gentlier awake,
   And tears begin to flow, and all the ache
   Grows milder with the witness of your light;
And human beings lie, subdued and worn
   By labor into weariness and sleep.
   I find beneath the sunlight hard to bear

That which obsesses me. Exhausted, torn,
   I fall upon my bed and through the deep
   Cavern of night cry out my whole despair.

              FREDERIC PROKOSCH

## SONNET VII

And so one sees all living matter perish
   As soon as its elusive breath has gone.
   You are the breath; I am the blood and bone.
   O heart, which I so desperately cherish,
Where have you vanished? Do not leave me lost,
   Pale and imperiled! O, come back again,
   Bring back this broken body from its pain,
   Return its precious and essential ghost!
But then, contrive it somehow without danger,
   O love, this wild and terrifying meeting,
   This hot return; and let me give my greeting
In calm and coolness to this mighty stranger;
   And let his warming loveliness enfold
   Me gently, who was once so bitter cold.

              FERDERIC PROKOSCH

## SONNET IX

As soon as I withdraw to take my rest
   And gently my lone bed receiveth me,
   My spirit with its burden sore opprest
   Forthwith betakes its sadness unto thee.
And then I seem within my tender breast
   To hold the happiness for which I thirst,
   For want of which, with heavy sighs distrest,
   I oft have sobbed as though my heart would burst.

O gentle sleep, O blest and blissful night,
  Ye kind dispensers of tranquillity,
  Beguile me in my dreams with false delight.
If I may not know love's reality,
  Grant me the semblance of it, that I may
  Possess in dream the boon I lack by day.

ALAN CONDER

## SONNET XIII

Oh were I faint with love upon the breast
  Even of him for whom you see me die:
  If, still with him, the world would not deny
  That I should live my poor last days at rest;
If, clasping me, he should say "Loveliest,
  Let us be happy";—confident that I,
  With him, would dare all storms of Destiny
  To sunder us while still of life possess'd:
If with my arms both clasped around him, close
  As ivy round the branch it overgrows,
  Death came in envy of the ease I had:
When sweetly he should cease my lips to kiss
  As my soul swooned on those sweet lips of his,
  How much were dying than my life more glad!

GEORGE WYNDHAM

## SONNET XIV

Yes, and as long as these poor eyes can bring
  Themselves to weep for that remembered hour,
  And while this voice can somehow find the power,
  After these sobs and sorrows, still to sing;
And while these fingers still can draw some new,
  Adoring music from these supple strings,
  And while this wild, incessant heart still brings
  Itself to think of you, and none but you:

While this is so, I have no wish to die.
But when I feel my fingers lying still,
My voice atremble, and my glances dry,
And when exhaustion drains away the will
To love intensely : let the night then fall
And cast its final darkness over all.

FREDERIC PROKOSCH

## SONNET XVIII

O kiss me yet again, O kiss me over
And over! Kiss me this time tenderly;
And this time let your passion enter me
And burn me through! I shall return, my lover,
Four more for every one you give me—yes,
Ten more if you desire it, still more tender.
Dreamy and drugged with kisses we shall wander
Through all our utter, intermingled bliss!
And so in each of us two lives have grown
Concealed in one; our lover's, and our own.
A paradox has gathered in my brain:
For while my life is disciplined and lonely,
My heart is ill, and can recover only
When it escapes, and breaks in two again.[15]

FREDERIC PROKOSCH

# Pierre de Ronsard
## (1524–1585)

Around the middle of the sixteenth century, a group of young men studying under the humanist scholar Dorat at the College de Coqueret in Paris discovered mutual interests and banded together to form the famous literary circle known as the Pléiade. Ardently studying classical literature, these young scholars admired the sublimities of the Greek and Latin poets and, comparing them with the poetry of Marot and his school, began a rebellion against the dilettantism of the formal French poetic tradition. Claiming for poetry a more serious status than that of a form of polite entertainment, the men of the Pléiade, with typical Renaissance enthusiasm and energy, devoted their talents to developing a new French literature, one which in imitation of the classical writers would include all the great genres hitherto neglected by French poets, which would create a new poetic language distinct from prose and worthy of its great themes, and which would be enriched by new and more sonorous rhythms.

Pierre de Ronsard, the acknowledged leader of the Pléiade, was born near Vendôme and at an early age began to travel with the French court in the capacity of a page. Soon stricken with illness, he lost his hearing, and, his career in the court thus curtailed, he turned his energies to humanist study at the College de Coqueret in Paris, where he became closely associated with Joachim du Bellay, Antoine de Baïf, and several others. Once his excellent poetic talent had been recognized, Ronsard was called back to the court to put himself at the services of royalty. At the death of Charles IX, however, Ronsard retired to an obscure refuge in the country of his birth, where, afflicted by illness, he continued to write until his death in 1585.

Ronsard's works include the *Odes*, his first publication, which appeared in 1550 and display both his original genius and his debt to Pindar; the *Amours de Cassandre* (1552), a book of sonnets and other short poems somewhat in the manner of Petrarch and addressed to a distant mistress; the *Hymnes* (1555), an attempt at poetry in a heroic and didactic vein, in imitation of Callimachus; the *Amours de Marie* (1557), a collection of love poems; the *Discours des misères du temps* (1562), and the *Remonstrance au peuple de France* (1563), in which he aimed at expressing national and patriotic themes; the first four cantos of a heroic poem, *La Françiade*, in which he attempted to imitate Homer but which he abandoned for more congenial subjects; the *Sonnets pour Hélène* (1578), love poems expressing the poet's somewhat belated passion together with his melancholy; and much other occasional and familiar verse.

Immense indeed was Ronsard's debt to classical writers; one cannot read his verse without hearing at every turn numerous echoes of Greek and Latin poets. An experimenter in metrics, Ronsard contributed to French literature not only a vast body of varied poetry but also a new tradition of themes and measures. Not the least of these contributions was his establishment of the alexandrine as the set line for serious poetry. Ronsard's poetic output established him as probably the foremost poet of the sixteenth century. Translated extensively, his poems found a warm reception everywhere, and he soon acquired an international reputation which was prominent enough that Queen Elizabeth of England was inspired to send him a valuable diamond in recognition of his talent.

## AND LIGHTLY, LIKE THE FLOWERS

"Ainsi qu'aux fleurs la vieillesse,
Fera ternir votre beauté."—

And lightly, like the flowers,
    Your beauties Age will dim,
    Who makes the song a hymn,
And turns the sweets to sour.


Alas, the chubby Hours
    Grow lank and gray and grim,
And lightly, like the flowers,
    Your beauties Age will dim.

Still rosy are the bowers,
    The walks yet green and trim.
    Among them let your whim
Pass sweetly, like the showers,
And lightly, like the flowers.

                    W. E. HENLEY


Let me decease within thine arms, my Dear,
    That shall suffice: for nothing would I know
    Of louder glory in the world than so,
    In kissing thee, to yield my breath even here.
He from whose heart Mar's fires have lickt out fear,
    Shall to the war, and, mad with the long show
    Of life and power, shall flaunt it for the blow
    His valour covets from a Spanish spear.
I, with less rage, ask but for this goodhap,
    Idly to die, Cassandra, in thy lap,
    After a hundred years, without a name:
For I do err, or there's more happiness
    Thus dying, than in daring to possess
    All of a short-lived Alexander's fame.

                    GEORGE WYNDHAM


## TO HIS YOUNG MISTRESS

Fair flower of fifteen springs, that still
    Art scarcely blossomed from the bud,
Yet hast such store of evil will,
    A heart so full of hardihood,
        Seeking to hide in friendly wise
        The mischief of your mocking eyes.

If you have pity, child, give o'er,
    Give back the heart you stole from me,
Pirate, setting so little store
    On this your captive from Love's sea,
        Holding his misery for gain,
        And making pleasure of his pain.

Another, not so fair of face,
  But far more pitiful than you,
Would take my heart, if of his grace,
  My heart would give her of Love's due;
    And she shall have it, since I find
    That you are cruel and unkind.

Nay, I would rather that I died,
  Within your white hands prisoning,
Would rather that it still abide
  In your ungentle comforting,
    Than change its faith, and seek to her
    That is more kind, but not so fair.

ANDREW LANG

Marie, arise, my indolent sweet saint!
  Long since the skylark sang his morning stave,
  Long since the nightingale, love's gentle slave,
  Carrolled upon the thorn his love-complaint.
Arise! come see the tender grass besprent
  With dew-pearls, and your rose with blossoms brave.
  Come see the dainty pinks to which you gave
  Last eve their water with a care so quaint.
Last eve you swore and pledged your shining eyes
  Sooner than I this morning you would rise,
  But dawn's soft beauty-sleep, with sweet disguising,
Still gently seals those eyes—that now I kiss
  And now again—and now this breast, and this,
  A hundred times, to teach you early rising!

CURTIS PAGE

"Who," cried the elders on the Trojan wall,
  When Helen passed, "dare of the ills complain
  Which by that beauty have no weight at all,
  Whose single glance outbids a world of pain?

And yet the wrath of Ares to forestall
    Were it not better to yield her up again
    Than see the port besieged, the ramparts fall,
    And all of Troas bloody with the slain?"
But that was old man's rede. King Menelaus
    Asked rightly her return whom rightly Paris
    Withheld, since both knew well it was the duty
Of young and old alike, although it slay us,
    To offer and to waste—if all miscarries—
    Country and goods and life itself for beauty.

HUMBERT WOLFE


## DEADLY KISSES

Ah, take these lips away; no more,
    No more such kisses give to me.
    My spirit faints for joy; I see
Through mists of death the dreamy shore,
And meadows by the water-side,
    Where all about the Hollow Land
Fare the sweet singers that have died,
    With their lost ladies, hand in hand;
Ah, Love, how fireless are their eyes,
    How pale their lips that kiss and smile.
    So mine must be in little while
If thou wilt kiss me in such wise.

ANDREW LANG


## ON HIS LADY'S WAKING

My lady woke upon a morning fair,
    What time Apollo's chariot takes the skies,
    And, fain to fill with arrows from her eyes
His empty quiver, Love was standing there:

I saw two apples that her breast doth bear;
  None such the close of the Hesperides
  Yields; nor hath Venus any such as these,
  Nor she that had of nursling Mars the care.
Even such a bosom, and so fair it was,
  Pure as the perfect work of Phidias,
  That sad Andromeda's discomfiture
Left bare, when Perseus passed her on a day,
  And pale as death for fear of death she lay,
  With breast as marble cold, as marble pure.

ANDREW LANG

## ROSES

I send you here a wreath of blossoms blown,
  And woven flowers at sunset gathered,
  Another dawn had seen them ruined, and shed
  Loose leaves upon the grass at random strown.
By this, their sure example, be it known,
  That all your beauties, now in perfect flower,
  Shall fade as these, and wither in an hour,
  Flowerlike, and brief of days, as the flower sown.
Ah, time is flying, lady,—time is flying;
  Nay, 'tis not time that flies but we that go,
  Who in short space shall be in churchyard lying,
And of our loving parley none shall know,
  Nor any man consider what we were;
  Be therefore kind, my love, whilst thou art fair.[16]

ANDREW LANG

*Quand vous serez bien vieille, au soir, à la chandelle,*

When you are very old, at evening
  You'll sit and spin beside the fire, and say,
  Humming my songs, "Ah well, ah well-a-day.
  When I was young, of me did Ronsard sing."

None of your maidens that doth hear the thing,
    Albeit with her weary task foredone,
    But wakens at my name, and calls you one
    Blest, to be held in long remembering.
I shall be low beneath the earth, and laid
    On sleep, a phantom in the myrtle shade,
    While you beside the fire, a grandame gray,
My love, your pride, remember and regret;
    Ah, love me, love, we may be happy yet,
    And gather roses, while 'tis called today.[17]

ANDREW LANG

## HIS LADY'S DEATH

Twain that were foes, while Mary lived, are fled;
    One laurel-crowned abides in heaven, and one
    Beneath the earth has fared, a fallen sun,
    A light of love among the loveless dead.
The first is chastity, that vanquished
    The archer Love, that held joint empery
    With the sweet beauty that made war on me,
    When laughter of lips with laughing eyes was wed.
Their strife the Fates have closed, with stern control,
    The earth holds her fair body, and her soul
    An angel with glad angels triumpheth;
Love has no more than he can do; desire
    Is buried, and my heart a faded fire,
    And for Death's sake, I am in love with Death.

ANDREW LANG

## HIS LADY'S TOMB

As in the gardens, all through May, the rose,
    Lovely, and young, and fair appareled,
    Makes sunrise jealous of her rosy red,
    When dawn upon the dew of dawning glows;

Graces and Loves within her breast repose,
   The woods are faint with the sweet odor shed,
   Till rains and heavy suns have smitten dead
   The languid flower, and the loose leaves unclose,—
So this, the perfect beauty of our days,
   When earth and heaven were vocal of her praise,
   The fates have slain, and her sweet soul reposes;
And tears I bring, and sighs, and on her tomb
   Pour milk, and scatter buds of many a bloom,
   That dead, as living, she may be with roses.

ANDREW LANG

## THE PARADOX OF TIME

Le temps s'en va, le temps s'en va, madame!
Las! le temps non: mais "NOUS nous en allons!"

Time goes, you say? Ah, no!
Alas, Time stays, *we* go;
   Or else, were this not so,
What need to chain the hours,
For Youth were always ours?
   Time goes, you say?—ah, no!

Ours is the eyes' deceit
Of men whose flying feet
   Lead through some landscape low;
We pass, and think we see
The earth's fixed surface flee:—
   Alas, Time stays,—we go!

Once in the days of old,
Your locks were curling gold,
   And mine had shamed the crow.
Now, in the self-same stage,
We've reached the silver age;
   Time goes, you say?—ah, no!

Once, when my voice was strong,
I filled the woods with song
   To praise your "rose" and "snow";
My bird, that sang, is dead;
Where are your roses fled?
   Alas, Time stays,—we go!

See, in what traversed ways,
What backward Fate delays
   The hopes we used to know;
Where are your old desires?—
Ah, where those vanished fires?
   Time goes, you say?—ah, no!

How far, how far, O Sweet,
The past behind our feet
   Lies in the even-glow!
Now on the forward way,
Let us fold hands, and pray;
   Alas, Time stays,—*we* go.

AUSTIN DOBSON

## CARPE DIEM

There is a time for all things, sweet!
   When we at church are kneeling
     We'll worship truly.
But when in secret lovers meet,
   Their wanton blisses stealing,
     We'll match them duly.

Why, then, oh why deny my will
   To kiss thy hair's soft beauty,
     Thy lips' dear roses?
When I would touch thy breast, why still
   Dost fain the nun's cold duty
     In cloister-closes?

For whom dost save thine eyes in sooth,
  Thy brow, thy bosom's sweetness,
    Thy lips twin-mated?
Dost think to kiss King Pluto's mouth
  When Charon's hateful fleetness
    Oars thee ill-fated?

Thine aspect shall be gaunt and dread,
  Thy lips, when Death has ta'en thee,
    All sicklied over.
Were I to meet thee 'mongst the dead
  I'd pass by and disdain thee,
    Thee, once my lover!

Thy skull shall know nor hair nor skin,
  Thy jowl the worms shall fatten,
    Erstwhile so winning;
Thou'lt have no other teeth within
  Thy jaws but such as batten
    In death's-heads grinning . . .

Sweet, while we live, oh! seize today,
  And every respite using,
    Spare not thy kisses!
Soon, soon, Death comes, and then for aye
  Thou'lt rue thy cold refusing
    And mourn lost blisses.[18]

CURTIS HIDDEN PAGE

## TO REMI BELLEAU

To think, Belleau, that such a man
As you translates Anacreon—
You drink so little! Did you see
The comet which not long since burst
And lit the sky? It foretold thirst,
Or I'm no use at prophecy!

These hot stars that in heaven blaze
Usher in parched and thirsty days
In order to make all men drink;
So drink, for after death we go
With other shades to drink below
At God knows what dark river's brink!

But no! On second thought, Belleau,
If you have set your mind to go
With the nine Muses on their mountain,
Keep on avoiding, as you do,
Bacchus and his unseemly crew,
Staying instead by learning's fountain.

And those who set out to combine
Venus with the God of Wine,
Say goodbye to sober sense.
Bacchus needs a pedagogue
To correct his fault and flog
Him well, as did Silenus once;

Or else the young girls who were there
To care for him, when Jupiter
From his burned mother took him up;
That these were Water-Nymphs is plain:
"For Bacchus damages the brain,
Unless the Nymph is in the cup."[19]

R. N. CURREY

## TO A FOUNTAIN

O lovely Bellerie,
Fountain as dear to me
As the nymphs, your daughters,
Who run away to hide
In your cool depths from the satyrs,
Chased to the very side
Of your protecting waters,

Still your eternal hands
Bless my paternal lands;
And I, your poet, this mead
And fresh green bank adorn
With a young suckling kid,
Each firstling of a horn
Just showing on his head.

In summer-time I doze
On your green banks, compose
On willow-shaded grass
These lines to send your fame
Out through the universe,
So that your gentle name
May live on in my verse.

The heat of the dog-star
May not burn up your shore;
Always your region yields
Close shade beneath the boughs
To shepherds from the folds,
Tired oxen from the ploughs,
And cattle from the fields.

For ever the princess
Of fountains, I address
Your hoarsely-murmuring
Rock-conduit as it jets
Endlessly-following
Water that foams and frets
Babbling and chattering.

                              R. N. CURREY


## EPITAPH ON RABELAIS

If it's true that Nature can
Raise new life from a dead man,
And if generation

Springs out of corruption,
Then a vine should issue forth
From the stomach and huge girth
Of our Rabelais who contrived
To keep on drinking while he lived,
Who, with his mighty throat sucked down
Far more wine, all on his own,
Through nose and mouth, in a bulp or two
Than a porker drinking milk can do,
Than Iris from the rivers, or
From the waves of the African shore.

Nobody in morning sun
Ever saw him sober; none
From sunset until late at night
Saw him anything but tight;
Without pause our Rabelais
Kept on drinking night and day.
When the fiery dog-days brought
Round the season of the drought,
Half-dressed, with his sleeves rolled up,
He'd lie down flat beside his cup
Among the glasses on the rushes
Among the richly-loaded dishes,
Sprawling there quite shamelessly
Floundering as messily
As a frog does in the mud;
Then, when drunk, he'd sing aloud
The praises of his good friend Bacchus,
How he came to be victorious
Over the Thebans, how his mother
With such warmth received his father,
That, instead of making love,
He just burned her up alive!

Sing of Gargantua and his mare
And the huge staff he used to bear;
Splendid Panurge; and the domains
Of those gaping Papimanes,

Their houses, customs, and strange laws;
Of Friar John of Antoumeures;
And the battles of Episteme;
But Death, who never drinks, took him,
The drinker, to the world below,
Where no other waters flow
Than the turbid streams that run
Down into wide Acheron.
Whoever happen to pass this way
Empty here a glass, I pray;
Pour out flagons, scatter cheese,
Legs of ham and sausages;
For if any feeling now
Animates that soul below,
These to lilies would be preferred
However freshly they were gathered![20]

R. N. CURREY

## ON THE CHOICE OF HIS SEPULCHRE

You grottoes and you fountains
That fall from rocks and mountains
And, gliding as you fall,
    Are musical;

You woods, you streams that wander
By verdant meadows yonder,
O river-bank, and lea,
    Hark, hark to me.

When Heaven and Time decide
That it were well I died
And left the sunlit mirth
    Of homely earth,

'Tis my desire none break
White marble for my sake,
That men may make more fair
    My sepulchre:

Not marble, but a tree
I'd have to shadow me,
With leafage ever green
    To mark the scene,

And from me may there spring
An ivy root, to cling
To me and wind me round
    Below the ground:

And may a winding vine
Adorn this grave of mine
That on all sides be made
    A spreading shade.

And thither will repair,
Commanded so each year,
The shepherds with their sheep,
    A tryst to keep:

And then these shepherd wights,
Having observed the rites,
Will thus bespeak a while
    The listening isle:

"Illustrious grave, the name
Thou bear'st is known to fame,
For all the universe
    Doth sing his verse

Who ne'er with envy burned
And all his life-long spurned
The begging of rewards
    From mighty Lords,

Who taught not men to brew
Love-potions, and who too
Did never make men versed
    In arts accurst;

But to our meads and wood
First brought the Sisterhood,
Who to his verses' sound
   Did foot their round.

For from his lyre his art
Drew song to charm the heart,
Immortalizing thus
   Our fields and us.

May manna from the skies
Fall ever where he lies,
And dewy balm of May
   Bathe him alway.

May grass grow round his grave
And murmuring waters lave
His sepulchre for ever,
   Ceasing never.

And we who count our own
His glory and renown
Will honour him each year
   As Pan he were."

The troop, in celebration,
Will then pour an oblation
Of milk and lamb's blood o'er
   My ashes, for

I shall be far away,
Where blesséd souls for ay
In their celestial home
   All blissful roam.

Nor hail nor snow can e'er
Disturb that halcyon air,
Nor thunderbolt infest
   That region blest:

There verdure goes on sighing
For ever, never dying,
Since in that clime supernal,
    Spring's eternal.

There Zephyr softly blows,
And there the myrtle grows
Myriad-hued and gay,
    In bloom for ay.

No madness there that brings
The lust of power to Kings
And lays a neighbour's state
    In waste through hate!

But brother-like there do
The happy dead pursue
The tasks they had on earth
    Ere their rebirth.

There shall I feel the fire
That filled Alcæus' lyre,
And, sweetest of the throng,
    Hear Sappho's song.

How those who hear them sing
Are filled with wondering,
And how their heart rejoices
    To hear those voices!

There tortured Tantalus
And weary Sisyphus
Forget, while listening fain,
    Their thirst and pain.

Only the lyre imparts
Such bliss to weary hearts,
Soothing the wounded spirit
    Doth she but hear it.

ALAN CONDER

# Joachim du Bellay
## (1522–1560)

The second great light of the Pléiade, Joachim du Bellay, from a noble family of Anjou, studied Greek and Latin under humanist scholars at the College de Coqueret in Paris, where he met Ronsard. Later, he accompanied his kinsman, Cardinal Jean du Bellay, to Rome, where the latter acted as the French ambassador. Returning to France in 1555, exhausted by his busy life with the ambassador, du Bellay retired to obscurity and a life solely dedicated to poetry, but, always of a frail constitution, he died young.

Du Bellay is known not only for his poetry but as the author of the prose treatise, the *Deffence et illustration de la langue françoise* (1549), the clarion call of the Pléiade in which the group's goal was proclaimed: to make the French language and literature the foremost in the modern world. Du Bellay's poetic works include a sonnet sequence, *L'Olive* (1549), in honor of Mlle de Viole, his platonic mistress, displaying his Petrarchism and his mastery of the sonnet form; the *Musagnaeomachie* (1549), a mythological allegory in the tradition of the ancients; the *Antiquitez de Rome* (1558), a series of sonnets about Rome, later translated into English by no less a poet than Edmund Spenser under the title *The Ruins of Rome*; the *Jeux rustiques* (1558), charming poems on a variety of subjects; the *Regrets* (1559), nostalgic personal reflections about the poet's native Anjou; and the *Poète courtisan* (1559), a satire on court poets, noted for its truthfulness and biting irony. Although his work is less varied and less forceful than that of Ronsard, du Bellay displays a talent which marks him as a major writer of the French Renaissance. Through his work flows a vein of lyricism and melancholy which is in many ways akin to that of the later romantic poets.

## L'OLIVE

### XIV

Sleep, of all gifts of Heaven held supreme,
   Sweeter than honey lay upon mine eyes,
   When lo, the treasure of Love's phantasies
   Passed to my soul through the white gates of dream.
Clasping her marble throat mine arms did seem,
   Mocking the ivy's amorous devise,
   To fasten round their alabaster prize
   As though such worth should sorrow's self redeem.
Already Love along my weary veins
   Shot the sharp fire of piercing fever-pains,
   And my soul wandered on her lips of rose,
Bound for the river of oblivion,
   When jealous of my joy, loud day too soon
   Opened the door of gentle sleep's respose.[21]

GEORGE WYNDHAM

## ON HIS DEAFNESS

When yet I might (as now I may no more)
   Taste the sweet honey of that gentle speech,
   You hid from me the face I did beseech
   And the dear eyes, whose livery I wore.
And now, when years have wrought upon me sore
   Till I am deaf, deaf as the wave-stunned beach,
   You send for me, when joy can never reach,
   The pale life left me on a darkling shore.
O random Fortune! Irony of woe!
   Only to see as if in painted show
   The face of her whose beauty makes me die;—
Only to touch the whiteness of her hand,
   To search her eyes, but not to understand
   The gentle voice that answers to my cry.

GEORGE WYNDHAM

## TO HIS FRIEND IN ELYSIUM

So long you wandered on the dusky plain,
  Where flit the shadows with their endless cry,
  You reach the shore where all the world goes by,
  You leave the strife, the slavery, the pain;
But we, but we, the mortals that remain
  In vain stretch hands; for Charon sullenly
  Drives us afar, we may not come anigh
  Till that last mystic obolus we gain.
But you are happy in the quiet place,
  And with the learned lovers of old days,
  And with your love, you wander evermore
In the dim woods, and drink forgetfulness
  Of us your friends, a weary crowd that press
  About the gate, or labor at the oar.[22]

ANDREW LANG

## A SONNET TO HEAVENLY BEAUTY

If this our little life is but a day
  In the Eternal,—if the years in vain
  Toil after hours that never come again,—
  If everything that hath been must decay,
Why dreamest thou of joys that pass away,
  My soul, that my sad body doth restrain?
  Why of the moment's pleasure art thou fain?
  Nay, thou hast wings,—nay, seek another stay.
There is the joy whereto each soul aspires,
  And there the rest that all the world desires,
  And there is love, and peace, and gracious mirth;
And there in the most highest heavens shalt thou
  Behold the Very Beauty, whereof now
  Thou worshipest the shadow upon earth.[23]

ANDREW LANG

## ROME

You, who behold in wonder Rome and all
  Her former passion, menacing the gods,
  These ancient palaces and baths, the sods
  Of seven hills, and temple, arch, and wall,
Consider, in the ruins of her fall,
  That which destroying Time has gnawed away—
  What workmen built with labor day by day
  Only a few worn fragments now recall.
Then look again and see where, endlessly
  Treading upon her own antiquity,
  Rome has rebuilt herself with works as just:
There you may see the demon of the land
  Forcing himself again with fatal hand
  To raise the city from this ruined dust.[24]

YVOR WINTERS

## HEUREUX QUI, COMME ULYSSE, A FAIT UN BEAU VOYAGE

Happy who like Ulysses, or that lord
  That raped the fleece; returning full and sage,
With usage and the world's wide reason stored,
  With his own kin can wait the end of age.
When shall I see, when shall I see, God knows!
  My little village smoke; or pass the door,
The old dear door of that unhappy house,
  That is to me a kingdom and much more?
Mightier to me the house my fathers made,
  Than your audacious heads, O Halls of Rome;
More than immortal marbles undecayed,
  The thin sad slates that cover up my home;
More than your Tiber is my Loire to me,
  Than Palatine my little Lyré there;
And more than all the winds of all the sea,
  The quiet kindness of the Angevin air.[25]

GILBERT K. CHESTERTON

## SONNET

I hate the money-lending avarice
  Of Florentines, the violent Siennese,
  The very rarely truthful Genoese,
  The sly Venetian's subtle artifice,
The Neapolitan's vanity, some vice
  That I've forgotten in the Ferrarese;
  I hate all Lombards and their treacheries,
  The cowardly Roman's unpreparedness;
I hate the surly Englishman, swaggering Scot,
  The talkative Frenchman, false Burgundian,
  The arrogant Spaniard and the German sot;
I hate some vice or other in every nation,
  And in myself a hundred vices find—
  But none I hate like a pedantic mind.[26]

R. N. CURREY

# Antoine de Baïf
## (1532–1589)

A friend of Ronsard and minor talent of the Pléiade, de Baïf is chiefly known as a scholar and erudite translator of Greek and Latin works. An advocate of linguistic fads, he promoted spelling reform, a phonetic orthography, and a metrical system based on that of classical quantitative verse. He lived much of his life in Italy, where he died, but spent sufficient time in France to persuade the king to found the Académie de Poésie et de Musique in 1570. De Baïf's poetry is excessively abstract and imitative of the classics, although it demonstrates that the poet had a perceptive ear and a penetrating mind.

### CARPE DIEM

Emperor and Turk, I wot,
With their schemes torment me not;
Hopes of making mighty gain,
Tempt not me who wealth disdain.
And still less do I desire
Fame and titles to acquire,
Or the pomp and gaudy show
Which the greatest monarchs know.

I my thought and care apply
To the day that passes by;
Fools are they who pine and fret
For what the future may beget.
Who tomorrow's fate can tell?

Like a master, quickly, well,
Forge me, Vulcan! without fail—
Not a steel-bright coat of mail
That will never break or yield;

Nor I ask an ample shield,
Nor a trenchant scimitar—
What have I to do with war?
Rather be thy skill displayed
In a cup of silver made;
And the goblet all around
Let not cruel war be found,
Nor of murder dreadful forms,
Nor the might of raging storms,
Nor the barren ocean shrouded,
By black threatning skies o'erclouded,
Nor depict the broken mast
In the raging billows cast:

But the pleasant clinging vine,
And its laughing grapes design,
And God Bacchus ivy-crowned,
Whom do jolly troops surround;
Goat-horned Satyrs who are dragging
The slow ass 'neath burden lagging,
On whom does Silenus ride,
Toppling oft from side to side.
And my love to represent,
Let thy chiefest skill be spent;
And be sure that Venus fair
And her cupids all be there.

HENRY CARRINGTON

# Vauquelin de la Fresnaye
## (1536–1607)

A lawyer from Normandy, Vauquelin de la Fresnaye was a follower of Ronsard who wrote graceful *Idylles* and *Satires*, much in the manner of Horace and in praise of country life. He also produced love sonnets and poems devoted to patriotic subjects in the style advocated by the Pléiade.

## O GENTLE BREEZE

O gentle breeze, whose incense-burdened breath
    Fills the night air with balm of thousand flowers!
    O smiling mead, where half in love with death
    Two parting lovers counted the sad hours!
O shadowy forest and swift-flowing stream,
    That saw at last their sorrows turn to bliss
    And their long severance ended in a kiss
    When love renewed their interrupted dream!
Now age has weaned them from love's wayward folly,
    And wisdom sanctifies their ancient fire,
    Blunting the too sharp edge of young desire:
Yet still they feel a gentle melancholy
    When some sweet chance brings back as in a dream
    This breeze, this wood, this mead, this flowing stream.

WILLIAM FREDERIC GIESE

# Phillippe Desportes
## (1546–1606)

Desportes is thought of as a court poet *par excellence*. Having traveled to Italy as secretary to the Bishop of Puy, he returned to Paris where he came under the patronage of the Duke of Anjou. When the Duke succeeded to the throne, Desportes became the richest abbot in France. He wrote much love poetry (*Amours de Diane, Amours d'Hippolyte, Amours de Cléonice, Amours diverses*), but late in his career he turned to religious poetry and produced a verse rendering of the Psalms. His poetry, which shows much influence from Italy and Spain as well as the Pléiade, is characterized by its grace and clarity. In addition, however, it is marked by an ingenuity which earns its author the title: precursor of *préciocité*. Incidentally, he had an enthusiastic following in England.

## VILLANELLE A ROZETTE

Rozette, because a little while
I stayed away, you've changed your heart,
And knowing of your fickle guile,
I was not slow with mine to part;
Never shall such frail loveliness
Again so move me from my bent:
We'll soon see, flighty shepherdess,
Which of the two will first repent.

The while in tears I waste away,
And curse my absence hour by hour,
You, who but loved by habit, play
At kissing your new paramour.

No nimble vane could pirouette
To yield the wind such quick consent:
We'll see, my shepherdess Rozette,
Which of the two will first repent.

Where are the sacred oaths and tears
Whose numbers choked our last good-bye?
Can proofs so sad of loving fears
Spring from a heart's inconstancy?
How false you are! May trustfulness
In you make all who trust lament!
We'll soon see, flighty shepherdess,
Which of the two will first repent.

He who stands where I stood before
Can hardly love you more than I;
And she I love hath greater store
Of beauty, love, and loyalty.
Take care of this new flame you've won,
With mine for all time I'm content,
And so, we'll try conclusion
Which of the two will first repent.

GEORGE WYNDHAM


## SONNET: DRESS YOUR GOLD LOCKS, ...

Dress your gold locks, make soft your azure eyes,
    Let your red lips enchanting projects feign;
    Call heaven to witness, heave deceitful sighs,
    Weep, act howe'er you will, your hopes are vain.
I will return no more, such frantic cries,
    So many days consumed in direst pain,
    To end in anguish when we met again,
    Will, for the future, guard me from surprise.
Experience teaches, grief has wisdom taught,
    How cursed the wretch by fickle woman caught,
    Entrap by luring speeches that beguile.

No, no! If by sweet words again abused,
    Pardon nor pity let me then receive:
    To err a second time is ne'er excused.

HENRY CARRINGTON


## INVOCATION

O Sleep! I bring thee this long-cellared wine,
And milk, and poppies dark, with crownèd heads,
To lure thee where the old crone Sibyline
Sits with her maids, pulling her last long threads
Of fresh-spun wool. Over the chill hearth bent,
With twisted thumb upraised and moistened lips
She plies her task. Softly her eyes eclipse,
Arrest her distaff, end her brabblement,
And let me all night, without harassment,
Still kiss and kiss that dimpled little maid,
Fond Ysabeau, who waits and waits, afraid.[27]

WILLIAM FREDERIC GIESE


## EPIGRAMME

Some four years ago I made Phillis an offer,
    Provided she would be my wh-re,
Of two thousand good crowns to put in her coffer,
    And I think should have given her more.

About two years after, a message she sent me,
    She was for a thousand my own,
But unless for an hundred she now would content me,
    I sent her word I would have none.

She fell to my price six or seven weeks after,
    And then for a hundred would do;
I then told her in vain she talk'd of the matter,
    Than twenty no farther I'd go.

T' other day for six ducatoons she was willing,
  Which I thought a great deal too dear.
And told her unless it would come for two shilling,
  She must seek a chapman elsewhere.

This morning she's come, and would fain buckle gratis,
  But she's grown so fulsome a wh-re,
That now methinks nothing a far dearer rate is,
  Than all that I offer'd before.

                              CHARLES COTTON

# Mathurin Régnier
## (1578?–1613)

Taking religious orders at the age of eleven, he became secretary to Cardinal de Joyeuse and a canon of Chartres Cathedral. But he led a dissolute life and his poetry did not follow religious lines. Perhaps because of his rebellious spirit, perhaps because he was a nephew of Desportes, he rejected the doctrines of Malherbe. His greatest success was in the field of satire, where he prepared the way for Molière.

## A CONFESSION IN BRIEF

Since sev'n sins from these our eyes
Bar the gates of Paradyse,
   Holy father, if truth's in me,
I'll abhor them everywhere,
An thou wilt but to me spare
   Haste and lust that so do win me.

These in me are Nature's flaw,
These nor precept, nay, nor law
   Nor your nimble speech can alter;
And when simple sorrowe might
Save me from my sinful plight,
   Whim would make my lips to falter.

I have tried to foil them oft
With a *Pater Noster* soft,
   With a Bible text to smother;
In the midst of combats fell,
Voices soothe mine ire and tell
   Howe kind Nature is their mother.

'Tis not God hath giv'n me these
To augment mine enemies,
    But a new Pandora sowing
With her own hand far and wide,
As a bane for human pride,
    This strange falsehood in me growing.

For no saint, howe'er devout,
Firm and zealous could put out
    Such a blaze of sinful fuel;
Carmelite, Celestine pure
Never could 'gainst such a lure,
    Keep unbroke a law so cruel.

Do thou then as I have claimed,
Soe that, firm and unashamed,
    I've a conscience clean within me,
As of old the Saints were knowne:
From the sev'n sins take alone
    Haste and lust that so do win me.

                    WILFRID THORLEY


# EPITAPH

I lived my life from day to day
Unthinking, yielding to its way,
Of nature's good law follower.
And therefore I ask wonderingly
Why death should dare to think of me,
Who never gave a thought to her.

                    IDA FASEL

# François Maynard
## (1582?–1646)

A magistrate, courtier, and one of the original members of the French Academy, he had a variegated career. He was noted for his gaiety and fondness for luxurious living. Probably at his best in his epigrams, but all in all a good poet, he is remembered chiefly as one of the few who pleased Malherbe. Though he labored over his sonnets, odes, and epigrams, his poetry has a certain grace along with its regularity. He used both the alexandrine and octosyllabic verse with dexterity.

## EPITAPH: TIME, WHICH DOES ALL CREATURES...

Time, which does all creatures kill,
   Has put the body underground
Of a certain bard whose quill
   Did both dead and living wound.

With his ink he blacked the name
Of the greatest kings whose fame
   Ne'er shall die nor be forgot;
And if 'gainst God he did not rise,
Uttering dreadful blasphemies,
   'Twas because he knew Him not.

HENRY CARRINGTON

Armand! I lose my vital heat,
   I see no longer as before,
I soon my ancestors shall meet
   Upon Cocytus' dismal shore.

There shall I follow in the train
    Of that illustrious king of France
Whose love did learned men sustain
    Through an age steeped in ignorance.

Soon as I join him where he stays,
    He will insist that I explain
What you are doing nowadays
    To heap disgrace on hated Spain.

With ease I shall at once obey
    By the fine record of your life,
And so the grief shall charm away,
    Recalled by Pavia's fatal strife.

But if he asks what post or place
    You gave me, how you helped to live,
What gifts bestowed, what acts of grace—
    What answer will you have me give?[28]

HENRY CARRINGTON

# Jean de Schélandre

## (1585?–1635)

Of a Protestant family, he began to write verses very early after the fashion of his master Ronsard. Opposed to Malherbe's insistence on formality, he refused to labor over his verses. His poems are vigorous and imaginative, and display that romantic sensitivity to nature and the love of conceits that characterized late sixteenth century French poetry. He also wrote for the stage. In some of his later dramas he ignored the unities and mixed tragedy and comedy in a way which indicates an acquaintance with Shakespeare, whose plays he may have seen during a visit to England in 1608.


## TO THE POETS OF OUR TIME

Wits of the present age, who please and shine,
    By airy subtleties and modish grace,
    Your words prosaic, each in ordered place
Force me to own you victors, and resign.

For me, I no more court the sisters nine,
    Gifts which from them I hold, new fashions chase,
    Yet may some stronger minds of older race
To your new sweets prefer my rougher line.

I have some coarser words, some rhymes deemed shallow.
But what wide glebe is found without a fallow?
    You may see Virgil limp, and Homer doze.[29]

**HENRY CARRINGTON**

# Jean de la Ceppède
## (1550–1622)

A native of Provence, a legal official, a devout Catholic, whose poetry is exclusively pious, his work had little audience from his own time until its recent revival by the present generation. He is one of a group of poets of the later sixteenth and early seventeenth centuries whose works have been rediscovered by an age which finds in them qualities much to its taste. Through strong images and strained, metaphysical paradox, his verse reveals a passionate spirituality. His obsession with the crucifixion and resurrection is evident in the following selections. In his agitated imagination familiar objects take on a fresh vividness: the wood, the nails, the crown of thorns, the stones (tomb), but above all else the blood. His principal works were: *Les Psaumes de la Penitence de David* (1594), and *Les Théorèmes Spirituels*, the latter containing about 500 sonnets.

## THÉORÈMES SPIRITUELS

My victorious King receives his vestments from mocking
Men at arms, but he is dressed inwardly
In a red royal tunic—so as conqueror
Of evil, prince of right, he stands in glory.
May I cry for him, for the purple and red,
That they might flow from me as tears
Yielding meaning, distilled from my contemplation
So that my being becomes a spring of his mystery.
Our sins are his color, lamb's wool
Stained red by the Father,
And so as Christ takes him as prince, he takes us,
And suffers them. O Christ, Holy Lamb, please hide
My red sins, hell's faggots for fire,
In my King's redeeming royalty.[30]

CLINTON LARSON

Love has given Him from paradise
For the red glory of our sins;
Wounds and spittle have lain under His crown of thorns;
Love has brought Mary the Mother to His tree,
Where He hangs from the hold of nails;
Love has brought Him to the sepulchre of stone;
Love has become His love—so great, so strong,
He attacks Hell and brings death to stone:
In His death's rigor He is your lover.

CLINTON LARSON

O Kingdom of Christ, you and He are one:
From the cross He lifts you to his throne;
He wears the diadem of thorns;
He bleeds himself pale and livid,
Empty for your ransom.
Today, in His body's stone, He summons you
To come and live in Him, in His chapels of mystery.
Come then, fair one, your groom asks it,
For He will bless you if you yield your heart to Him:
He will keep it in His living stone;
He will wrest it living from His own death's stone.[31]

CLINTON LARSON

O Cross, the old horror and fear of you are gone;
Christ has redeemed you from the wrath of God.
His blood becomes your elixir at Golgotha,
Where it fell to the earth it redeemed,
And so you are changed where you grow
From wormwood to moly; you are polished
Smooth, the Church of the elect.
Fair tower of David, where the shields of God
Repose on your doubled ramparts,
All men, and I, come to you, refuge!
You hold the gates of hell ajar;
Your image across them crosses me.
May you keep me from their captivity!

CLINTON LARSON

Great Sun, flame of Christ,
You have passed through four houses of the Zodiac:
Through Virgo, where Christ was born of flesh
From His soul, matched and matchless;
Through the Waterbearer, when He sorrowed
In tears, blameless; through the Bull,
When He offered His body on the gallows.
Now he enters the house of the Lion
With a mane of light whose beams
Enflame the hemispheres, and His voice
Is the shaking thunder, the roar from the grave
That brings the world of beasts to the yoke
Of His redemption.[32]

CLINTON LARSON


O Phoenix, cherished bird of Arabia,
You are the symbol of Christ the Hero.
He, like you, lies unenslaved among the dead.
You die on a scented pyre;
He dies on a tree that offers heaven its perfume.
Your ashes are his marrow;
You bear your ashes to an altar in the burning desert.
Christ, so resurrected, against the azure sky
And the vaults of stars You raise your tree of light.

CLINTON LARSON

# Jean de Sponde
## (1557–1595)

Known during his life as a translator, humanist, and jurist, he became converted to Catholicism late in life. Like several of his eccentric contemporaries, he has been rediscovered only in our century. He wrote *Sonnets d'amour* and poems of religious experience: *Sonnets et stances de la mort*; the long poem, *Stances du sacré banquet et convive de Jésus-Christ*; and *Méditations sur les Pseaumes avec un essai de quelques poèmes chrestiens*. He writes with passion and an ornateness that represents in striking fashion the metaphysical trend in late French Renaissance poetry. And yet there is a vast difference between his poetry and that of La Ceppède, with his visions of Christ's bleeding wounds. Sponde views the human situation broadly and with eloquent pessimism.

## SONNETS D'AMOUR III

Whoever were to stand in the heavens, and lower then his sight
    Upon the wide display of this dry element,
    He would believe all this to be only a single
    Mark, a mark still hidden by a cloudy veil:
But if he contemplate, from here, beyond that blue curtain,
    That crystal circle, that golden firmament,
    He would judge that his eyes' voyage across the skies is
      infinitely vast,
    And that such grandeur is, to us, totally unknown.
Thus of this great heaven, where love has guided me so sure,
    Of this great heaven of love o'er which my eye is stretched:
    If I unbend a little my keen attention to the other,
To the other loves, I see under a night's pall
    The world of Epicurus, to atoms now reduced:
    Their love all of earth, and mine celestial.[33]

ROBERT NUGENT

## SONNETS D'AMOUR XXVI

The winds groaned in the air, darkest cloud
   Upon darkest cloud was piled and hid the daylight from us,
   The depths of Hell were lifted to the skies,
   The sea with mountains, and the world with storms, was
     swelled:
When I saw a bird, leaving our shore,
   Fly to the very middle of these raging waves,
   Place there the straws gathered from her nest
   And suddenly calm the sea's frothy anger.
And so did love to me: like a Halcyon
   It lodged the other day within my passion
   And filled my unfortunate soul with fortune's good.
After the distress, at last, it gave me a quiet mind:
   But the sea falls calm but once a year,
   And the calmness of my soul will be there forever.[34]

ROBERT NUGENT

## SONNETS DE LA MORT IV

For whom so many travails? for yourself? whose breath
   Beats in the breast and bears its languor out?
   Your designs are far from the end of their strength,
   And you are very near your trouble's final rest.
I grant you still a certain hold on life's span,
   Which of itself flows—Time's uncertain rigor;
   Ah, finally you are to lose this fruit and this labor:
   The mountain is more often struck by thunder than the plain.
These envied scepters, these cast down treasures,
   Haughty field of the camp of your proud virtues,
   Are the dispute and the envy of avaricious death.
But why this care? but why this distress?
   Can you really define this life's course?
   The flight of life, the race towards death.[35]

ROBERT NUGENT

## SONNETS DE LA MORT V

Alas! count your days: the days which have gone
   Are already dead for you, those which are yet to come
   Shall all die at the moment of their newborn dawn,
   And half of life is by half Death's kingdom.
These proud desires, piled up pell-mell,
   This furious heart that your arm implores,
   This untamable arm that your heart adores:
   Death tortures them and brings them both to trial.
A thousand waves, a thousand reefs, impede your way;
   You break across, but at last, with no appeal or stay,
   You will be the plunder of the reefs and the waves.
An hour waits for you, a moment spies
   Upon you, unnatural executioners of your own lives,
   Who live your days in travail, and who die a death that gives
     no ease.

ROBERT NUGENT

## SONNETS DE LA MORT

Yet we must die, and though proud life might dare
   To laugh at death, it still will feel death's flay.
   The suns will blast these flowers of a day
   And time will crack this little phial of air;
This candle which now casts its smoky glare
   Will gutter, to its own green wax a prey,
   The colors in this painting will decay,
   And waves, too, break on beaches, frothy, bare.
I have had bright lightning blind my eyes
   And heard its thunder growling in the skies
   Where storms have charged the driven atmosphere.
I have watched snows melt in floods, then dry;
   Seen roaring lions tamed to rageless fear:
   Live, men, make life your all, yet you must die.

JOHN R. GALT

## SONNETS DE LA MORT

Who, who are these whose fawning hearts, debased,
   Abjectly covet fame and worldly hoards?
   Who are the servants, who the noble lords;
   The black-souled and the alabaster-faced?
These fraudulent, mad masquers who would waste
   Their time to flatter those the court rewards,
   And these who thrust with ineffective swords
   Once more at heavens they cannot ungrace?
Who are the schemers tacking far from land,
   Fawners on life and traitors to life's end
   Whose star is their own gain, their wind mere whim?
I, too, would fear death, sailing this same sea,
   Did I not know that life is, although dim,
   The beacon leading to eternity.

JOHN R. GALT

## SONNETS DE LA MORT

All swells against me, tempts me, and assails:
   The world, the flesh, and that revolted Prince
   Whose wave, whose power and deceit torments
   And overwhelms me, Lord; whose spell prevails.
What ship, what purpose, what deaf ear avails
   That You provide for danger, frailty, sense
   Which dazzles us? Your templed immanence,
   Strong voice and mighty hand which never fails?
For what? Oh God, I often feel the war
   This rebel angel wages still with Your
   Own temple, hand, and voice: My flesh, this world.
But yet Your altar, hand, and voice will be
   Ship, strength, and ear which break the spell for me
   And turn each wave, each onslaught that is hurled.[36]

JOHN R. GALT

# Jean-Baptiste Chassignet
## (1570?–1635)

Like Sponde and La Ceppède, he is a rediscovery of our century. His early work, *Le Mépris de la vie et Consolation contre la mort* (1594), contains over 400 sonnets dealing predominantly with the theme of mortality, on which he reflects with imaginative and varied comparisons. In 1601 came *Paraphrases sur les douze petits prophètes*, and in 1613 *Paraphrases sur les psaumes*. He lived his life in obscurity and deeply felt creativity, his sole inspiration the Bible, which he transformed to poetry that was grave, correct, and often, through metaphors, deeply moving, and died while working on the Book of Job.

## HIS SCORN OF LIFE AND CONSOLATION FOR DEATH

As little children fear a spectral shade,
   A phantom, or a mask, so, too, do we
   Fear death and in our hearts feel it to be
As it is painted: frightful, sad, decayed.
As honest artists, or those who degrade:
   Engravers, sculptors, or false painters, see
   Death and represent it falsely, we
Define it, sweet or awful, as portrayed.
These apprehensions, torturing our minds,
   Drive us ahead of them like yearling hinds
   Fleeing before a wolf; we have no space
To see it clearly: let us leave such dreams,
   Then we will find death other than it seems,
   With gentle touch, and with a pleasant face.

JOHN R. GALT

# Théophile de Viau
## (1590–1626)

A poet who had much in common with his friend Saint-Amant, he regrettably dissipated his gifts in varied and often violent activities. His part in a licentious publication and his reputation as leader of freethinkers resulted in arrest, banishment, and finally death from hardships suffered. His tragedy *Pyrame et Thisbe* was a successful and lyrical play reminiscent of the Elizabethans. Although an enemy of Malherbe, he could write in classical form; but, like several others of his generation, he was a romantic who, in his feeling for nature, his musical sensitivity, and surrealistic suggestiveness, anticipated later poetic styles. To be sure, at times he succumbed, like the others, to the affectations of preciosity. Five volumes of his poems were published during his life.

## ODE

Before me, where a raven croaks,
Deep shadow sets my sight at loss;
Two weasels and two foxes cross
The narrow path my passing chokes;
My horse goes lame and nearly stops;
My epileptic servant drops;
I hear the violent thunder's birth;
Hear Charon calling me to him.
A shape, arising, spectral, dim
Reveals the center of the earth.

This stream flows backward to its source;
Up a belfry climbs an ox;
Blood runs streaming out of rocks;
An asp takes a she-bear by force;

On an ancient tower's crest
A serpent tears a vulture's breast;
A fire, deep in ice, burns hot;
The sun takes on a blackened pall;
I see the moon about to fall;
That tree has left its rooted spot.[37]

JOHN R. GALT

## TO CORINNA

In this unpeopled shady valley
The stag that bays the murmuring stream
Bounds lightly from some verdant alley
To spy the water's silvery gleam.

A naiad dwelling by the spring
Throws open wide each evening
Her door of shining crystal made
And sings a joyful serenade.

Here silence deep and shadows dim
Amid the clustered elm-trees hover,
While amorous Zephyrs rock each limb
And every leaf with kisses cover.

Come, my Corinna, come and lie
At ease upon this mossy bed,
Or if you fear some envious eye,
We'll choose this hollow grot instead.

Here love has built a fragrant bower,
Here Venus' self has set her shrine,
And in this haunt of vine and flower
No feet shall tread but yours and mine.

How I love your lawless tresses,
That wander daintily remiss,
Touching your cheek with warm caresses
Till I grow jealous of their kiss.

O lovely lips of rose and amber,
Lips to melt the heart of Jove,
Here where the honeysuckles clamber,
How can ye speak of aught but love?

O dainty fingers, snowy white!
If by the streamlet's mossy brink
Some god should stray, in his delight
He'd kiss them and forget to drink.

Nay, hide those lily hands away,
Nor in the brook your beauty glass;
In my fond eyes your charms survey,
And let the god unheeded pass.

Here where pale myrtles dot the ground,
And peeping violets feed the sight,
And waters make a pleasant sound,
We'll sit and kiss from morn till night.

Shrill the chaffinch and the linnet
In the rosebush tune their lay,
With a trembling passion in it
Born of springtide and the May.

Come, then, come, my trembling dryad!
By this music-making stream,
With the lark we'll form a triad,
And we'll sing of love's sweet dream.

I will bathe my eager fingers
In the billows of your hair,
Like a devotee who lingers,
Saying o'er and o'er his prayer.

Fear no harm from Cupid's wiles,
Listen to the love I plead,
And your answer in your smiles
And your blushing cheek I'll read.

My Corinna, let me kiss you,
There's no witness near but Love;
Sol's bright arrows here will miss you:
This is Cupid's sacred grove.

Gossip Zephyrs overhead
Watch us in our leafy bed
While we whisper, hand in hand,
Things no Zephyrs understand.[38]

WILLIAM FREDERIC GIESE

# *François de Malherbe*
## (1555–1628)

Unofficial laureate of the court of Henry IV and of the Queen Regent, Marie de Medicis, dictator of the school of "new" poetry, Malherbe exercised great influence over the first generation of the seventeenth century and, indeed, through the entire century. He voiced the doctrine that poetry must be regarded as a craft demanding slow, careful workmanship. Opposed to the Pléiade, Italianism, inspiration, and freedom of form, opposed to spontaneity and affectation, he insisted upon purity of poetic diction and a stricter regulation of rhyming. In other words, he pointed in the direction of correctness, anticipating the classicists of the second half of the century.

In his own poetry, after his theories and his style were developed, he achieved an impeccable style and lofty expression, but he lacked warmth and was not distinguished as a lyrist.

## CONSOLATION TO M. DU PÉRIER

Du Perier, must thy grief eternal be?
   And the distressful plaints
Which thy paternal love incessantly
   Repeats pass all restraints?

This blow—thy daughter to the grave consigned
   By death decreed for all—
Is it a maze, whence thine entangled mind
   May not its steps recall?

I know what charms did thy lost child commend,
   And I shall ne'er attempt
To soothe thy sorrow, as a heartless friend,
   With words that breathe contempt.

But she was of the earth, where things most fair
　　Still find the saddest lot,
And Rose the little span that roses share
　　Of life exceeded not.


Say, had your prayers been granted, and suppose
　　Your darling had obtained,
With hair, age-whitened o'er, her course to close,
　　What then would she have gained?


Think you she would, if old, in heaven's fair court
　　A dearer welcome have?
Or with less pain funereal dust support
　　And worm that haunts the grave?


No; soon as Atropos has closed her shears,
　　And soul from body sped,
'Ere Charon's bark is won, age disappears
　　And follows not the dead.


Death sternness hath to which nought else compares;
　　And though we loud complain,
Remorseless as she is she stops her ears,
　　And lets us plead in vain.


The poor man in his cottage 'neath the thatch
　　Under her law she brings;
The guard that o'er the Louvre keeps his watch
　　Saves not from her our kings.


'Gainst her to murmur, or our patience lose,
　　Is folly at the best;
The only wisdom is God's choice to choose—
　　This only gives us rest.[39]

HENRY CARRINGTON

## TO LOUIS XIII

I yield unto the conquering hand of age;
Only my mind, unbated in its course,
Can show even yet upon my latest page
　　Its primal force.
The Muses came to crown my infant brow
With gracious wreaths of never-fading bays;
I had their favors young, I have them now
　　In my last days.
So shall you learn how great a gift is mine,
How great my skill; and from my Muse's wings
Shall flash such rays as never yet did shine
　　On crownèd kings.
Whether your martial feats my song inspire
Or in my verse your royal goodness shine,
What bard is there so vain to think his lyre
　　Can equal mine?
Amphion, who a city raised from naught,
And won the plaudits of the universe,
Though great his fame, no greater marvel wrought
　　Than my proud verse.
My lines shall fill the world with thy renown;
The very peoples of the Nile shall bring,
When this they read, their fairest flowers to crown
　　Louis our king.

WILLIAM FREDERIC GIESE

# Honoré d'Urfé
## (1567?–1625)

Born at Marseille of an only family, he spent his youth in his château at Forez. For his part in the troubles of the Ligue, he was at first imprisoned and later banished. Unoccupied, he began *L'Astrée*, the lengthy Arcadian romance on which he continued to work for the remainder of his life.

*L'Astrée* was published in parts from 1610–27, the first two parts appearing in 1610, the third in 1619. The fourth was edited by his secretary in 1627, and the fifth was added by his secretary from notes he left. Each of the five parts or volumes is divided into twelve books. In prose and verse, this prototype of a flood of romantic fiction of the century especially delighted its feminine readers from Mme. de Rambouillet to Mme. de Sevigné. But men such as Boileau and La Fontaine also spoke of it admiringly, and Rousseau made a pilgrimage to Urfé's castle. It shows the influence of preciosity and was the precursor of the sentimental novel. Some "Stances" are given here.

## SONG OF THE INCONSTANT HYLAS
### Out of Astrea

If one disdain me, then I fly
Her cruelty, and her disdain;
And e'er the morning gild the sky,
Another mistress do obtain.
    They err who hope by force to move
    A woman's heart to like; or love.

It oft falls out that they, who in
Discretion seem us to despise,
Nourish a greater fire within,
Although perhaps conceal'd it lies,
    Which we, when once we quit our rooms,
    Do kindle for the next that comes.

The faithful fool that obstinate
Pursues a cruel beauty's love,
To him, and to his truth ingrate
Idolater does he not prove?
    That from his pow'rless idol, never
    Receives a med'cine for his fever.

They say the unweary'd lover's pains
By instance meet with good success;
For he by force his end obtains:
'Tis an odd method of address,
    To what design so e'er 't relate,
    Still, still to be importunate.

Do but observe the hourly fears
Of your pretended faithful lover,
Nothing but sorrow, sighs, and tears,
You in his cheerfull'st looks discover;
    As though the lover's sophistry
    Were nothing but to whine and cry.

Ought he by a man's name be stil'd,
That (losing the honour of a man)
Whines for his pippin, like a child
Whipp'd and sent back to school again,
    Or rather fool that thinks amiss,
    He loves, but knows not what love is!

For my part I'll decline this folly,
By others' harms (thank fate) grown wise,
Such dotage begets melancholy,
I must profess love's liberties;
    And never angry am at all
    At them who me inconstant call.[40]

CHARLES COTTON

## Vincent Voiture
### (1597?–1648)

A prominent public servant, he served at court and was sent on missions to Italy and Spain. He was a brilliant conversationalist, a leading figure in the salon of the Hôtel de Rambouillet, an original member of the French Academy. His letters show his wit as well as his serious side. Preciosity is present in his work, but he uses it with conscious playfulness. His touch is spontaneous and delicate in the manner of the Italians whom the *Précieuses* admired. He used a variety of forms—*stances*, *épîtres*, *chansons*, sonnets, epigrams—but it was for his revival of the rondeau that he was especially noted. The irony of some of his epistles gives a foretaste of Voltaire.

### RONDEAU: IN GOOD PLAIN FRENCH...

In good plain French your words devoutly rise
More solemn than a monkey could devise;
   Your soul aye finds so little that doth please,
    We well might think our France and all her sees
Turned round your reverend worship pivot-wise.

For every matter you have bigot sighes,
For all our wickedness teares fill your eyes;
   You hide your Spanish heart in homilies
        Of good plain French.

Then leave our State untroubled of your cries;
A worthy sailor-man the rudder plies:
   For, if we must speak frankly at our ease,
    Although your mind is full of subtleties,
That you're a blockhead we all realize
        In good plain French.

WILFRID THORLEY

On the way from Fontenay
Along the high road to Gournay,
Composing verses without plan,
For whim alone he did obey,
Voiture, the cold, unfeeling man,
His feigned love attempted to display.

The nymphs of forests and of streams,
Listening to his plaintive themes,
Poured forth their laughter unrepressed;
But a Faun who heard him too,
This to the Dryads did suggest:
"Perhaps his declaration is too true."

JUDITH MCDOWELL

## EVENING BEAUTY

With roses crowned, the nymph that I adore
    Walked in the evening glow across the lawn,
    Her cheeks and eyes so bright that all men swore
    'Twas not my love but reappearing dawn.
The earth to greet her sprouted thousand flowers,
    The birds on every bough held jubilee,
    And paling stars forgot to count the hours,
    Deeming new day was rising from the sea.
The sun forspent, that hovered on the deep,
    Infused new splendors in his golden beams
    And bade his fiery chariot eastward sweep,
Unbarred by Neptune and the ocean streams,
    Till, love-bedazed yet fearing her disdain,
    He seaward plunged and dared not come again.

WILLIAM FREDERIC GIESE

# Tristan l'Hermite

## (1601?–1655)

François l'Hermite, sieur de Solier, called "Tristan l'Hermite," lived a life of adventure and pleasure. He was best known as author of a number of tragedies, one of them, *Mariamne*, rivaling Corneille's *Le Cid* in popularity. He also wrote an autobiographical novel, *Le Page disgracié*. His poems on nature, while less original than Théophile's, have the same evocative power and perceptiveness. They anticipate the Symbolists and show how deep was the French impulse to romanticism in an age striving at the same time for classical correctness of form. Like most of the writers of his generation, he cultivated preciosity, yet unmistakably he combines sincere feeling with it.

### THE BRACELET

Now Love be prais'd! that cruel fair,
　　Who my poor heart restrains
　　Under so many chains,
Hath weav'd a new one for it of her hair.

These threads of amber us'd to play
　　With every courtly wind;
　　And never were confin'd;
But in a thousand curls allow'd to stray.

Cruel each part of her is grown;
　　Nor less unkind than she
　　These fetters are to me,
Which to restrain my freedom, lose their own.

THOMAS STANLEY

# Antoine-Girard de Saint-Amant
## (1594–1661)

Antoine-Girard (also spelled Gérard, Giraud), who claimed to be sieur de Saint-Amant, was a convert to Catholicism who combined a military and diplomatic career with a life of pleasure in Paris and Rouen. He was an original member of the French Academy and friend of Théophile de Viau. Among his works are several collections of poetry which show his love of life in the witty Gallic spirit exemplified by Rabelais and Régnier. A poet in the Cavalier vein, he is also a precursor of nineteenth century French romanticism. His *La Solitude* makes use of all the trappings of the mysterious—a ruined castle, tombs, a ghost, the wild charm of nature. He was the author of five volumes of poetry and a dull epic, *Moyse sauvé*, which he called an *idylle héroique*.

## THE ALPINE WINTER

These particles of fire which glisten in the snow,
    These sparks of azure, gold, and crystal, flakes of light,
    Which Winter wears like oriental garments bright,
    And seems like white hair tossing in a gusty blow.
This heavenly cotton drape with which the peaks are dressed;
    This bright transparency of silver, of worth near
    To gold; this air which suits, so healthy and so clear,
    The vital spirit: these sweet gleams my eyes attest.
This season pleases me. I like its cold embrace;
    Its robes of innocence, its pure and open face
    Can somewhat hide the crimes of which earth bears such trace.
Therefore, th' Olympian's view of Winter's not unkind;
    His rage has spared it and no thundering bolt from space,
    To desolate its days, has ever Jove consigned.

ROSE E. BURCKHARDT

## THE ENJOYMENT

Far from the court's ambitious noise
Retir'd, to those more harmless joys
Which the sweet country, pleasant fields,
And my own court, a cottage, yields;
I liv'd from all disturbance free,
Though prisoner (Sylvia) unto thee;
Secur'd from fears, which others prove,
Of the inconstancy of Love;
A life, in my esteem, more blest,
Than e'er yet stoop'd to Death's arrest.

My senses and desires agreed,
With joint delight each other feed:
A bliss, I reach'd, as far above
Words, as her beauty, or my love;
Such as compar'd with which, the joys
Of the most happy seem but toys:
Affection I receive and pay,
My pleasures knew not Grief's allay:
The more I tasted I desir'd,
The more I quench'd my thirst was fir'd.

Now, in some place where Nature shows
Her naked beauty, we repose;
Where she allures the wand'ring eye
With colours, which faint art outvie;
Pearls scatter'd by the weeping morn,
Each where the glitt'ring flowers adorn;
The mistress of the youthful year
(To whom kind Zephyrus doth bear
His amorous vows and frequent prayer)
Decks with these gems her neck and hair.

Hither, to quicken Time with sport,
The little sprightly Loves resort,
And dancing o'er the enamel'd mead,
Their mistresses the Graces lead;

Then to refresh themselves, repair
To the soft bosom of my fair;
Where from the kisses they bestow
Upon each other, such sweets flow
As carry in their mixéd breath
A mutual power of life and death.

Next in an elm's dilated shade
We see a rugged Satyr laid,
Teaching his reed, in a soft strain,
Of his sweet anguish to complain;
Then to a lonely grove retreat,
Where day can no admittance get,
To visit peaceful solitude;
Whom seeing by repose pursu'd,
All busy cares, for fear to spoil
Their calmer courtship, we exile.

There underneath a myrtle, thought
By Fairies sacred, where was wrought
By Venus' hand Love's mysteries,
And all the trophies of her eyes,
Our solemn prayers to Heaven we send,
That our firm love might know no end;
Nor time its vigour e'er impair:
Then to the wingéd God we sware,
And grav'd the oath in its smooth rind,
Which in our hearts we deeper find.

Then to my dear (as if afraid
To try her doubted faith) I said,
"Would in thy soul my form as clear,
As in thy eyes I see it, were."
She kindly angry saith, "Thou art
Drawn more at large within my heart;
These figures in my eye appear
But small, because they are not near,
Thou through these glasses seest thy face,
As pictures through their crystal case."

Now with delight transported, I
My wreathéd arms about her tie;
The flattering Ivy never holds
Her husband Elm in stricter folds:
To cool my fervent thirst, I sip
Delicious nectar from her lip.
She pledges, and so often past
This amorous health, till Love at last
Our souls did with these pleasures sate,
And equally inebriate.

Awhile, our senses stol'n away,
Lost in this ecstasy we lay,
Till both together rais'd to life,
We re-engage in this kind strife.
Cythaera with her Syrian boy
Could never reach our meanest joy.
The childish God of Love ne'er tried
So much of love with his cold bride,
As we in one embrace include,
Contesting each to be subdu'd.[41]

THOMAS STANLEY

## THE ORGY

Friends, our lives are lost in rhyme,
Let's not continue killing time;
Bacchus invites us here to lead
Quite a different life indeed.
Let's leave Apollo a fop unsung;
Let's desecrate his lyre with dung.
Plague on the Muses of Parnassus,
If maids they be, they are not lasses;
Plague on consecrated creeks,
Drawing pencils and fiddle sticks;
By any other name poetic
Inspiration is frenetic.

Laval, I still call Pegasus
A horse in the last analysis;
Who follows him and follows his course
Follows and is himself a horse.
    Good Lord! Outside look how it rains!
Let's make it rain inside our veins
With wine, which is to say with laughter,
And that's the very word we're after.
Let's sing and dance and carry on,
Let's drink until the night is gone,
So that tomorrow's sunrise will
Find us all at table still.
Away with slumber and repose;
For when the tomb and death enclose
Our sorry bones with others such,
Alas, we shall but sleep too much.
Let's drink this sweet juice of the vine;
I see Faret and his design
To make his bosom worthy of
This deity, and I approve.
    Bacchus! Behold our bacchanal,
By thy sainted mug, I shall
Draw a rough draft of that cup
And without water drink it up.
By thine ivy coronet,
By the most famous cabaret,
By thy thirst so formidable,
By thy health indomitable,
By thine honored revelries,
By thy howling bacchantes,
By the cymbal, by the drum,
By banquet boards for all who come,
By the blessed Lent thus ended,
By this goblet, great and splendid,
By thine orgies' pipes and flutes,
By thy glorious attributes,
By thy sighs from belches sprung,
By the smoked beef of this tongue,
By thy cohorts, plotting slyly,

By this bisque renowned so highly.
By each blushing drunken mug,
By the majesty of this jug,
By the shots not fired but drunk,
By goats like us in lewdness sunk,
By skoal! good health! and clinck of glass,
By old Silenus on the ass,
By the satyrs that attend thee,
By thy great wench Ariadne,
By thy conquests manifold,
By this cheese both ripe and old,
By all innocent delights,
By thy high and holy rites,
By thy panthers, black and savage,
By this hanging length of sausage,
By tobacco, thy sole perfume,
By the loveliest grapes in bloom,
By thy colors, white and red,
By this ham with spices spread,
By the pot that is thy bell,
By this grilled meat seasoned well,
By this place so fresh and sweet,
By this olive which I eat,
By this orange, gay passport,
By Gillot, thy pet, in short,
Receive us in thy happy band,
These honest knights with glass in hand,
And to prove thyself divine,
Never leave us without wine.[42]

CHRIS RICHARDS

# Pierre Corneille
## (1606–1684)

One of the great dramatists of a brilliant century of drama in France, a veritable "classic," Corneille wrote more than thirty plays, the best known being *Le Cid*, *Horace*, *Cinna*, *Polyeucte*, and *Les Menteurs*. In his early years he was well known and admired at the celebrated salon of la Marquise de Rambouillet. In the field of lyric poetry, he is distinctly a minor figure, inclining to reason and rhetoric rather than feeling, but he is capable of turning a witty piece for an occasion.

## STANZAS TO THE MARQUISE

Think, Marquise! what if my face
Show a wrinkle here and there?
You at my age will, Your Grace,
Also show some signs of wear.

Times spares none; if he imposes
Marks of age upon me now,
Soon too he will blight your roses
Just as he now seams my brow.

Subject to the planets' law,
Day to night turns, youth to age:
I was once what you now are:
You will reach my present stage.

Yet I have a certain charm,
Potent in its properties,
That absolves me from alarm,
Great though be Time's ravages.

Though your charms be loved by men,
My attractions, that you scorn,
May be youthful even when
Those that you vaunt are outworn.

They may keep alive the glory
Of such eyes as I found fair:
Future men will read my story
And believe what's written there.

By our far descendants, who
To my writings will give credit,
Beauty will be granted you
Just so far as I'll have said it.

Ponder on it, fair Marquise!
Greybeards may offend the eye,
Yet 'tis worth your while to please
Greybeards of such stuff as I.[43]

ALAN CONDER

# GUIRLANDE DE JULIE

The Hôtel de Rambouillet, home of the Marquise de Rambouillet, was the intellectual center of Paris society in the first half of the seventeenth century. The marquise, a woman of intelligence and charm, received people of rank and writers of distinction, creating the first authentic salon. It was there that *préciocité* was cultivated and brought into fashion.

*Guirlande de Julie* was a handsome vellum book, decorated by the floral painter Nicolas Robert and written by the calligrapher Nicolas Jarry. It contained 91 poems, chiefly madrigals, contributed by nineteen frequenters of the Hôtel de Rambouillet. It was presented to Julie d'Angennes, daughter of the marquise, on her Saint's day, May 22, 1641, by the Duc de Montausier, whom she subsequently married.

# Charles de Sainte-Maure, Duc de Montausier

## (1610–1690)

A distinguished gentleman who served Louis XIV and supervised the education of the Dauphin, he was a *habitué* of the Hôtel de Rambouillet. After fourteen years of courtship, he married Julie, daughter of the Marquise de Rambouillet. His literary recognition rests chiefly on his role in the creation of the *Guirlande*.

### GUIRLANDE DE JULIE
### MADRIGAL

Recevez, ô Nymphe adorable,
Dont les cœurs reçoivent les lois,
Cette Couronne plus durable
Que celles que l'on met sur la tête des Rois.
Les fleurs dont ma main la compose
Font honte à ces fleurs d'or qu'on voit au firmament;
L'eau dont Permesse les arrose
Leur donne une fraîcheur qui dure incessamment;
Et tous les jours ma belle Flore,
Qui me chérit et que j'adore,
Me reproche avecque courroux
Que mes soupirs jamais pour elle
N'ont fait naître de fleur si belle
Que j'en ai fait naître pour vous.

MONTAUSIER

Receive, oh Nymph adorable,
From whom our hearts receive their law,
This Garland, far more durable

Than crown we place upon the kingly brow.
These flowers which my hand composes
Will shame the golden flowers of the sky.
The dew Consent show'rs on these posies
Gives them a freshness that will never die.
Now Flora fair, whom I adore,
And who befriended me of yore,
Reproaches me as one untrue,
Because for her my sighs ne'er brought
To life a flower so finely wrought
As these I here present to you.

HAROLD M. PRIEST

## LE NARCISSE

Je consacre, Julie, un narcisse à ta gloire;
Lui-même des beautés te cède la victoire.
Étant jadis touché d'un amour sans pareil,
  Pour voir dedans l'eau son image,
  Il baissait toujours son visage
Qu'il estimait plus beau que celui du soleil.
Ce n'est plus ce dessein qui tient sa tête basse;
C'est qu'en te regardant, il a honte de voir
  Que les dieux ont eu le pouvoir
De faire une beauté qui la sienne surpasse.

MONTAUSIER

Julie, I pledge thee this Narcissus fair;
Thy beauty he concedes beyond compare.
One time enamored by consuming love,
  Spying his image in the pond,
  He lavished on it kisses fond,
Deeming it fairer than the sun above.
No more is it for that his head hangs down;
'Tis that in seeing thee he's shamed to find
  That the gods their art combined
To frame a beauty greater than his own.

HAROLD M. PRIEST

# Jean Desmarets de Saint-Sorlin
## (1595?–1676)

He held various high administrative offices and was an original member of the Academy. Besides being a lyric poet, he was a dramatist and a polemical writer anticipating Chateaubriand. He wrote two epics on Christian and national themes and defended their use against Boileau's objections in *Art poétique*. His romance *Ariane* is a story of Rome under Nero. Among his comedies is *Les Visionnaires*, which gave Molière material for *Les Femmes savantes* and which may have been suggested by the elegant and intellectual Mme. de Rambouillet. His lyrics, which exhibit a certain grace and power, often have religious subjects.

### LA VIOLETTE

Franche d'ambition, je me cache sous l'herbe,
Modeste en ma couleur, modeste en mon séjour;
Mais, si sur votre front je puis me voir un jour,
La plus humble des fleurs sera la plus superbe.

DESMARETS


With no pretentions, in the grass I hide,
My color modest and my place so low;
But if one day I can adorn your brow,
The humblest flower will be most glorified.

JUDITH MCDOWELL

# Claude de Malleville
## (1597–1647)

Secretary to several distinguished people, finally King Louis XIII, he became one of the original members of the French Academy. Although he is now remembered principally for his contribution to *Guirlande de Julie*, his poetry was highly regarded in his own time, and a sonnet of his, *La Belle Matineuse*, was considered the equal of Voiture's on the same subject. He was not always the *précieux* trifler but could also achieve effective realism or lyric melancholy.

### LA COURONNE IMPÉRIALE

Bien que de la Rose et du Lis
Deux rois d'éternelle mémoire
Fassent voir leurs fronts embellis,
Ces fleurs sont moindres que ta gloire;
Il faut un plus riche ornement
Pour récompenser dignement
Une vertu plus que royale;
Et, si l'on se veut acquitter,
On ne peut moins te présenter
Qu'une couronne impériale.

MALLEVILLE

The Lily and the Rose may be
Two monarchs of eternal name
That show their heads most splendidly,
But lesser theirs than your high fame;
A richer wreath we must afford,
Your virtue justly to reward,
A virtue pure yet queenly too;
And if to laud is our intent,
No less a gift must we present
Than an Imperial Crown for you.

JUDITH MCDOWELL

# Jean Ogier de Gombauld
## (also Gombaud, Gombault)
## (1570–1666)

One of the founders of the French Academy as well as a frequenter of the Hôtel de Rambouillet, he wrote a pastoral (verse) drama *Amaranthe*, and a prose romance *Endymion* as well as tragedies, which are now forgotten. His volumes of verse are *Poésies* (1646), and *Sonnets* (1649). The sonnet form was his particular forte. With other *habitués* of the Rambouillet salon, he contributed to the *Guirlande de Julie*.

## L'AMARANTE

Je suis la fleur d'amour qu'amarante on appelle
Et qui viens de Julie adorer les beaux yeux.
Roses, retirez-vous, j'ai le nom d'immortelle!
Il n'appartient qu'à moi de couronner les dieux.

GOMBAULD


I am the flower of love, that Amaranthus mild,
Here off'ring tribute to my Julie's eyes so bright.
Pale roses, now withdraw; for I'm "immortal" styled.
To crown immortal gods I claim as my sole right.

HAROLD M. PRIEST

# SPANISH POEMS

# *Anonymous*

## GALLEYS OF SPAIN

Ye galleys of our land
   Arrest your oars again,
That he, my love, may rest,
   Who drags your heavy chain.

Bright galleys! on the surge
   Ye bear with every stroke,
The surges of my thoughts,
   Which fear and love awoke.
Upon the ocean's breast
   Its fair winds move again;
So let my lover rest
   Who drags your heavy chain.

The waters of the sea
   Though cold, inflame my soul;
My love's pure light would glow
   E'en at the icy pole.
That love on whirlwind's breast
   Would fly across the main,
To let my lover rest
   Who drags your heavy chain.

Oh wait! bright galleys now,
   In some fair harbour wait,
Or guard the narrow pass
   Of some not-distant strait;
Or, at the maid's behest,
   In tranquil port remain,
That he, my love, may rest,
   Who drags your heavy chain.

The winter hours draw nigh;
  Come, galleys, then, and stay,
In cheerful solitude,
  Within a sheltered bay;
There ye may anchor best,
  For there no dangers reign—
So let my lover rest
  Who drags your heavy chain.[1]

JOHN BOWRING

# Juan del Encina
## (1468–1529?)

Leaving the University of Salamanca to serve the Duke of Alba in 1493, he was present at the siege of Granada, which he celebrated in his *Triunfo de Fama* in Italy in 1498. In Rome in the early years of the sixteenth century, he became a favorite of Pope Alexander VI, the father of Cesare and Lucrezia Borgia. He was ordained a priest about 1515 and appointed prior of the monastery at León. Before he was twenty-five, he composed over 170 lyrics, sixty-eight of which together with the music he wrote for them can be found in Asenjo Barbieri's *Cancionero Musical.* His lyrics alternate between elaborately figured conceits and simple devotional poems. Also a writer of eclogues, he created real flesh and blood Spanish shepherds in place of the traditional figures. As a religious dramatist he began the movement which ended with Calderon's *Auto Sacramentales.* He was also noted for his elegant secular dramas.


### CHORUS

Let us give ourselves to pleasure,
   Care will follow
   With no need for beck or hollo.

Let us then enjoy the day,
Take a rest from weary toil,
Let no grief our laughter spoil
But dismiss it far away.
Far and far off let it stay,
   Care will follow
   With no need for beck or hollo.

Let us join the search for pleasure,
Bid a long farewell to trouble;
They will find their trials double
Who their ills and sorrows treasure.
Welcome joys without a measure,
    Care will follow
    With no need for beck or hollo.

From our woes we'll flee apace
With all the strength that in us lies;
Every worry we'll despise,
Still the path of gladness trace,
After pleasure lightly race,
    Care will follow
    With no need for beck or hollo.

ENVOY

Let us always joyous be,
Gay and full of laughter ever;
From sad thoughts ourselves dissever,
Part from them right merrily.
After pleasure let us flee,
    Care will follow
    With no need for beck or hollo.

                    BEATRICE GILMAN PROSKE

MINGO'S DISCOURSE

Look you, Gil, at dawn
Cool is the country air;
The huts give shadow where
A burning sun has shone,

And he who lays him down
Among the flocks to sleep
Will find repose as deep
As any lord in town.

With what a pleasant sound
The cricket blithely sings!
How sweet the piping rings!
No sweeter tune is found.

With what delight the panting
And thirsty shepherd kneels
And to his parched throat feels
The water coolness granting

From fount or current slanting
That over pebbles rushes
Where sound of laughter gushes!
What pleasure more enchanting?

BEATRICE GILMAN PROSKE

# Gil Vicente
## (1470?–1536)

He was a Portuguese dramatist who wrote in his native language
but also in Spanish. By trade he was a goldsmith. As a literary man he
followed and imitated Encina, composing some forty-three dramas—
religious, comic, and tragi-comic. His plays were full of religious and
social criticisms which were highly original in his day. The songs in
his plays, which were full of sincerity and passion and were written in
graceful lyric stanzas, cannot always be authenticated as original; for
he is thought sometimes to have adapted popular airs. However, the
selection "Grace and beauty has the maid," from his play *Auto da
Sibilla Cassandra*, is known to be his. His poetry reflects a profound
insight into the human spirit.

## CANTIGA

Muy graciosa es la doncella,
¡cómo es bella y hermosa!

Digas tú, el marinero,
que en las naves vivías,
si la nave o la vela o la estrella
es tan bella.

Digas tú, el caballero,
que las armas vestías,
si el caballo o las armas o la guerra
es tan bella.

Digas tú, el pastorcico,
que el ganadico guardas,
si el ganado o las valles o la sierra
es tan bella.

Grace and beauty has the maid,
Could anything more lovely be?

Sailor, you who live on ships,
Did you ever see
Any ship or sail or star
As beautiful as she?

Knight of war, in armour clad,
Did you ever see
Horse or arms or battlefield
As beautiful as she?

Shepherd, you who guard your flock,
Did you ever see
Cattle, vale or mountain range
As beautiful as she?

ALICE JANE MCVAN

## SONG

If thou art sleeping, maiden,
   Awake and open thy door,
'Tis the break of day, and we must away
   O'er meadow, and mount, and moor.

Wait not to find thy slippers,
   But come with thy naked feet:
We shall have to pass through the dewy grass
   And waters wide and fleet.

HENRY WADSWORTH LONGFELLOW

## BALLAD OF FLÉRIDA

It was the month of April
Before the dawn of May,
When the lilies and the roses
Their gladdest hues display,

On the fairest night serene
That heaven could conceive
When Flérida the lovely
Infanta took her leave.

Within her father's garden
To the trees she spoke and said,
"Never shall I see you more
Until the day I'm dead,

"Nor nightingales' sweet singing
Among the branches hear.
Farewell, O water cold,
Farewell, O water clear.

"God keep you all, my flowers,
Which once my glory were;
I go to foreign lands
Since fate has called me there.

"And if my father seek me,
Who loved me well and long,
Say it's love that leads me,
That mine was not the wrong.

"So urgent was his call
He swayed me by his power.
Alas, I cannot see my way,
None warned me in that hour."

Then spoke the knight Don Duardos,
"My love, pray weep not so.
In the pleasant land of England
Clearer waters flow.

"And brighter gardens blossom,
And thou may'st walk therein.
Thou shalt have three hundred maidens
All born of noble kin.

"Palaces of silver
Shall be thy dwelling place;
Hyacinth and emerald
In the hangings interlace.

"The rooms are paved with gold
Which out of Turkey came;
Enameled legends tell
My story and my name.

"They tell the smart of wounds
Thou gavest me that day
When fronting Primaleón
I struggled in the fray.

"Lady, thou didst slay me,
Of him I had no fears."
Flérida heard him speaking
And dried away her tears.

And they went down to the galleys
Of Don Duardos's pride;
A fleet of fifty were they
All sailing on the tide.

To the gentle sound of rowing
The Infanta fell asleep
In the arms of Don Duardos
Who well his own might keep.

All men who now draw breath
Learn wisdom from my tale:
O'er power of love and death
There's none that can prevail.[2]

BEATRICE GILMAN PROSKE

# Garcilaso de la Vega
## (1503–1536)

After joining the royal bodyguard in 1521, he found favor with Emperor Charles V. He fought with distinction at the Battle of Pavia, but as a result of a court intrigue he was exiled for a short time to an island on the Danube. Later he served in the Spanish embassies in Italy, principally at Naples. At the age of thirty-three he was killed while leading a storming party at Muy. A Spanish Sir Philip Sidney, he personified all of the graces of the Renaissance gentleman, and was at once the hero of a legend and the idol of a nation.

As Wyatt and Surrey were to do in England, Garcilaso, together with his friend Boscán, introduced poetry in the manner of the Italian Renaissance into Spain. A poet of grace, sensibility, and emotional depth, he has been hailed by poets and critics as one of the most gifted of Spanish lyrists. One of his finest works is his Eclogue I. His best love poems sprang from his passion for a Portuguese lady, Isabel Freire, who married a Spanish nobleman, then died in childbirth. This bare plot gives us sufficient information to read his poignant sonnets understandingly.

## SONNET

Fair Naiads of the river, that reside
    Happy in grottos of rock crystal veined
    With shining gems, and loftily sustained
    On columns of pure glass, if now ye glide
On duteous errands, or weave side by side
    Webs of fine net-work, or in groups remove
    To hear and tell romantic tales of love,
    Of genii, Fays and Tritons of the tide,—

Awhile remit your labours, and upraise
  Your rosy heads to look on me. Not long
  Will it detain you. Sweet'ners of my song,
For pity hear me, watering as I go
  With tears your borders, and for such short space,
  In heavenly notes sing solace to my woe!

JEREMIAH H. WIFFEN

## SONNET X

## ON FINDING SOME KEEPSAKES OF HIS DEAD MISTRESS

Oh precious treasures, which to my grief I found,
  (Precious and joyous as long as God so willed)
  Combined within my memory do you build
  A league to open ever more my wound.
Who would have said, at that time when around
  Me throbbed a world with pleasure filled,
  That it would be upon the morrow killed
  And there where I found joy grief would abound?
Since in one short hour from me you stole
  All the great good which gradually you gave,
  Take from me now the sorrow that you left;
If not, I shall suspect that, like a knave,
  With joyous wine you often filled my bowl
  Only to lead me slyly to my grave.

WALTER T. PATTISON

## SONG III

Now go I quietly
Nor weary you with pleading;
From my deathbed, silence, speeding,
More eloquent shall be.

An evil thing it was
That my vows your spirit troubled,
And the injury was doubled
Since they nothing helped my cause.

Though tears my eyes may dim,
No plaint shall ease my crying;
Who speaks no word at dying,
His death shall plead for him.

BEATRICE GILMAN PROSKE

# Saint Teresa of Jesús
## (1515–1588)

Other designations by which she is known are Teresa of Avila, Teresa Sanchez de Cepeda Davila y Ahumada. At the age of sixteen she entered the Carmelite Convent. A highly practical woman, she rose to a position of high authority in her order and was responsible for starting numerous religious foundations as well as instituting important religious reforms. Offsetting the practical in her nature, there developed an intense mysticism for which she was recognized, even celebrated during her lifetime. As a consequence, she was ordered by her superior to write her autobiography and other works describing the development of the spiritual life of the soul. Her primary works were in prose: *Vida*, *Castillo Interior*, and *Conceptos del Amor de Dios*. The lyrics, an uncertain canon varying from 35 to 49, were written either for a religious occasion or after a religious ecstasy. Her style is extremely unadorned, but gives continual glimpses of intense religious ecstasy and passion. Her basic poetic theme concerned the complete annihilation of the individual in a mystical union with divine love.

She is recognized as a guiding spirit in the school of religious mystics of the sixteenth century, whose doctrines were extremely elaborate and subtle, as expounded in the prose works of Saint Teresa and St. John of the Cross. However, for the general reader it is enough at first to recognize that for these writers religious devotion could best be expressed in terms of earthly love. This is by no means a novel or strange ambiguity, but the treatment here is at once more direct and more tense than is ordinarily found.

## GOD SUFFICES

Let nothing affright you,
Let nothing dismay,
For God does not change
Though things pass away.

With patience one gains all he may assay.
The one who has God
Will lack in no way.
God suffices for aye.

MILDRED E. JOHNSON

## LET MINE EYES SEE THEE

Let mine eyes see Thee,
Sweet Jesus of Nazareth,
Let mine eyes see Thee,
And then see death.

Let them see that care
Roses and jessamine;
Seeing Thy face most fair
All blossoms are therein.
Flower of seraphim,
Sweet Jesus of Nazareth,
Let mine eyes see Thee,
And then see death.

Nothing I require
Where my Jesus is;
Anguish all desire,
Saving only this;
All my help is His,
He only succoureth.
Let mine eyes see Thee,
Sweet Jesus of Nazareth,
Let mine eyes see Thee,
And then see death.[3]

ARTHUR SYMONS

# ON THE WORDS "DILECTUS MEUS MIHI"

I have yielded utterly,
And so changed the heart I give,
That my Love lives but for me
And for Him I live.

When the blessed hunter's wound
Left me fallen and subdued,
In the arms of love I swooned,
And was there imbued
With new life that has renewed
And so changed the heart I give
   That my Love lives but for me
   And for Him I live.

Lifted high with love His dart
Wounded me, and by its aid
One with the Creator's heart
Was my spirit made,
And by no other love is swayed
Since to God myself I give,
   And my Love lives but for me
   And for Him I live.[4]

JESSIE READ WENDELL

# VERTIENDO ESTA SANGRE

See, His blood He's shedding:
*Dominguillo, why?*
*I have no reply.*

Why is it, I ask you,
Why in justice' name?
For the child is guiltless,
Free from sin and shame.

Wherefore does He love me?
I have no reply.
Yet He yearns to save me:
*Dominguillo, why?*

Must His cruel torments
At His earth begin?
Yes, for He is dying
To remove our sin.
What a mighty Shepherd
Have we, by my fay!
*Dominguillo, eh!*

You have not yet seen Him:
Such an innocent?
"No but I've been told by
Brasil and Llorent."
We must surely love Him
From this very day,
*Dominguillo, eh?* [5]

                    E. ALLISON PEERS


## EN LAS INTERNAS ENTRAÑAS

Within my heart a stab I felt—
A sudden stab, expecting naught;
Beneath God's standard was it dealt
For goodly were the deeds it wrought,
And though the lance hath wounded me,
And though the wound be unto death,
Surpassing far all other pain,
Yet doth new life therefrom draw breath!

How doth a mortal wound give life?
How, while life-giving, yet doth slay?
How heal while wounding, leaving thee
United to thy God alway?

Celestial was that hand, and though
With peril dire the fray was fraught,
I came forth victor o'er the lance
And goodly were the deeds it wrought.[6]

FATHER BENEDICT ZIMMERMAN


# LINES BORN OF THE FIRE OF LOVE FOR GOD

Empty of life I live, and wait
With hope another life so high,
I die because I do not die.

By union of the love in me
And His, in which I live,
I make my God my captive,
And thus my heart is free:
But from my soul I cry
For His captivity;
I die because I do not die.

How long this mortal life,
How hard is such exile,
This prison and these chains
In which the soul is trapped.
Only to hope and wait to leave
Causes me such grief and pain;
I die because I do not die.

How bitter is the life in which
I cannot know my Lord!
And though His love be sweet
The waiting is not so;
My Lord, please lift from me
This burden heavier than steel;
I die because I do not die.

Only confidence that I
Must die enables me to live;
Because that life in death
Assures me of my hope:
Oh, life born in death,
For whom I wait, do not delay;
I die because I do not die.

Observe how strong is love;
Life, be not troubled now,
For you alone are such
That by your loss you are regained;
Come now, sweet death who are
But swift and easy, come;
I die because I do not die.

Life, whom I can give
To God who lives in me,
You shall not lose yourself
If in His grace you be;
In death I wish to conquer you,
For He alone is my need;
I die because I do not die.

What life is there for me
Without Thy presence here,
But to suffer a greater death
Than I have ever seen?
A pitiful, sinful soul would be
My self deprived of Thee;
I die because I do not die.

The fish who leaves the sea
No further comfort needs,
And he who leaves this life, at last
Is favored by the gift of death;
Is there so mournful a death,
As that in which I live?
I die because I do not die.

When I begin to find relief,
To see Thee in the Sacrament,
Still it causes me regret,
That I can see but not possess;
I cannot see Thee as I wish,
And all is grief increased;
I die because I do not die.

When I enjoy myself, my Lord,
With hopes of seeing Thee,
Yet know the peril of Thy loss,
My painful grief is doubled:
Living with such a fear,
And hoping as I wait,
I die because I do not die.

Oh, take me from this death,
My Lord, and give me life.
Do not imprison me
In mortal bonds so strong:
Oh, see I die to look on Thee
And cannot live unless Thou'rt here;
I die because I do not die.

Now shall I cry for death
And grieve that I do live,
Because, through my own sin
It seems is death withheld.
My Lord, when shall it be,
When I shall say in Truth,
I die because I do not die.[7]

SHIRLEY WHITE JOHNSTON

# Fra Miguel de Guevara
## (1585?–1646?)

A missionary friar in Mexico, Fra Miguel learned various languages of the natives to further his work among the Indians. He wrote a manual for studying one of the dialects: "Doctrinal Art and Method for Learning Matlalzingo in Order to Administer the Holy Sacrament."

## TO CHRIST CRUCIFIED

The promises of heaven Thou givest me
    Are not what moves me, Lord, to love Thee so,
    Nor am I moved by threat of hellish woe
    To keep from breaking Thy divine decree.
*Thou* movest me, O Lord; I'm moved to see
    Thee nailed upon a cross with many a blow
    And made a cruel mockery and show;
    Thy ignominious death is what moves me.
I'm moved by Thy great love in such a way
    That if there were no heaven I'd love Thee still,
    And if there were no hell, I'd still not stray.
To gain my love, Thou dost not have to pay;
    If what I hope for Thou couldst not fulfill,
    I'd love Thee even as I do today.[8]

MILDRED E. JOHNSON

# Fray Luis Ponce de León
## (1528?–1591)

When about fifteen years of age he entered the Augustinian order.
Trained in philosophy and theology at the University of Salamanca,
he was named professor there in 1561 and held that post through the
rest of his life, with one interruption. In 1572 he was imprisoned on a
charge of heresy, ostensibly for translating "The Song of Solomon"
into Castilian. In his commentary he interpreted this poem to be an
emblematic eclogue which poetically foreshadowed the Divine
Espousal of the Church with Christ. In December, 1576, he was
acquitted of heresy and permitted to return to his teaching at the
university. *Los Nombres de Christo*, his most famous work, was in
prose. By means of a Platonic dialogue he discussed the mystical meaning of the symbolic names of Christ, The Mount, The Shepherd, The
Bridegroom, The Prince of Peace, *etc.* Though he considered his
poetry as a mere amusement, under the orders of his superior he collected his verse, but his death in 1591 prevented its publication. It was
finally given to the public in 1631 by Francisco de Quevedo as a
counterblast to *culteranismo*. Another literary achievement was his
1588 edition of the works of Saint Teresa of Jesús, with whom he had
had a long and deep spiritual friendship.

His poetry, which is simple and contemplative, conveys a mood of
serenity which contrasts him with his fellow mystics. Also he gives
more attention to the glory of imagined flight than of spiritual embraces.

## ODE TO FELIPE RUIZ

When from this prison drear,
Philip, may I take flight into the sky,
And in the farther sphere,
Above the Earth most high,
Pure truth without concealment may descry?

In my new life elate,
Converted into light of radiant sheen,
At one and separate,
What is and what hath been
Shall I see and its true origin unseen.


There 'twill be mine to see
How the divine power the foundations laid
With such skilled accuracy
That stable, undismayed,
Earth's heaviest element therein is stayed;


And there shall I behold
The pillars that prop Earth everlastingly,
The boundary-marks that hold
In check the angry sea,
In prison fixed for it by Heaven's decree;


Why the Earth trembles, why
The waters of the deep sea rage and swell,
Whence in grim strife to vie
The north wind comes, what spell
Causes the Ocean waves to ebb and well;


Where rise the crystal springs,
And who to the great rivers' ceaseless flow
Their store of water brings;
Of icy cold and snow
And summer heat the causes I shall know;


Who in the air sustains
Water on high, the forge of lightning flash,
The dwelling of the rains
Shall I see, and how God's lash
Furls the treasured snow, and whence the thunders
          crash.

Look, on a summer day
When through the air a veil of grey is thrust,
Day's face grows dark in play
Of mad north-west wind's gust,
And lightly to the sky is whirled the dust;


God moves amid the cloud,
Guiding his aery chariot swift and bright,
With dreadful thunder loud
And flashing fire's light:
Men bow themselves, Earth trembles in affright.


The roofs are washed with rain,
And rushing streams pour down from all the hills:
At his lost labour vain
And the fields' flooded drills
The peasant's heart dismayed amazement fills.


And thence uplifted, I
The motions shall behold of lofty Heaven,
All that moves naturally
And that by force is driven,
And to the signs and fates what cause is given;


And who the stars inspires
And kindles with a beauty radiant, clear,
Their efficacious fires;
Why Great and Little Bear
To bathe themselves in Ocean ever fear.


I shall see where the sun,
The light and fountain of our life, abides,
Why is so swiftly run
His course of wintertides,
And why in the long nights his ray he hides;

Yea, in the highest sphere
Those dwellings of delight shall I behold:
Motionless they appear,
Fashioned of light and gold,
The mansions that the spirits blest enfold.[9]

AUBREY F. G. BELL

## THE LIFE OF THE BLESSED

Region of life and light!
Land of the good whose earthly toils are o'er!
Nor frost nor heat may blight
Thy vernal beauty, fertile shore,
Yielding thy blessed fruits for evermore!

There, without crook or sling,
Walks the Good Shepherd; blossoms white and red
Round his meek temples cling;
And, to sweet pastures led,
His own loved flock beneath his eye is fed.

He guides, and near him they
Follow delighted; for he makes them go
Where dwells eternal May,
And heavenly roses blow,
Deathless, and gathered but again to grow.

He leads them to the height
Named of the infinite and long-sought Good,
And fountains of delight;
And where his feet have stood,
Springs up, along the way, their tender food.

And when, in the mid skies,
The climbing sun has reached his highest bound,
   Reposing as he lies,
   With all his flock around,
He witches the still air with numerous sound.

   From his sweet lute flow forth
Immortal harmonies, of power to still
   All passions born of earth,
   And draw the ardent will
Its destiny of goodness to fulfill.

   Might but a little part,
A wandering breath, of that high melody
   Descend into my heart,
   And change it till it be
Transformed and swallowed up, O love! in thee:

   Ah! then my soul should know,
Beloved! where thou liest at noon of day;
   And from this place of woe
   Released, should take its way
To mingle with thy flock, and never stray.[10]

WILLIAM CULLEN BRYANT

# Luis Vaz de Camoëns
## (1524–1580)

A native of Portugal and one of the chief glories of Portuguese literature, Camoëns is also recognized for some excellent verse in Spanish. Educated at the University of Coimbra, he went to Lisbon in 1544, where he started writing drama and lyric poetry. During this time he was involved in a hopeless love affair with Catarina de Attayda, who was to be the object of much of his love poetry throughout his life. By 1547 he had also authored three highly successful comedies. For the next two years he served in the army in North Africa where he lost the sight of his right eye. In 1552 he left Portugal and spent the next eighteen years of his life in the Far East at Goa, Macao, and Mozambique, alternating as either an official or as a prisoner for peculation and debt. In 1570 he returned to Lisbon in the direst poverty, and in the spring of 1572 he published *The Lusiads*, his national epic glorifying the Portuguese. Pensioned for this masterpiece, he wrote little else until his death in 1580.

## ON THE DEATH OF CATARINA DE ATTAYDA

Those charming eyes within whose starry sphere
    Love whilom sat, and smiled the hours away,—
    Those braids of light, that shamed the beams of day,—
    That hand benignant, and that heart sincere,—
Those virgin cheeks, which did so late appear
    Like snow-banks scattered with the blooms of May,
    Turned to a little cold and worthless clay,
    Are gone, forever gone, and perished here,—
But not unbathed by Memory's warmest tear!
    Death thou hast torn, in one unpitying hour,
    That fragrant plant, to which, while scarce a flower,

The mellower fruitage of its prime was given;
  Love saw the deed,—and as he lingered near
  Sighed o'er the ruin, and returned to heaven!

R. F. BURTON

## ON REVISITING CINTRA AFTER THE
## DEATH OF CATARINA

Apparel of green woods and meadows gay;
  Clear and fresh waters innocent of stain,
  Wherein the field and grove are found again,
  As from high rocks ye take your downward way;
And shaggy peaks, and ordered disarray
  Of crags abrupt, know that ye strive in vain,
  Till grief consent, to soothe the eye of pain,
  Shown the same scene that Pleasure did survey.
Nor as erst seen am I beheld by you,
  Rejoiced no more by fields of pleasant green,
  Or lively runnels laughing as they dart;
Sown be these fields with seeds of ruth and rue,
  And wet with brine of welling tears, till seen
  Sere with the herb that suits the broken heart.

RICHARD GARNETT

# Baltasar de Alcázar
## (1530–1606)

Born in Seville, a member of a noble family, he followed a military career primarily at sea. He was noted in the Sevillian school for the grace and malice of his lyrics, which were both original and ingenious. Using the old Spanish metrics, he wrote with humor and gusto, especially on epicurean subjects. As a devoted student of Martial, he wrote stinging epigrams, racy jests, and gay romances. It did not occur to him to publish his poems, but some of them were collected and printed in *Flores de Poetas* in 1605.

## TRES COSAS

Three things have chained my heart in love
That equally do please:
The fair Inez, a well-smoked ham,
And aubergines in cheese.

Friends, this Inez of whom I speak
Has such a hold on me
That I must hate all else but her.
Who can her equal be?

For one whole year she ruled my sense,
A task within her means,
Until she served for lunch one day
Smoked ham and aubergines.

Inez, victorious at first,
No longer keeps that role.
My judgment gone, these three main things
Share equally my soul.

Not measure, weight, nor taste of each
Can help me find the means
To judge between the fair Inez
And ham and aubergines.

Now Inez boasts a beauty rare,
But Aracena ham,
With aubergines and Spanish cheese,
Makes other foods a sham.

So equal are these three in weight
That all are sure to please;
Alike are all the three to me,
Inez, the ham and cheese.

At least this matter of new loves
Will force Inez to free
Her favors much more cheaply now
And sell herself to me.

Wherefore if reason stirs her not
I still have other means;
A slice of ham smoked in the fire,
Au gratin aubergines.[11]

WAYNE ROLLINS

# Fernando de Herrera
## (1534–1597)

Sometimes referred to as "El Divino," he was the leading poet of the Sevillian school. He added to the style of Garcilaso and the Italian school a studied elegance of expression pointing toward *culteranismo*. His poetry exhibited brilliant imagination, sonorous expression, and harmony of words. The greater number of his poems were Petrarchan and sang of his Platonic love for Leonora Gelves, who is addressed in the poems as Doña Luz. His greatest lyrics were his patriotic songs, in which he extolled Spain and the True Faith with high fervor in strong Biblical cadences. Among these are "Ode to Don Juan of Austria," "Song of Victory at Lepanto," and "Ode on the Death of Don Sebastian of Portugal," considered by many to be among the greatest poems in Spanish literature. A phrase frequently encountered is "Herreran magnificence."

### IDEAL BEAUTY

O Light serene! present in one who breathes
   That love divine, which kindles yet restrains
   The high-born soul—that in its mortal chains
   Heavenward aspires for love's immortal wreaths!
Rich golden locks, within whose clustered curls
   Celestial and eternal treasures lie!
   A voice that breathes angelic harmony
   Among bright coral and unspotted pearls!
What marvelous beauty! Of the high estate
   Of immortality, within this light
   Transparent veil of flesh, a glimpse is given;
And in the glorious form I contemplate
   (Although its brightness blinds my feeble sight)
   The immortal still I seek and follow on to Heaven![12]

HENRY WADSWORTH LONGFELLOW

# TO DON JUAN DE AUSTRIA

Deep sea, whose thundering waves in tumult roar,
   Call forth thy troubled spirit—bid him rise,
   And gaze, with terror pale, and hollow eyes,
   On floods all flashing fire, and red with gore.
Lo! as in list enclosed, on battle-floor
   Christian and Sarzan, life and death the prize,
   Join conflict: lo! the batter'd Paynim flies;
   The din, the smouldering flames, he braves no more.
Go, bid thy deep-toned bass with voice of power
   Tell of this mightiest victory under sky,
   The deed of peerless valour's highest strain;
And say a youth achieved the glorious hour,
   Hallowing thy gulf with praise that ne'er shall die,—
   The youth of Austria, and the might of Spain.[13]

EDWARD CHURTON

# Saint John of the Cross
## (1542–1591)

San Juan de la Cruz, whose full name was Juan de Yepes y Álvarez, is called the *Ecstatic Doctor* in the Catholic Church for his mystical life and writings. He entered a Carmelite monastery in 1563 and became a famous leader in the order. Following the example, advice, and encouragement of Saint Teresa of Jesús, he introduced many monastic reforms within his order. An intensely mystical person, he wrote not only poetry but also much prose. Among his prose works perhaps the most famous is *Subida de Monte Carmelo*. He also composed lengthy glosses on many of his poems. He found mysticism the highest expression of man, since by contemplation man becomes one with God. All of his writings were deeply imbued with the metaphors of "The Song of Songs." In his verse he developed the language of amorous symbolism perhaps to its highest point with a sense of physical ravishment, of daring abandon. His words become symbols of inexpressible thoughts, unbearable ecstasy, too subtly sensuous for adequate translation. His two most famous poems are "The Spiritual Canticle" and "The Dark Night of the Soul."

## DARK NIGHT OF THE SOUL

In an obscure night,
With anxious love inflamed,
O happy lot!
Forth unobserved I went,
My house being now at rest.

In that happy night,
In secret seen of none,
Seeing nought but myself,
Without other light or guide
Save that which in my heart was burning.


That light guided me
More surely than the noonday sun
To the place where he was waiting for me
Whom I knew well,
And none but he appeared.


O guiding night!
O night more lovely than the dawn!
O night that hast united
The lover with his beloved
And charged her with her love.


On my flowery bosom,
Kept whole for him alone,
He reposed and slept:
I kept him, and the waving
Of the cedars fanned him.


Then his hair floated in the breeze
That blew from the turret;
He struck me on the neck
With his gentle hand,
And all sensation left me.


I continued in oblivion lost,
My head was resting on my love;
I fainted at last abandoned,
And, amid the lilies forgotten,
Threw all my cares away.[14]

DAVID LEWIS

## O FLAME OF LIVING LOVE

O flame of living love,
That dost eternally
Pierce through my soul with so consuming heat,
Since there's no help above,
Make thou an end of me,
And break the bond of this encounter sweet.

O burn that burns to heal!
O more than pleasant wound!
And O soft hand, O touch most delicate,
That dost new life reveal,
That dost in grace abound,
And, slaying, dost from death to life translate!

O lamps of fire that shined
With so intense a light,
That those deep caverns where the senses live,
Which were obscure and blind,
Now with strange glories bright,
Both heat and light to His beloved give!

With how benign intent
Rememberest thou my breast,
Where thou alone abidest secretly;
And in thy sweet ascent,
With glory and good possessed,
How delicately thou teachest love to me![15]

ARTHUR SYMONS


## VERSES WRITTEN UPON AN ECSTASY OF HIGH CONTEMPLATION

I enter'd in—I knew not where—
And, there remaining, knew no more,
Transcending far all human lore.

I knew not where I enter'd in.
'Twas giv'n me there myself to see,
And wondrous things I learn'd within,
Yet knew I not where I could be.
I tell not what was shown to me:
Remaining there, I knew no more,
Transcending far all human lore.

That was the lore, all else above,
Of perfect peace, devotion deep.
In that profound retreat of love
The path direct I learn'd to keep.
Such secret knowledge did I reap
That, stammering, I could speak no more,
Transcending far all human lore.

Herein so deeply was I vers'd,
Thoroughly absorb'd and borne so high,
So far my senses were immers'd
That destitute of them was I.
My soul was dower'd from on high
With power of thought that thought no more,
Transcending far all human lore.

He that in truth attains to this
Is lost to self upon the earth.
All that, before, he counted his
Appears to him of little worth.
His knowledge comes anew to birth,
Yet, resting there, he knows no more,
Transcending far all human lore.

The nearer I approach'd the cloud
The less I understood its light,
That, howso darksome was its shroud,
Illumin'd all the gloomy night.
Wherefore a soul that knows that sight
Can never compass knowledge more,
For this transcends all human lore.

This wond'rous knowledge knowing naught
Is of a power so sov'reign high
That wise men's reasoning and thought
Defeat it not, howe'er they try.
Ne'er can their intellect come nigh
This power of thought that thinks no more,
Transcending far all human lore.

Built on so excellent a plan
This summit of true knowledge is
That neither wit nor power of man
Can ever reach such heights of bliss.
He that can climb as high as this
Through knowledge that can know no more
Shall aye transcend all human lore.

Would ye unto this summit climb?
Then know wherein its nature lies.
'Tis an experience all-sublime,
God's Self reveal'd before our eyes.
His grace alone the means supplies
Whereby man understands no more,
Yet far transcends all human lore.

E. ALLISON PEERS

## SPIRITUAL CANTICLE

*Songs between the Soul and the Spouse*

### BRIDE

1. Whither hast thou hidden thyself, And hast left me, O Beloved, to my sighing?
   Thou didst flee like the hart, having wounded me: I went out after thee, calling, and thou wert gone.

2. Shepherds, ye that go Yonder, through the sheepcotes, to the hill,
   If perchance ye see him that I most love, Tell ye him that I languish, suffer and die.

3. Seeking my loves, I will go o'er yonder mountains and banks; I will neither pluck the flowers nor fear the wild beasts; I will pass by the mighty and cross frontiers.

4. O woods and thickets Planted by the hand of the Beloved! O meadow of verdure, enamelled with flowers, Say if he has passed by you.

5. Scattering a thousand graces, He passed through these groves in haste, And, looking upon them as he went, Left them, by his glance alone, clothed with beauty.

6. Ah, who will be able to heal me! Surrender thou thyself now completely. From today do thou send me now no other messenger, For they cannot tell me what I wish.

7. And all those that serve Relate to me a thousand graces of thee, And all wound me the more And something that they are stammering leaves me dying.

8. But how, O life, dost thou persevere, Since thou livest not where thou livest, And since the arrows make thee to die which thou receivest From the conceptions of the Beloved which thou formest within thee?

9. Since thou hast wounded this heart, Wherefore didst thou not heal it? And wherefore, having robbed me of it, hast thou left it thus and takest not the prey that thou hast spoiled?

10. Quench thou my griefs, Since none suffices to remove them, And let mine eyes behold thee, Since thou art their light and for thee alone I wish to have them.

11. Reveal thy presence And let the vision of thee and thy beauty slay me; Behold, the affliction of love is not cured Save by thy presence and thy form.

12. O crystalline fount, If on that silvered surface Thou wouldst of a sudden form the eyes desired Which I bear outlined in my inmost parts!

13. Withdraw them, Beloved, for I fly away.

SPOUSE
Return thou, dove,
For the wounded hart appears on the hill At the air of thy flight, and takes refreshment.

14. My Beloved, the mountains, The solitary, wooded valleys,
The strange islands, the sonorous rivers, The whisper of the amorous breezes,

15. The tranquil night, At the time of the rising of the dawn,
The silent music, the sounding solitude, The supper that recreates and enkindles love.

16. Drive us away the foxes, For our vineyard is now in flower,
While we make a bunch of roses, And let none appear upon the hill.

17. Stay thee, dead north wind. Come, south wind, that awakenest love;
Breathe through my garden and let thy odors flow, And the Beloved shall pasture among the flowers.

18. O nymphs of Judaea, While mid the flowers and rose-trees the ambar sends forth perfume,
Dwell in the outskirts And desire not to touch our thresholds.

19. Hide thyself, dearest one, And look with thy face upon the mountains,
And desire not to speak, But look upon her companions who travels mid strange islands.

20. Birds of swift wing, Lions, harts, leaping does,
Mountains, valleys, banks, waters, breezes, heats, And terrors that keep watch by night.

21. By the pleasant lyres And by the sirens' song, I conjure you,
Cease your wrath and touch not the wall, That the Bride may sleep more securely.

22. The Bride has entered Into the pleasant garden of her desire,
And at her pleasure rests, Her neck reclining on the gentle arms of the Beloved.

23. Beneath the apple-tree, There wert thou betrothed to me;
There did I give thee my hand And thou wert redeemed where thy mother had been corrupted.

24. Our flowery bed, Encompassed with dens of lions,
Hung with purple and builded in peace, Crowned with a thousand shields of gold.

25. In the track of thy footprint The young girls run along by the way.

At the touch of a spark, at the spiced wine, Flows forth the Divine balsam.

26. In the inner cellar, of my Beloved I have drunk, And, when I went forth over all this meadow,

   Then knew I naught And lost the flock which I followed aforetime.

27. There he gave me his breast; There he taught me a science most delectable;

   And I gave myself to him indeed, reserving nothing; There I promised him to be his bride.

28. My soul has employed itself And all my possessions in his service:

   Now I guard no flock nor have I now other office, For now my exercise is in loving alone.

29. If, then, on the common land, From henceforth I am neither seen nor found,

   You will say that I am lost; That, wandering love-stricken, I lost my way and was found.

30. With flowers and emeralds Gathered in the cool mornings

   We will make the garlands flowering in thy love And interwoven with one hair from my head.

31. By that hair alone Which thou regardest fluttering on my neck,

   Beholding it upon my neck, thou wert captivated, And wert wounded by one of mine eyes.

32. When thou didst look on me, Thine eyes imprinted upon me their grace;

   For this cause didst thou love me greatly, Whereby mine eyes deserved to adore that which they saw in thee.

33. Despise me not, For, if thou didst find me swarthy,

   Now canst thou indeed look upon me, Since thou didst look upon me and leave in me grace and beauty.

34. The little white dove Has returned to the ark with the bough,

   And now the turtle-dove Has found the mate of her desire on the green banks.

35. In solitude she lived And in solitude now has built her nest,

   And in solitude her dear one alone guides her, Who likewise in solitude was wounded by love.

36. Let us rejoice, Beloved, And let us go to see ourselves in thy Beauty,

   To the mountain and the hill where flows the pure water; Let us enter farther into the thicket.

37. And then we shall go forth To the lofty caverns of the rock which are well hidden,
    And there shall we enter And taste the new wine of the pomegranates.

38. There wouldst thou show me That which my soul desired,
    And there, at once, my life, wouldst thou give me That which thou gavest me the other day.

39. The breathing of the air, The song of the sweet philomel,
    The grove and its beauty in the serene night, With a flame that consumes and gives no pain.

40. For none saw it, Neither did Aminadab appear,
    And there was a rest from the seige, And the cavalry came down at the sight of the waters.[16]

E. ALLISON PEERS

## OTHER VERSES WITH A DIVINE MEANING

To win love's chase, I took my way
And full of hope, began to fly.
I soar'd aloft and soar'd so high
That in the end I reach'd my prey.

To gain at last right royally
The battle when the flight was o'er,
So far aloft I had to soar
That my own self I could not see.
So fiercely strove I on that day
My strength grew faint and weak indeed
But love suffic'd for all my need
And in the end I reach'd my prey.

The dreadful force of dazzling light
Blinded me as aloft I flew;
The greatest gain that e'er I knew
Was made in blackness of the night.

But love it was that won the day;
Blindly, obscurely, did I fly;
I soar'd aloft and soar'd so high
That in the end I reach'd my prey.

The farther upward did I go
In this great chase of love so high
The baser, humbler soul was I,
The more exhausted did I grow.
"No hope!" was all that I could say,
But, as I sank and sank so low,
Higher and higher did I go,
And in the end I reach'd my prey.

In ways no mortal can explain
I made a thousand flights in one,
For he that hopes to reach the sun
His heart's desire shall surely gain.
Naught had I hoped for but this day
And hope impell'd me up to fly.
I soar'd aloft and soar'd so high
That in the end I reached my prey.

E. ALLISON PEERS

## OTHER STANZAS WITH A DIVINE MEANING CONCERNING CHRIST AND THE SOUL

A shepherd-boy his grief is brooding o'er,
Alone, uncomforted, disconsolate.
His thought is fix'd upon his heart's true mate;
His breast with love is stricken very sore.

He weeps not for some love-wound giv'n of yore,
For no such thing could pain and grieve him so,
E'en though it overcharg'd his heart with woe.
He weeps because she thinks of him no more.

And so, because she thinks of him no more
—That shepherd-maid of his, so fair to see—
He lets his alien foes treat cruelly
The breast that love has stricken very sore.

"Woe," cries the shephered-boy, "Woe be in store
For him that's come betwixt my love and me,
So that she wishes not to know or see
This breast that love has stricken very sore."

Then climbs he slowly, when much time is o'er,
Into a tree, with fair arms wide outspread.
And, clinging to that tree, forthwith is dead.
For lo! his breast was stricken very sore.[17]

                          E. ALLISON PEERS

# Miguel de Cervantes Saavedra
## (1547–1616)

The greatest of all Spanish authors was born at Alcala de Henares in 1547. Twenty years later he was a student at the University of Madrid. During 1569 he travelled throughout Italy as the chamberlain of Cardinal Acquaviva, and the following year he enlisted as a solider. In 1571 he fought valiantly in the Battle of Lepanto, where he was permanently maimed by two shots in his chest and one in his left hand. He fought also at Novarino, Tunis, and Goletta. On the voyage back to Spain he was captured by pirates and spent the next five years as a prisoner in Algiers. Ransomed in 1580 he returned to his native land to a life of hardships and struggle. As the deputy commissary officer for the great Armada, he was unjustly excommunicated and briefly imprisoned for the misconduct of his subordinate. In 1605 Cervantes published the first part of *Don Quixote*, and ten years later he issued the second part. He died at Madrid in 1616. Aside from his masterpiece he was noted for his pastoral romance *Galatea*, the *Novelas Exemplares* and various comedies and interludes. His poem "Viaje del Parnaso" gives the key to most of his other lyrics which are scattered throughout *Don Quixote* and his plays. In it he praises and scorns the various poetic usages of his day. His lyrics are light and clever and frequently burlesque the subjects and techniques of his fellow poets.

Ye trees and shrubs, each plant
In this place that grows,
So tall and green, not scant,
Do I tire you with my woes
As for my love I pant?
Let not my grief disturb
You, even though it be a
Thing that might perturb.

Don Quixote cannot curb
His tears for Dulcinea
  del Toboso.

Here is the place to which
The lover most loyal far
Hath fled from a beauteous witch,
Under an evil star.
To wander he has an itch;
Love drags him every way,
Which certainly cannot be a
Very good thing, I should say.
Don Quixote his tears doth spray
By the kegful for Dulcinea
  del Toboso.

Seeking adventure he goes
Among the barren rocks;
Cursing his many woes
And fortune's cruel knocks,
He flounders in Love's throes.
Held by no gentle rein,
It must ever be a
Lash that adds to his pain.
Don Quixote, sorrowful swain
Weeps for his Dulcinea
  del Toboso.[18]

      SAMUEL PUTNAM

Love's mariner am I,
Sailing Love's own deep sea,
Bereft of hope, forlorn;
No haven waits for me.
 And yet, my course I steer
By a bright and gleaming star
Palinurus never sighted—
I behold its light afar.

I know not whither it leads;
No other thought have I
Than to fix my soul's gaze upon it,
Let all the rest go by.
    A maiden reserve uncalled for,
An unheard of modesty:
These the dark clouds that cover
My star of ecstasy.
    O star so bright and gleaming,
I tell thee with bated breath:
To lose forever the sight of thee
Would surely be my death.[19]

                        SAMUEL PUTNAM


Oh, could my "was" an "is" become,
I'd wait no more for "it shall be";
or could I the future now but see,
and not this present, dour and glum.

### GLOSS

All things must pass away at last,
and so, the blessing that was mine,
fair Fortune's gift, it also pass'd,
ne'er to return, though I repine;
my skies are wholly overcast.
Long hast thou seen me at thy feet,
O Fortune fickle, Fortune fleet;
but make me happy once again
and I'd forget my present pain,
could but my "was" and "is" now meet.

No other pleasure do I crave,
no other palm or warrior's prize,
such triumph as befits the brave;
all that I ask: those happier skies
to which my memory is a slave.

Would'st thou but give this gift to me,
O Fortune, then perchance I'd see
this fire of mine—O priceless boon!—
consume me less, and if 'twere soon,
I'd wait no more for "it shall be."

Impossible the thing. I ask,
since Time, once gone, none can recall;
for to accomplish such a task,
no power on earth but is too small.
No more beneath those skies I'll bask.
Swift doth he come and swiftly flee,
nor doth return, light-footed he!
and well I know it is not right
to seek to stay Time in his flight;
turn past to present—futile plea!

My life is anxious, filled with gloom;
and living thus 'twixt hope and fear,
is naught but death's familiar doom;
better to lie upon my bier
and seek the door to pain's dark room.
It seemeth me, it would be sweet
to end it now, thus life to cheat;
but living long and living longer,
the fear within grows ever stronger
of that dread "shall be" I must greet.[20]

SAMUEL PUTNAM

O thou above who in thy bed,
'Tween sheets of linen fine,
With outstretched legs dost sleep all night,
Ah, 'tis for thee I pine!

O thou, La Mancha's bravest knight,
The purest, when all is told,
Thy virtue and thy noble worth
Outweigh Arabia's gold!

Then, hear the plaint of gentle maid
Aweary with desire,
Who in the light of thy twin orbs
Doth feel her heart catch fire.

Seeking adventures, thou dost roam,
To others bringing woe;
Wounds thou dost deal, deniest balm:
No mercy wouldst thou show.

Tell me, O valiant-hearted youth—
God prosper thine emprise!—
Wast born 'mid Jaca's barren crags
Or 'neath the Libyan skies?

And was it serpents suckled thee?
Thy nurses, who were they,
In forest wild, dark mountain cave,
Amongst the beasts of prey?

Ah, well may Dulcinea boast,
The plump and sturdy lass,
That she a tiger fierce hath tamed
And doth all maids surpass.

For this, her fame shall spread abroad
From Jarama to Henares,
From Pisuerga to Arlanza,
From the Tagus to Manzanares.

How gladly would I change with her,
Give a petticoat to boot,
My gayest one with golden fringe,
To win my hapless suit.

Oh, to be clasped within thine arms
Or sit beside thy bed,
Fondly caress thee with my hand,
And scratch thy scurvy head!

But I am asking far too much,
Ah, no, it is not meet;
Most humbly I should be content
Playing with thy feet.

What coifs I'd bring thee, wert thou mine,
And silver slippers, too,
And damask breeches, Holland capes:
With gifts like these I'd woo!

What finest pearls of gallnut size;
Unrivaled they would be
Thus, each "La Sola" would be called
For want of company.

Then, gaze not from Tarpeian rock
Upon this kindling blaze.
Manchegan Nero, spare thy wrath
Ere it my heart doth raze.

I'm but a child, a virgin young,
Just three months past fourteen;
By God and on my soul I swear,
'Tis all of life I've seen.

I am not lame, I do not limp,
I'm whole of limb and sound;
My lily locks thou may'st perceive,
Go trailing on the ground.

My mouth is wide, my nose is flat,
These faults I'll not deny,
But topaz teeth my beauty save,
Exalt it to the sky.

My voice thou knowest to be sweet,
If thou dost hear me now;
My build is middling, a little less,
It is not bad, I vow.

And these and all my other charms
Thy quiver hath won for thee.
Altisidora is my name;
This house is home to me.[21]

SAMUEL PUTNAM


## EPITAPH

Below there rests the knight,
Ill-errant, battered, sore,
Whom Rocinante bore
On his wanderings, left and right.
Sancho Panza, if you inquire,
Lies also within this span,
The most faithful little man
E'er followed the trade of squire.

SAMUEL PUTNAM


## EPITAPH

Here Dulcinea doth lie,
Who was plump and high of bust;
Now she is ashes and dust,
For horrid death passed by.
She was of noble race,
Truly a highbred dame,
The great Don Quixote's flame
And the glory of this place.

SAMUEL PUTNAM

# Luis de Góngora y Argote
## (1561–1627)

Born in Cordova in 1561, the son of a minor city official, Góngora became one of the most controversial figures in the history of Spanish poetry. At sixteen the boy was sent to the University of Salamanca to study law; but the young Góngora took little interest in legal studies, and shortly after taking his B.A. degree, boldly declared himself a professional poet.

By 1585 he had won some local reputation as a poet of promise. In 1590, by a stroke of good fortune, Góngora obtained a lay sinecure which enabled him to devote more time to his art and to visit the capital when he so desired. There he won immediate acclaim as an engaging wit and a poet of considerable skill.

In 1605 Góngora took holy orders and was ordained a priest, though he never took his pious vocation very seriously. Probably because of his social grace and literary gifts rather than for reasons of genuine piety, Góngora rose in clerical ranks to become the private chaplain of Philip IV. After a period of declining mental powers he died of apoplexy in 1627.

As the critics are quick to point out, Góngora was actually two poets: one a happy traditionalist, the other a radical innovator. His early poetry is distinguished by a refined wit and a subtle elegance, with just a touch of Herreran pomp and magnificence. Sometime after his arrival in court, Góngora embraced both the art of *conceptisma*, a poetic method involving the deliberate opacity of thought and idea, and *culteranismo*, characterized by linguistic obscurity, strained syntax, Latinized neologisms, and elaborate metaphor, a product of Herrera and the Sevillian school. About 1609, Góngora began experimenting with these two techniques, combining the attributes of both into a synthetic form, afterwards known as "Gongorism." Spanish Gongorism is akin to, though not quite identical to Marinismo, *préciocité* and Metaphysical poetry.

The influence of the new poetry can hardly be exaggerated. With the publication of Góngora's *Polifemo y Galatea* and *Soledades*, the literary world of Spain was rocked to its foundations; the works created a storm of protests as wits like Lope de Vega and Francisco de Quevedo delivered sharp polemics against this decadent new poetry. But partly through the approbation of Philip and his literary clique and partly because of the poet's unmistakable talent, "Gongorism" prevailed and lived to influence the poetry of Spain for nearly a century thereafter. Subsequently a reaction set in and it became the object of ridicule—the worst type of poetry ever perpetrated. Only in the twentieth century has it been restored to some stature along with the school of Donne and with baroque art generally.

## THE ROSEMARY SPRAY

The flowers upon the rosemary spray,
Young Maid, may school thy sorrow;
The blue-eyed flower, that blooms to-day,
To honey turns to-morrow.

A tumult stirs thy tender breast,
With jealous pain true-hearted,
That he, whom thy first love hath bless'd
From thee hath coldly parted.

Ungracious boy, who slights thy love,
And overbold disdaining
To ask forgiveness, and remove
The cause of thy complaining.

Hope, come and drive those tears away!
For lovers' jealous sorrow,
Like dewy blue-eyed flower on spray
To honey turns to-morrow.

By thine own joy thou wast undone:
A bliss thou couldst not measure,
Like star at dawn too near the sun,
Eclipsed thee by its pleasure.

Walk forth with eyes serene and fair;
The pearls, that deck the morning,
Are wasted in the day's fierce glare;
With calmness tame his scorning.

Disperse those clouds that but dismay;
Distrust that jealous sorrow:
The blue-eyed flower, that blooms to-day,
To honey turns to-morrow.[22]

EDWARD CHURTON

## THE ROSE OF LIFE

Blown in the morning, thou shalt fade ere noon:
    What boots a life which in such haste forsakes thee?
    Th'art wondrous frolick being to die so soon:
    And passing proud a little color makes thee.
If thee thy brittle beauty so deceives,
    Know then the thing that swells thee is thy bane;
    For the same beauty doth in bloody leaves
    The sentence of thy early death contain.
Some clown's coarse lungs will poison thy sweet flower
    If by the careless plow thou shalt be torn:
    And many Herods lie in wait each hour
To murther thee as soon as thou art born,
    Nay, force thy bud to blow; their tyrant breath,
    Anticipating life, to hasten death.[23]

SIR RICHARD FANSHAWE

## THE COUNTRY BACHELOR'S COMPLAINT

Time was, ere Love play'd tricks with me,
    I lived at ease, a simple squire,
And sang my praise-song, fancy free,
    At matins in the village quire. . . .

I rambled by the mountain side,
  Down sylvan glades where streamlets pass
Unnumber'd, glancing as they glide
  Like crystal serpents through the grass. . . .


And there the state I ruled from far,
  And bade the winds to blow for me,
In succour to our ships of war,
  That plough'd the Briton's rebel sea;


Oft boasting how the might of Spain
  The world's old columns far outran,
And Hercules must come again,
  And plant his barriers in Japan. . . .


'Twas on St. Luke's soft, quiet day,
  A vision to my sight was borne,
Fair as the blooming almond spray,
  Blue-eyed, with tresses like the morn. . . .


Ah! then I saw what love could do,
  The power that bids us fall or rise,
That wounds the firm heart through and through,
  And strikes, like Caesar, at men's eyes.


I saw how dupes, that fain would run,
  Are caught, their breath and courage spent,
Chased by a foe they cannot shun,
  Swift as Inquisitor on scent. . . .


Yet I've a trick to cheat Love's search,
  And refuge find too long delay'd;
I'll take the vows of Holy Church,
  And seek some reverend cloister's shade.

EDWARD CHURTON

## NOT ALL SWEET NIGHTINGALES

They are not all sweet nightingales
That fill with songs the flowery vales;
But they are little silver bells,
Touched by the winds in the smiling dells;
Magic bells of gold in the grove,
Forming a chorus for her I love.

Think not the voices in the air
Are from the wingèd Sirens fair,
Playing among the dewy trees
Chanting their morning mysteries;
Oh, if you listen, delighted there,
To their music scattered o'er the dales,
They are not all sweet nightingales,
That fill with song the flowery vales;
But they are little silver bells,
Touched by the winds in the smiling dells;
Magic bells of gold in the grove,
Forming a chorus for her I love.

Oh! 'twas a lovely song—of art
To charm—of nature to touch the heart;
Sure 'twas some shepherd's pipe, which played
By passion fills the forest shade;
No! 'tis music's diviner part
Which o'er the yielding spirit prevails.
They are not all sweet nightingales,
That fill with song the flowery vales;
But they are little silver bells,
_Touched by the winds in the smiling dells;
Magic bells of gold in the grove,
Forming a chorus for her I love.

In the eye of love, which all things sees,
The fragrance-breathing jasmine trees—

And the golden flowers—and the sloping hill—
And the ever melancholy rill—
Are full of holiest sympathies,
And tell of love a thousand tales.
They are not all sweet nightingales,
That fill with songs the cheerful vales;
But they are little silver bells,
Touched by the wind in the smiling dells,
Bells of gold in the secret grove,
Making music for her I love.

JOHN BOWRING

## ROMANCE

The loveliest girl in all our country-side,
Today forsaken, yesterday a bride,
Seeing her love ride forth to join the wars,
With breaking heart and trembling lips implores:
"My hope is dead, my tears are blinding me,
Oh let me walk alone where breaks the sea!

"You told me, Mother, what too well I know,
How grief is long, and joy is quick to go,
But you have given him my heart that he
Might hold it captive with love's bitter key,—
My hope is dead, my tears are blinding me.

"My eyes are dim, that once were full of grace,
And ever bright with gazing on his face,
But now the tears come hot and never cease,
Since he is gone in whom my heart found peace,
My hope is dead, my tears are blinding me.

"Then do not seek to stay my grief, nor yet
To blame a sin my heart must needs forget;
For though blame were spoken in good part,
Yet speak it not, lest you should break my heart.
My hope is dead, my tears are blinding me.

"Sweet Mother mine, who would not weep to see
The glad years of my youth so quickly flee,
Although his heart were flint, his breast a stone?
Yet here I stand, forsaken and alone,
My hope is dead, my tears are blinding me.

"And still may night avoid my lonely bed,
Now that my eyes are dull, my soul is dead.
Since he is gone for whom they vigil keep,
Too long is night, I have no heart for sleep.
My hope is dead, my tears are blinding me,
Oh let me walk alone where breaks the sea!"

JOHN PIERREPONT RICE

## LET ME GO WARM

Let me go warm and merry stil';
And let the world laugh, an' it will.

Let others muse on earthly things,—
The fall of thrones, the fate of kings,
    And those whose fame the world doth fill;
Whilst muffins sit enthroned in trays,
And orange-punch in winter sways
The merry sceptre of my days;—
And let the world laugh, an' it will.

He that the royal purple wears,
From golden plate a thousand cares
    Doth swallow as a gilded pill;
On feasts like these I turn my back,
Whilst puddings in my roasting-jack
Beside the chimney hiss and crack;—
    And let the world laugh, an' it will.

And when the wintry tempest blows,
And January's sleets and snows
    Are spread o'er every vale and hill

With one to tell a merry tale
O'er roasted nuts and humming ale,
I sit, and care not for the gale;—
   And let the world laugh, an' it will.

Let merchants traverse seas and lands,
For silver mines and golden sands;
   Whilst I beside some shadowy rill,
Just where its bubbling fountain swells,
Do sit and gather stones and shells,
And hear the tale the blackbird tells;—
   And let the world laugh, an' it will.

For Hero's sake the Grecian lover
The stormy Hellespont swam over;
   I cross, without the fear of ill,
The wooden bridge that slow bestrides
The Madrigal's enchanting sides,
Or barefoot wade through Yepes' tides;—
   And let the world laugh, an' it will.

But since the Fates so cruel prove,
That Pyramus should die of love,
   And love should gentle Thisbe kill;
My Thisbe be an apple-tart,
The sword I plunge into her heart
The tooth that bites the crust apart;—
   And let the world laugh, an' it will.[24]

HENRY WADSWORTH LONGFELLOW


LOVE IN REASON

I love thee, but let love be free:
   I do not ask, I would not learn,
What scores of rival hearts for thee
   Are breaking or in anguish burn.

You die to tell, but leave untold,
　　The story of your Red-Cross Knight,
Who proffer'd mountain-heaps of gold
　　If he for you might ride and fight;

Or how the jolly soldier gay
　　Would wear your colours, all and some;
But you disdain'd their trumpet's bray,
　　And would not hear their tuck of drum.

We love; but 'tis the simplest case:
　　The faith on which our hands have met
Is fix'd, as wax on deeds of grace,
　　To hold as grace, but not as debt.

For well I wot that nowadays
　　Love's conquering bow is soonest bent
By him whose valiant hand displays
　　The largest roll of yearly rent. . . .

So let us follow in the fashion,
　　Let love be gentle, mild, and cool:
For these are not the days of passion,
　　But calculation's sober rule.

Your grace will cheer me like the sun;
　　But I can live content in shades.
Take me: you'll find when all is done,
　　Plain truth, and fewer serenades.[25]

EDWARD CHURTON


## THE NATIVITY OF CHRIST

Today from the Aurora's bosom
A pink has fallen,—a crimson blossom;
And oh, how glorious rests the hay
On which the fallen blossom lay!

When silence gently had unfurled
Her mantle over all below,
And crowned with winter's frost and snow,
Night swayed the sceptre of the world,
Amid the gloom descending slow,
Upon the monarch's frozen bosom
A pink has fallen,—a crimson blossom.

The only flower the Virgin bore
(Aurora fair) within her breast,
She gave to earth, yet still possessed
Her virgin blossom as before;
The hay that colored drop caressed,—
Received upon its faithful bosom
That single flower,—a crimson blossom.

The manger, unto which 'twas given,
Even amid wintry snows and cold,
Within its fostering arms to fold
The blushing flower that fell from heaven,
Was as a canopy of gold,—
A downy couch,—where on its bosom
That flower had fallen,—that crimson blossom.[26]

HENRY WADSWORTH LONGFELLOW

# CLEAR HONOR OF THE LIQUID ELEMENT

Clear honor of the liquid element,
　Sweet rivulet of shining silver sheen!
　Whose waters steal along the meadows green,
　With gentle step, and murmur of content!
When she, for whom I bear each fierce extreme,
　Beholds herself in thee,—then Love doth trace
　The snow and crimson of that lovely face
　In the soft gentle movement of thy stream.

Then, smoothly flow as now, and set not free
   The crystal curb and undulating rain
   Which now thy current's headlong speed restrain;
Lest broken and confused the image rest
   Of such rare charms on the deep-heaving breast
   Of him who holds and sways the trident of the sea.[27]

HENRY WADSWORTH LONGFELLOW

## SONNET

Yesterday a human deity, today a bit of dust;
   Yesterday an altar, today a tomb, Oh mortals!
   Plumes, though they be eagle plumes,
   Are still plumes, who does not know this errs much.
The bones that this sepulchre encloses today,
   Would, were they not embalmed in oriental spices,
   Give ample proof of corruption to mortals;
   Let reason make clear what this marble hides.
The Phoenix, that had Lerma yesterday for her Arabia
   Is now a maggot in worm's meat,
   And serves as a warning to persons of understanding.
If the ocean can engulf a whale
   What shall it avail a boat to have lights in the cabin?
   Dust unto dust, for thus all beings must.[28]

ELISHA KANE

## SONNET

The planking of the vessel torn apart,
   Pious yet cruel sign of wreckage
   Of the holy temple with its tattered curtains
   Caused these hangings to be set on the walls.
Having pardoned the injuries of the weather
   And the violence of the stormy stars of Orion,
   I assemble the scattered flocks
   On the expansive banks of the Betis.

I shall again be a shepherd, since a mariner
  God will not have me be, for with his darts he urges on
  The winds of the south and the waters of the ocean;
Making, to the melancholy though savage sound
  Of that bitch, now wild mistress,
  A yearning to the wild beasts and to the cruel rocks.[29]

ELISHA KANE


## SONNET

Dear Geese, whose haunt is where weak waters flow,
  From rude Castilian well-head, cheap supply,
  That keeps your flowery Vega never dry,
  True Vega, smooth, but somewhat flat and low;
Go; dabble, play and cackle as ye go
  Down that old stream of gray antiquity;
  And blame the waves of nobler harmony,
  Where birds, whose gentle grace you cannot know,
Are sailing. Attic wit and Roman skill
  Are theirs; no swans that die in feeble song,
  But nursed to life by Heliconian rill,
Where Wisdom breathes in Music. Cease your wrong,
  Flock of the troubled pool: your vain endeavour
  Will doom you else to duck and dive for ever.[30]

EDWARD CHURTON


## WHEN DON LUIS WAS IN CUENCA

I saw highland maidens dancing
Among the Júcar trees
To the sound of stony waters
And of branches in the breeze.
Not in that white circle
The nymphs who dwell in waters,
Nor sprites the woodland worships,
Diana's forest daughters.
These maids are from Cuenca
And bring it honour meet,

A hill two rivers kiss
To kiss their dancing feet.
In merry groups they weave,
Hand in white hand advance
In clasp of friendship, changing
With the figures of the dance.
　　How beautiful the highland girls,
　　How beautifully they dance!

Brighter than sun their curls,
Less gold Arabia hoards,
Some garlanded with flowers
And some with silver cords.
Gowned in tints of heaven
If not in those of hope,
Blue woolens that with sapphire
And priceless emerald cope.
Each foot (when flying skirts
Permit the feet to show)
Bound with pretty ribbons,
Is mother-of-pearl and snow.
Their graceful movements raise
In honest arrogance
The crystal of the column
In straight and slender stance.
　　How beautiful the highland girls,
　　How beautifully they dance!

One holds ivory tablets
Between her fingers white,
Instruments the muses
Might envy when they strike.
The water checks its flowing
And still is every bird
While all the leaves hang motionless
To let her song be heard.

　　　Cuenca girls
　　　To pine groves chance,

Some for pine nuts,
Some to dance.
They crack pine nuts,
The dancing girls,
Two nuts together
Or with their pearls.
Arrows of love's
Inheritance,
Some for pine nuts,
Some to dance.

The sightless god
From a leafy tree
Begs the sun's eyes
That he may see.
Over eyes of the sun
You will see them advance,
Some for pine nuts,
Some to dance.[31]

ALICE JANE MCVAN


## THE SOLITUDES

The highwater mark of Gongorism, a *cause célèbre*, this poem has been greatly admired by some and vehemently condemned by others. It was planned as a work in four parts but was left incomplete when Góngora had finished only one full section and a part of the second. It is a little over 2000 lines long.

Though the poem must strictly be classed as narrative, it reveals no plot. A young man, despondent for love, has left his home, is shipwrecked, and wanders through strange country. The rustic scenes he passes and the encounters with shepherds and fisherfolk make up the story. He witnesses a folk festival, a country dance, a rustic wedding; old men tell him tales or offer words of homely philosophy. However, along with this unpromising material, Góngora has written a poem rich in descriptions of untamed nature and accounts of the charm of primitive folk that, like the traditional pastoral, reflects a yearning for escape from the realities of city and court. The finest passages are lyric, descriptive, or (occasionally) reflective.

The essence of the work derives from its style, which is highly ornamented and often excessively obscure. Its vocabulary is Latinate and often recondite; metaphors are crowded, sometimes interlocking, often far-fetched. Eschewing plain statement, he employs epithets and every species of substitution—metonymy, synecdoche. To these difficulties we can add that it is full of classical allusions which may not be readily apprehended by many readers. Altogether it is about as difficult for the uninitiated as the poetry of—say—John Donne or T. S. Eliot. It may not have the depth of Donne or Eliot, but it surpasses either in sheer brilliance.

## THE FIRST SOLITUDE

It was the flowery season of the year
In which Europa's perjured robber strays[32*]
—Whose brow the arms of the half-moon adorn,
The sun the shining armour of his hide—
Through sapphire fields to feast on stellar corn,
When, fitter cupbearer than Ganymede
For Jupiter, the lovesick boy gave tears
(Absent, disdained and shipwrecked) to the tide
And winds, which moved by his complaining lays
As to a second Arion's harp gave heed.

A pitying limb from mountain pine, opposed,
The constant enemy to Notus' strife,
Became no puny dolphin on that day
To the unthinking traveller who reposed,
Trusting to miserable boards his life,
And to an Ocean's Lybia his way.

Close by a headland, crowned
With sheltering feathers and dry rushes, he,
Engulfed before, then spewed up by the sea,
(Covered with foam, with seaweed girded) found
  A hospitable rest,
Where built the bird of Jupiter his nest.

*Notes for this long selection have been made at points where the difficulties occur.

And, having kissed the sand,
The fragment from the shivered hull he gave
As offering to the rocks, now from the wave
    Safe, and restored to land;
    For even boulders rude
Are flattered by the marks of gratitude.

. . . . . . . . . . . . . . . . . . . . . . . . . . . . . . . .

### AN IDYLLIC SCENE

When remora to his footsteps was his ear [33]
By sweet canorous instrument constrained,
Which, fingered by a mountain maiden near
Above a streamlet from complaining hoarse,
Silenced the ripples it had near restrained.

And by this mountain girl there was another,
Who, to her human, liquid crystal gave;
Her hand, sweet aqueduct for such a wave,
Equalled the one but far outdid the other.
    From the green margin, one
Roses transferred and lilies to her hair,
And, by the bloom of colour or the fair,
Seemed, if no tinted dawn, a flowering sun.

The coal black slates between her fingers white
Another skilled one wounded, and I doubt
If any rocks could calmly hear her out.
While to the rude sonorous harmonies,
There, yet another mountain-girl in sight
—With luscious movements but with honest eyes—
By dancing caused the forest to arise.

. . . . . . . . . . . . . . . . . . . . . . . . . . . . . . . .

### ON SAILING THE WIDE OCEAN

The youth saluted all with courtesy,
    And then (admired was he
As well as answered by the mountaineers)
Shade from the boulders he solicited.

A politic old man, with white hairs grave,
　　With eyes brim full of tears,
Who recognized in his attire the wave,
(The burning sun could not absorb the stain
Cerulean, on his garments to remain
　　Always) as follows said:—

"What fiercest tiger or most wild wild boar[34]
Disgracing even the Hyrcanian shore
Was foster-parent to that ploughman dark,
The first to furrow in an evil hour
The spumy country in ill-destined bark,
　　Vague Clytie of the breeze[35]
Transformed to canvas rather than a flower?
Beechwood his scales, this sea-born monster, know,
To shores divided by the seven seas
　　Has introduced more woe
　　Than all the arms and hates
The Hellene fleet brought to the Phrygian gates.

"Nautical industry that mineral found[36]
Which, as the ivy to the rocks, is bound
To the bright metal circling angry Mars;
Solicits too the diamond that glows
On the nocturnal cloak about our sphere
　　And to the pole most near;
With virtue strange to this most constant star
　　Distant, the stone will turn;
Though farther North it is no constant stay,
Either towards the balcony of rose
(That beautiful Aurora has revealed)
Inclining now, or else to where lie sealed
　　In cold cerulean urn
　　The cinders of the day.

"The winged oak, by the attractive worth
Of this hard faithful lover of the North,
Can double now the most tempestuous cape,
Nor island, fugitive, its track escape.

"Tiphys the first unwieldy vessel steered,
  Then Palinurus more;
And it was through that inland sea they veered,
Almost a tank in the surrounding shore,
  Whose famous strait
Is pent up by the twin herculean gate.

"Covetousness the pilot is to-day
Of wandering forests not of shifting trees,
She Neptune (agèd father of the seas,
Of whose proud realm on the diurnal way
—Born in the waves and in the waves to die—
The sun itself discerns no boundary),
Has left whiteheaded now with his own foam,
The utmost limits of the Earth to roam.

"Three fir trees late of this all-powerful one [37]
(Where hitherto no other sailor trod)
Wrested his trident from the watery god,
Kissing the turquoise curtains that the West
Has drawn around the azure couch of rest
  Of the declining sun.

"The flying vipers from the Carib bow [38]
—Shading the sun and poison to the wind—
Have not the ever-waving banners harmed,
That glorious still, routed the fierce winged foe
The isthmus with a hundred feathers armed;
This land their proper limit has assigned
Unto the (crystal serpent) ocean tides,
And from the head, crowned by the North, divides
The tail the South with stars antarctic scaled.

"And other ships to southern zones have sailed,
In the new sea, and there have freely gained
The snowy daughters of the lovely shell,
The homicidal metals found as well
That Midas' touch less copiously obtained.

"It could not now this element suffice
In spumy cliffs to imitate the land,
To lead the grampus or to enlist the whale,
Or to defame, by whitening, the sand
With wreckage of the first rash enterprise
(Marks that the vulture, even, pitying sees)
So that such lamentable signs as these
Against the future efforts should prevail.

"Thou, Covetousness, thou,
The second Charon of the Stygian deep,
All open graves the envying sea may keep,
Destined to hold thy bones, disdainest now.

"That Cape whose mountain Eolus assigned
As prison new for every furious wind,
For Boreas puffing through two hundred lips,
For Auster never slackening in speed,
Was doubled well by thy persistent ships;
   The promontory decreed
   Cape of Good Hope indeed.

"Frustrate the astronomic prophecies
   And sailors' lore of old,
Calms, shipwrecks conquered 'neath the zone that lies
The nearest to the sun, thy ships have pressed
Onward to kiss the kingdoms of the Dawn,[39]
Whose purple seas the clearest pearls supply,
   Whose secret mines can bring
The noblest settings—for such gems—of gold:
To penetrate the aromatic lawn,
   That builds both pyre and nest
For the Arabian bird, whose outstretched wing
Uncurves a flying rainbow in the sky.

"The crystal zodiac for a glorious pine[40]
(The wandering rival of Apollo's car)
   The element became,
   Four hundred days the same

Couch for the night it was and dais for day,
Till the elusive hinge of silver fine [41]
This bark discovered on the western way:
Hinge that unites, one ocean, the two seas,
Whether the carpet of the morning star
It kisses, or the rocks of Hercules.
    And now this vessel Fame
For future glory hangs as votive rod
In the dank temple of the ocean god
    With Victory for name.


"That fixed armada in the eastern sea [42]
Of islands firm I cannot well describe,
Whose number, though for no lasciviousness
But for their sweetness and variety,
The beautiful confusion emulate
When in the white pools of Eurotas rose
The virginal and naked hunting tribe,
—Whose cliffs the polished ivory express,
Whose limbs the Parian marble imitate—
Well might Actaeon lose himself for those!


"But leave the wood of islets in their foam, [43]
Fragrant producers of the perfume sweet,
Egypt, the ancient source of this delight,
Delivered unto Nilus' mouths—to greet
    The gluttony of Greece—
No spiky cloves but spurs to appetite,
—For till their importation into Rome
Cato was temperate and chaste Lucrece—;
In seas uncertain let it stay, my friend,
Where with my riches I was forced to part,
There worse, my son was doomed to meet his end,
His memory a vulture in my heart."
. . . . . . . . . . . . . . . . . . . . . . . . . . . . . . . . . . . .

A RUSTIC FESTIVAL

A spacious circle pleasant centre made
To more road-ends than planet to its rays,
With alder-trees and poplars white about;
   And there the Spring essayed
—In April's glory shod and clad in May's—
To draw the sparks of wavy crystal out
From a hard flint that the narcissi crowned.
   The joining cross-roads here
A shady meeting place the peasants near,
And pleasant goal the distant cowherds found,
   So that each separate way
More weary than the weary traveller lay.


   The thirsting maidens all
Inclined toward the crystal concert there,
Like foolish quails to the decoying call
That imitates their voice, and hides in green,
Among the unripe wheaten ears, the snare.
Musical leaves the smallest branches clad
Of poplars that stood combing their green hair;
But now no zephyrs nor sweet nightingales
Could for a moment keep the mountain lad,
   For music, gentle gales,
   And flowers thankless, seen
The fresh grass of the peaceful place to tread
As though the burning Lybian sand it were,
The pearly serpents scattered by the spring
Worse than the snakes of Pontus reckoning,
And for his feet and for his lips he fled.


Thereon all passed, arranged the company,
As at the Equinox we furrowing see
   The high seas of the air
   No flying galleys' hulls
   But the swift-sailing gulls,
Sometimes like moons that either wax or wane
Distant the extremes of their band they bear,

At other times winged characters they feign
Upon the sky diaphanous to write
As parchment, for the feathers of their flight.

The maidens paused beneath the vaults of shade
   In the fresh painted glade,
Reclining on green carpets there, that grew
With tints the looms of Sydon never knew.

. . . . . . . . . . . . . . . . . . . . . . . . . . . . . . . . . . . . . . .

### WEDDING HYMN

#### *Semichorus I*

Come Hymen come, for here to thee we bring
With eyes but without wings a god of love,
Whose unshorn locks that sweetly hang above
Conceal the down upon his visage fair;
His down the flowers of a youthful spring,
And sunbeams from his forehead are his hair.
A boy he loved her, but adores to-day
This Psyche of the village, nymph to wage
For parchèd Ceres. Join her now, we pray,
Who in the twilight of her second age
Uncertain is, join in thy yoke to stay
   At his desire sincere,
   Come Hymen, Hymen here.

#### *Semichorus II*

Come Hymen come, where in the morning skies
Of candid roses, day is now foretold
By such a beautiful young virgin, she
—Herself the Aurora of her sovereign eyes—
Could warm with her two suns Norwegian lands,
And whiten Ethiopia with two hands.
April carnations, early rubies, see
As many as are set in hair of gold,

With flowers that chain the lovers' necks—behold
The links of concord in the chain of rose—
These to her cheeks, that modesty disclose,
  The purple spoil appear,
Come Hymen, Hymen here.


### Semichorus I

Come Hymen come, and may each wingèd son
Of every lovely nymph the woods can shew
Render no common feathers to the air;
Some, from the silvered quivers that they bear,
Shoot musket roses, orange blossom snow;
Let others keep the hamlet safe from one,
The most unlucky of nocturnal fowls,
That flies too slowly and ill-boding howls;
And in their flight let some crown silently
The marriage-bed, while the lascivious bee
From virginal acanthus sips the rare
  Hyblaean nectar there,
Come Hymen, Hymen here.


### Semichorus II

Come Hymen come, the flying steeds and pied
(For azure eyes with lashes of fine gold
Compose their plumes)—the goddess high shall lead,
The greatest glory of the sovereign choir;
And let her guarantee the bonds indeed
Only to be dissolved when they grow old;
She who is Juno now unto our bride
In varying months shall chaste Lucina be,
To greet their threshold so repeatedly
That the world shall her, new Niobe, admire,
But no white marble's ill fecundity
  And cliff to Lethe near,
Come Hymen, Hymen here.

*Semichorus I*

Come Hymen come, our agriculture heap
With plenty that from friendly stars is due,
A progeny robust, so that their hand
Shall tame wild bulls, and a red sea of grain
Shall liberally flood the stubborn land;
Let too the young and flowery green plain
Be hoary turned by many flocks of sheep,
And all the pasture worn in hours few;
They to Minerva liquid gold shall strain,
And, wedding elms unto the vineyard trees,
Bacchus, with vine shoots crowning Hercules,
   Even the club shall rear,
   Come Hymen, Hymen here.

*Semichorus II*

Come Hymen come, and may she also pay
To Pales as to Pallas pledges sweet,
A mother then, hardly a girl to-day.
With wandering lilies some the forest greet;
A thousand lambs whose wavy wool shall dress
The shining crystals of the streamlet slow;
Others Arachne, arrogant and vain,
Shall modestly, accusingly, display
On their white stuff, but never to express
The thefts and amorous wiles of Jove below;
Oh let them hold the shining golden rain
   And the white swan in fear,
   Come Hymen, Hymen here.

EDWARD MERYON WILSON

# Lope de Vega
## (1562–1635)

Lope Felix de Vega Carpio was a true son of the Renaissance. Of humble birth and an early orphan, he surmounted these obstacles to become one of the leading figures of the Golden Age and Spain's most prolific literary genius. With no formal education whatsoever, Lope managed to acquire a knowledge of Latin and an excellence in the aristocratic arts of fencing, dancing and singing, while still in his teens. At thirteen he was writing plays and poems.

Despite the almost unbelievable fecundity of his pen, de Vega found time for an exciting if somewhat scandalous life. Twice married, once to Isabel de Urbina, and after her death to Juana de Guardo, he also carried on numerous liaisons with various women of the court. Among these was his affair with Micaela de Lujan, who bore him two children: a son Lope Felix and a daughter Maria, who followed in the footsteps of her mercurial father and wrote admirable lyric verse. He was also, at different times, a successful soldier, a sailor with the invincible Armada, and a priest.

Following the death of his second wife, Lope turned with characteristic zeal to the life of religious piety. Despite lapses into carnal sins which almost wrecked his career as a priest, he remained a devout son of the church until his death in 1635.

The excesses of his life are surpassed only by the quantity and quality of his writing. His work constitutes an entire literature in itself. His plays alone far outnumber the combined works of the English Elizabethans. It is estimated that he wrote between 1800 and 2200 plays or dramatic pieces in addition to his non-dramatic works. Discounting such an exaggerated figure, there are still known to be over five hundred plays whose authenticity is unquestioned. This means that Lope wrote over one million five hundred thousand lines of dramatic verse, not counting his epic and lyric poetry, or his novels.

Lope's fame rests largely upon his contribution to Spanish drama, but this reputation is enhanced still further by his skill as a lyric poet.

Included here are two of his religious poems, at least one of which reflects the inner struggle and divided loyalty of his soul.

## TOMORROW

Who am I thus Thy friendship to procure?
   What interest in me, Lord, dost Thou pursue
   To wait outside my door, all drenched with dew
   And somber nights of winter thus endure?
What hardness made me keep my heart secure
   Against Thy entrance! What strange madness grew,
   That cold of the ingratitude I knew
   Could dry the wounds upon Thy feet so pure!
How many times the angel o'er and o'er
   Said, "Soul, go to your window; He is nigh;
   Behold with how much love He does implore!"
How many times I said, O Lord most high,
   "Tomorrow I will open wide the door,"
   And on the morrow made the same reply!

MILDRED E. JOHNSON

If her forehead was not snow,
   It was a sky above two arches,
   Which, to the rain of my eyes,
   Predicted fair weather.
In whose shadow were seen
   Two beautiful and azure suns,
   Sapphires and precious stones
   From these that weep portraits;
Although from them chaste love
   Then made two reprints
   That served me for mirrors
   They were false glasses.[44]

ELISHA KANE

# Francisco Gomez de Quevedo y Villegas
## (1580–1645)

A man of wealth and learning, Quevedo served for a time as a diplomat in Italy under Viceroy Osuna; but he preferred a life of letters to the service of his country, and after his unfortunate experience in Italy, where he was forced to share his patron's disgrace, he carefully avoided courtly circles. Implacable and quick tempered, his caustic wit eventually got him in trouble with the king; and when he insulted the king's favorite, the Count Olivares, he was imprisoned in the monastery St. Mark in León.

He is said to be Spain's great poet of death and time. In these two realities he saw the destiny and fate of man. For all of his pessimism, however, his poetry is tempered with a strong current of orthodox religious zeal. A wit, a satirist, an ardent stoic, Quevedo lived at a time when Spanish prestige was failing. Blaming this decline on corruption in government, the parasitism of the upper classes, and the vainglorious pride of his countrymen, he assailed every type of human foible with an almost Swiftian indignation. Though principally a prose writer, he achieved success in several kinds of verse from intense love lyrics to hilarious burlesques.

## THE FLY

*Out of the wine-pot cried the Fly,*
*Whilst the grave Frog sate croaking by,*
Than live a wat'ry life like thine,
I'd rather choose to die in wine.

### I

I never water could endure,
Though ne'er so crystalline and pure.
Water's a murmurer, and they
Design more mischief than they say,

Where rivers smoothest are and clear.
Oh there's the danger, there's the fear;
But I'll not grieve to die in wine,
That name is sweet, that sound's divine.

*Thus from the wine-pot, etc.*


## II

Dull fish in water live, we know,
And such insipid souls as thou;
While to the wine do nimbly fly,
Many such pretty birds as I:
With wine refresh'd, as flowers with rain,
My blood is clear'd, inspir'd my brain;
That when the Tory boys do sing,
I buzz i' th' chorus for the king.

*Thus from the wine-pot, etc.*


## III

I'm more belov'd than thou canst be,
Most creatures shun thy company;
I go unbid to ev'ry feast,
Nor stay for grace, but fall o' th' best:
There while I quaff in choicest wine,
Thou dost with puddle-water dine,
Which makes thee such a croaking thing.
Learn to drink wine, thou fool, and sing;

*Thus from the wine-pot, etc.*


## IV

In gardens I delight to stray,
And round the plants do sing and play:
Thy tune no mortal does avail,
Thou art the Dutchman's nightingale:

Would'st thou with wine but wet thy throat,
Sure thou would'st leave that dismal note;
Lewd water spoils thy organs quite,
And wine alone can set them right.

*Thus from the wine-pot, etc.*

### V

Thy comrades still are newts and frogs,
Thy dwelling saw-pits, holes, and bogs:
In cities I, and courts am free,
An insect too of quality.
What pleasures, ah! didst thou but know,
This heav'nly liquor can bestow:
To drink, and drown thou'dst ne'er repine;
The great Anacreon died by wine.

*Thus from the wine-pot, etc.*[45]

PHILIP AYRES

## TO A NOSE

There was a man well fastened to a nose—
    A nose superlative did he escort;
    An executioner or scribe, in short,
    A sword well barbed and sharp against its foes.
It was a sundial badly out of pose,
    It was a musing alchemist's retort,
    An elephant with trunk upraised in sport,
    More nose than Roman Ovid did expose.
It was a fighting galley's pointed beak,
    It was a pyramid on Egypt's pate,
    Twelve tribes of noses in one nose sublime
An infinite nose of noses, so to speak,
    Very much of a nose it was, a nose so great
    That in the face of Annas 'twere a crime.[46]

JEAN WILLARD BURNHAM

## SONNET: DEATH WARNINGS

I saw the ramparts of my native land,
    One time so strong, now dropping in decay,
    Their strength destroyed by this new age's way
    That has worn out and rotted what was grand.
I went into the fields; there I could see
    The sun drink up the waters newly thawed;
    And on the hills the moaning cattle pawed,
    Their miseries robbed the light of day for me.
I went into my house; I saw how spotted,
    Decaying things made that old home their prize;
    My withered walking-staff had come to bend.
I felt the age had won; my sword was rotted;
    And there was nothing on which to set my eyes
    That was not a reminder of the end.[47]

JOHN MASEFIELD

# Pedro Calderon de la Barca

## (1600–1681)

Calderon was the last of the great dramatists of Spain's Golden Age. The son of a prosperous and aristocratic family, he was educated at Jesuit schools and at the University of Salamanca. Hair-splitting subjects such as law, logic, and theology claimed his attention, and he seemed admirably suited for either a legal or a theological career. Instead he chose to be poet and courtier. His lyrics, written mainly for his plays, often reveal a mannerist quality. Concerning his plays, Ernest Mérimée has observed: "His drama is one of the most *lyrical* that exists. . . . In far higher degree than the aspiring lyrists of his time he possessed in brain and ear and veins what he himself, in truly Spanish phrase, styled *la música de la sangre.*"

## SONNET

Those flakes of fire, brilliant sparks of light,
   Receive their shining radiance from the sun
   With hints of more; and thus, their life begun,
   Lasts but as he shows pity with his might.
And so, though beautiful those blooms of night,
   Their lustrous gleam is but a passing one;
   For stars a life-time in one night is run,
   As flowers live an age in one day's flight.
That fleeting spring is image of our life,
   From it our ill, our good do we perceive,
   By when the sun goes down or it doth rise.
How long may man expect to live in strife,
   What change is there that he may not receive
   From star that night by night is born and dies?[48]

ELEANOR L. TURNBULL

# THE DYING EUSEBIO'S ADDRESS TO THE CROSS

Tree, whereon the pitying skies
Hang the true fruit love doth sweeten,
Antidote of that first eaten,
Flower of man's new paradise,
Rainbow, that to tearful eyes
Sin's receding flood discloses—
Pledge that earth in peace reposes,
Beauteous plant, all fruitful vine.
A newer David's harp divine,
Table of a second Moses;—
Sinner am I, therefore I
Claim thine aid as all mine own,
Since for sinful man alone,
God came down on thee to die:
Praise through me thou hast won thereby,
Since for me would God have died,
If the world held none beside.
Then, O Cross! thou'rt all for me,
Since God had not died on thee
Let me die without confession.
I, repenting my transgression,
Will not the first robber be
Who on thee confessed to God;
Since we two the same path trod,
And repent, deny not me
The redemption wrought on thee.[49]

D. F. MCCARTHY

# Sister Marcela de Carpio de San Felix
## (1605–1688)

Marcela de Carpio was a daughter of the great dramatist Lope de Vega. At the age of seventeen she entered the convent of the Trinitarians in her home town, where she remained for sixty-six years until her death in 1688. She wrote a quantity of lyric poems and short dramatic pieces which were enacted within the convent, as is shown by the fact that she left in the convent library a 460 page quarto manuscript containing her lyrics and her plays. No complete edition of her works had been printed until the twentieth century.

## AMOR MYSTICUS

Let them say to my Lover
That here I lie!
The thing of His pleasure,
His slave am I.

Say that I seek Him
Only for love,
And welcome are tortures
My passion to prove.

Love giving gifts
Is suspicious and cold;
I have all, my Belovèd
When thee I hold.

Hope and devotion
The good may gain;
I am but worthy
Of passion and pain.

So noble a Lord
None serves in vain,
For the pay of my love
Is my love's sweet pain.

I love Thee, to love Thee,—
No more I desire;
By faith is nourished
My love's strong fire.

I kiss Thy hands
When I feel their blows;
In the place of caresses
Thou givest me woes.

But in Thy chastising
Is joy and peace.
O Master and Love,
Let Thy blows not cease.

Thy beauty, Belovèd,
With scorn is rife,
But I know that Thou lovest me
Better than life.

And because Thou lovest me,
Lover of mine,
Death can but make me
Utterly Thine.

I die with longing
Thy face to see;
Oh! sweet is the anguish
Of death to me!

JOHN HAY

# NOTES TO THE POEMS

# NOTES ON ITALIAN POEMS

PETRARCA, *Rime*

1  "In Vita 3." Historically important, this sonnet records Petrarch's first sight of Laura on Good Friday of 1327. Alternative versions of the poem are offered here for comparison. Occasionally throughout the book this practice will be followed. The first is a literal prose translation, the second a verse rendering.

2  "In Vita 14." An interesting example of an inverted structure. The poet means to say that he searches in the faces of the crowd the resemblance of her face eagerly, as a pilgrim eagerly seeks the image of his Lord. The first eleven lines portray the pilgrim's hard journey, and it is only in the final tercet that the poet and his quest are introduced.

3  "In Vita 69." The opening line of the original poem presents one of the frequent puns on the name Laura, a device which is not translatable. Incidentally, because of Laura's golden locks, blond tresses became fashionable throughout Renaissance poetry.

4  "Canzone, *Chiare, fresche e dolci acque.*" Of the 365 poems in the *Canzoniere*, most are sonnets; but there are forty-eight poems in other forms, chiefly the *canzoni*, a type akin to the ode. In this canzone he speaks with deep affection of the rural scenes around Vaucluse which were associated with his meetings with Laura.

5  "Canzone, *Italia mia.*" One of a few poems in Petrarch's collection not related to the poet's love story. This poem was exceedingly popular during the century before the Risorgimento because it described so aptly the conditions of Italy enslaved. It may have been the war which broke out in 1344 between the d'Este and Gonzaga families that stirred Petrarch to write this canzone, or he may have had reference to a war between Venice and Milan in the 1350's. Actually any decade of the century could have provided the background of grievances brought about by the employment of foreign mercenary forces.

6  "In Vita 102." Chaucer's free adaptation of a sonnet, expanded to twenty-one lines. This and three of the following poems (104, 113, 156) illustrate a type of playful conceit, displaying more ingenuity than genuine feeling, a pattern too often associated with the Petrarchan school because it was so easily and so frequently imitated—"more honored in the breach than the observance."

7  "In Vita 157." A symbolic piece, uncommon among Petrarch's poems,

indicating a premonition of the death of Laura. The hind represents Laura, the emperor Christ, according to accepted Italian exegesis. The jewelled collar recalls an account of the finding of such a collar in a game preserve of the Roman emperors, inscribed: *Noli me tangere Caesaris sum.* Wyatt's poem is a free adaptation rather than a translation and is employed to dramatize a situation at the English court. *Noli me tangere*, in this instance, is an admonition to keep hands off the damsel (Ann Boleyn) who is marked for her emperor (Henry VIII).

8   "In Morte 1." Petrarch's continued glorification of Laura after death follows the precedent set by Dante in his *Vita Nuova.*

9   "In Morte 2." The coincidence of the death of Laura and that of Giovanni della Colonna, a dear friend, is elegized here. In the opening line of the Italian, the names are referred to indirectly through common nouns.

10  "In Morte 42." Milton expresses a similar feeling, though not for the same reason.

> "Seasons return, but not to me returns
> Day, or the sweet approach of Ev'n or Morn,
> Or sight of vernal bloom, or Summer's Rose,
> Or flocks, or herds, or human face divine; ..."

11  "In Morte 86." A retraction, recalling the opening sonnet. He prays God to forgive his waste of life and to help him make the rest of his days more pious.

### BOCCACCIO

12  "Ballata." A song from the *Decameron.* This and the poems following by Poliziano and Lorenzo de' Medici represent a *type* of Renaissance lyric which flourished, especially in the fifteenth century, an easy, graceful song of love, with a setting of meadows and spring flowers. The author knows no compulsion for novelties, for astonishing his readers. Pure lyricism is enough.

### STROZZI

13  "On Buonarroti's Statue of 'Night'". A compliment to the life-like quality of "Night," one of the prominent figures on the tomb of Giuliano de' Medici in Florence.

### MICHELANGELO

14  "To Night." A reply to Strozzi's poem above.

15  "David." It is not entirely certain that Michelangelo intended that these fragmentary verses should be combined in a single poem, for though found on the same sheet, they are not written as a continuous piece.

Girardi's note reads: "Written on the right side of a sheet containing, on the left, two sketches of a David, probably the David ... in bronze for Pietro di Rohan, and a study of a right arm for the David in marble; between September 1501 and August 1502. In verses 1-3 perhaps Michelangelo means to say David fought with strength, I with the power of a genius, Verse 4 is the first verse of sonnet 269 of Petrarca." Cf. Petrarch, *In Morte* 2.

The inscription with its archaic spelling reads:

> Dauicte cholla fromba
> e io chall' archo,
> Michelagniolo.
> ........................
> Roct' è l'alta cholonna e'l uer[de lauro].

16 "On the Painting of the Sistine Chapel." A sonnet "with tail." According to an Italian practice, the poet may add to a standard sonnet a section consisting of a half-line (rhyming with the preceding line) plus a couplet with a new rhyme. New "tails" may be added at the discretion of the author.

  The poem voices the resentment of Michelangelo for the years spent on his back on a scaffold painting the ceiling of the Sistine Chapel. To us it is ironical that he disliked this assignment and completed the work under duress.

17 "The Lover and the Sculptor." This sonnet, one of the best known by Michelangelo, echoes the concept of the foregoing lyric.

18 "The Artist and His Work." The thought that a work of art may outlast its creator—a familiar theme, which becomes peculiarly impressive as the mind turns to the works of Michelangelo—is revolved in the sestet to the promise of enduring fame for the beloved one through the artist's creation. Shakespeare writes:

> "So long as men can breathe or eyes can see,
>   So long lives this, and this gives life to thee."

The effectiveness of the final tercet is marred by the free rendering of the final phrase, "For her 'twas wise to pine." The Italian, ... *e com' amarvi io non fui stolto*, reads literally, "and how in loving you I was not stupid."

19 "Beauty and the Artist." A violent statement of the intensity of feelings in the man and the artist.

20 "You Have a Face." One of the rare, absurd pieces in which the author burlesques the conventional figures of poetry in hilarious fashion. Dashed off in a spirit of the broadest kind of humor, it is careless of any kind of sequential development.

21    "Madrigal." One of the best Platonic statements of the relation of earthly to heavenly beauty.

22    "Danger of Loss Eternal." His resolution taken, only to be withdrawn.

23    "Love Lifts to God." One of an important group of poems addressed to his handsome young friend, Tommaso de' Cavalieri. This and the two following, "Love, the Light-Giver," and "Love's Entreaty," expressed in Platonic terms, reflect the happy mood of mutual affection. Later this tone is changed to disappointment because of the friend's indifference.

24    "Just As a Silkworm." The customary pattern of a poem of endearment to a man, employing the language which could be equally appropriate for an address to a lady, is broken at last by the reference to the hairy chest of the object of devotion.

25    "Just as an Empty Form." The figure of the goldsmith's mold, or cast, is given an unexpected turn, suggestive of the metaphysical sensibility.

26    "Love Is a Refiner's Fire." The terrifying energy of fire, which clearly fascinated Michelangelo, is a recurring figure in his poems.

27    "If My Rough Hammer." A somewhat complex poem because of the shifting significance of the metaphorical hammers, now referring to God and now to his lost love. It is similar to the kind of imagery employed by George Herbert.

28    "Dante." This sonnet pays high tribute to another great Florentine artist. Michelangelo's sympathy for Dante may have been enhanced by his own rebuffs by the leaders and citizens of Florence. The roughness and strength of Dante's language in *Inferno* is the nearest counterpart in Italian poetry to the pervading style of Michelangelo's verse.

29    "On Rome in the Pontificate of Julius II." This diatribe against Rome and especially the papal court in which the author served is one of the comparatively rare commentaries on social and political affairs among his poems.

30    "When Contracting, the Lash." A curious observation of visual phenomena, resembling nothing in poetry so much as certain passages in Dante.

31    "Why Should It Come So Seldom?" A hermetic piece treating inspiration, though whether it is concerned with love or art is not clear. The preference for day over night expressed in the last lines is not consistent with some of his other lyrics, as is seen in the two poems following.

32    "Light and Darkness." This sonnet is distinguished for figurative patterns, both fresh and startlingly vivid.

33    "A Prayer for Purification." A representative of a considerable group of poems of contrition. The deep earnestness, coupled with the

staccato rhetoric of this and the following poem reminds the reader of Donne's *Holy Sonnets*: "Batter my heart . . . :"

34  "On the Brink of Death." Deeply repentant, now he regrets the life he has devoted to art. This is a theme reiterated in numerous of his later poems. Although Petrarch and several other writers expressed these sentiments before him, we nevertheless cannot question his sincerity.

### DELLA CASA

35  "To Sleep." This theme, the plea for repose, became familiar throughout the poetry of the age. Notable treatments are by Desportes in French, by Sidney and Daniel in English. Shakespeare finally gave the theme its most famous expression in the speech of Macbeth, "Sleep no more . . ."

### TANSILLO

36  "The Philosophic Flight." This sonnet has sometimes been ascribed to Giordano Bruno. Even Symonds, the author of the translation quoted here, assigns it to Bruno. However, the preponderance of evidence indicates that it was by Tansillo.

### BERNI

37  "Portrait." Weary of the cliché compliments of innumerable poets, the author here creates a burlesque piece by attaching familiar adjectives or epithets to the wrong objects. Though the conclusion differs, the pattern of regurgitation is reminiscent of Shakespeare's "My mistress' eyes are nothing like the sun."

### STAMPA, *Rime*

38  "Oh Night." Here the familiar theme, the praise of night, is given a frankly erotic turn, recalling Ariosto "Capitolo VIII."

39  "Deeply Repentant." One of the poems of her last period, recalling the latter poems of Petrarch and Michelangelo.

### TASSO

40  "Aurora." In his verses to Laura Peperara, he employs the familiar Petrarchan device of punning on the name Laura. Note the next to the last line of the Italian.

41  "The Happiness of a Flea." This unexpected subject for a love poem inevitably reminds us of Donne's "The Flea," which is of later date.

42  "To Lucrezia d'Este." A graceful compliment in praise of the Duchess of Urbino, his long-time friend, whose beauty does not diminish with advancing age.

43 "The Golden Age." A song from the pastoral drama *Aminta*. This poem is generally regarded as one of the finest treatments of the classical golden-age theme in Renaissance literature.

44 "To Madame Lucrezia d'Este, Duchess of Urbino." The Ulysses reference is the episode in the *Odyssey* relating how the hero, cast ashore on the island of Phaeacia, was discovered by Nausicaa and conducted to her father's palace. In the closing lines, Tasso's compliment to the duchess echoes lines of the *Aeneid* (I, 330–32) from the scene in which Aeneas recognizes Venus, though she appears in the guise of a mortal: *O dea certe*, O goddess surely.

This sonnet and the four which follow it in the text represent the numerous poems which the poet addressed to various influential personages, supposed to be his friends, appealing for relief from his confinement in Santa Anna.

GUARINI

45 "The Microcosm." Readers familiar with Donne will recall his "I am a little world made cunningly" as well as his fondness for "sublunary."

MARINO

46 "Apollo and Daphne." A free translation which has turned a sonnet into a poem of four quatrains. This treatment of the classical myth invites comparison to Bernini's statue on the same subject, one of the best examples of Mannerism to be found.

47 "Christo Smarrito." Sherburne's translation is an exceptionally free one. In the first place he has condensed 150 lines into 82. Also he has altered the form from a stanzaic pattern to octosyllabic couplets. The opening stanza reads:

> *Sospirava e spargea*
> *largo di pianto un fiume*
> *la Dea, la vera Dea,*
> *madre di vero nume,*
> *ricercando il suo cuore,*
> *il suo smarrito e fuggitivo Amore.*

In this passage a characteristic device has been omitted in the translation. Marino refers to the mother and son as goddess and god, as if he were speaking of Venus and Cupid. One other significant omission seems worthy of comment. The line in which the Virgin speaks of Christ as both her spouse and son is not reproduced. In other respects, the translation renders the spirit of the poem with reasonable fidelity. The most extensive condensation is in Mary's soliloquy, which Sherburne shortened by 52 lines.

48 "She Washed His Feet with Her Tears." A fine example of the employment of the Metaphysical sensibility, partly in its expression of religious feeling through the language of carnal love and partly that "the
most heterogeneous ideas are yoked by violence together."

CAMPANELLA

49 "The People." An enunciation of a democratic concept of society startling to encounter at the beginning of the seventeenth century. It
seems about a century and a half ahead of its time.

REDI

50 "Bacchus in Tuscany." The fragments of translations presented here are
not in the order of their appearance in the original. The first passage
translated by de' Lucchi stands near the beginning (ll. 11–30); the
second passage by de' Lucchi appears near the end of the poem.
Leigh Hunt's two passages belong to the first third of the total work.

## NOTES ON FRENCH POEMS

MAROT

1 "Epitaph on Jean Veau." This jocose epitaph is built entirely around a
pun on the name of the dead child.

SCÈVE, *Délie*

2 "In the April of My Age." This reflects the Petrarchan opening for a
long series of love poems: the poet was pierced by Love's dart when,
being off his guard, he spied his lady for the first time.

3 "Some Delight in Telling Stories." The poem rises to a striking conclusion: others may express their love in eloquent declarations; all I
can manage to utter is "Pity, pity, pity." His assertion is in some
measure belied by the 400-odd poems he wrote on the theme of his
love.

4 "Let Silence or Speech Be Permitted." One important significance of
the title of his book, the association of the name Delia (*Délie*) with
Diana, is here introduced. The difficult phrasing of the opening lines
demonstrates a characteristic of Scève's style, compact expression of
involved thought.

5 "Like Hecate You Will Make Me Wander." Hecate is another name for
Diana under one of her numerous manifestations: i.e., as goddess of
the realms of the dead.

6 "If It Is Love, Why then Does He Kill Me?" The opening suggests a
familiar convention after the pattern of Petrarch. However, the poem,
instead of producing the anticipated list of "contrarieties," dwells
solely on the death-in-life conceit.

7   "Bound to the Caucasus." A striking use of a figure from classical
    mythology. The identification of Prometheus is clear to the informed
    reader from the first, even though Prometheus is not named until the
    last line.

8   "The Happiness of Our Happiness." The living-dying paradox, one of
    Scève's favorite themes, is here given an unmistakably erotic applica-
    tion.

9   "If with Her Hand." An unexpected turn in the last four lines.

10  "I by Myself, She in Another's Arms." In accordance with the doctrine
    of Courtly Love, he condemns the embraces of the marriage bed as
    alien to "true love."

11  "All Judgment of this Infinity." The poem is especially marked by
    indirect and contorted phrasing. In several instances an adjective or
    adverb stands for a noun. I have purposely rendered this poem in as
    literal a translation as possible in order to reveal this quality.

12  "Longer than a Platonic Century." The Great Year of the World, or
    the Platonic Year, signifies the period of the precessional revolution
    of the equinoxes: i.e., 36,000 centuries. This is a difficult, enigmatic
    piece. A shift from the second to third person is unexpected. The
    closing passage is not exactly Platonic.

13  "Lady, You Are the Body." Donne-like, he plays with, analyses, ex-
    tracts the essence out of a metaphor.

14  "The White Dawn." Closes with a startling figure from the embalmer's
    trade. This again suggests a kinship with Donne.

LABÉ

15  "Sonnet XVIII." Singularly unmannered in most of her work, she is not
    much interested in paradoxical statement or complex relations. This
    poem is an exception.

RONSARD

16  "Roses." One of the familiar themes of classical as well as Renaissance
    lyrics: a love-lesson through the example of the fading rose. Cf. Ben
    Jonson's, "I sent thee late a rosy wreath. . . ."

17  "When You Are Very Old." This is probably Ronsard's best known
    poem, at least to English readers. It has been translated many times
    (Cf. Notes on Translation), and the first line was taken over directly
    in a well-known sonnet by Yeats. Although the original is in Alexan-
    drine (12 syllable) lines, almost all of the English translations employ
    our standard sonnet line, iambic pentameter.

        The reminder to the lady that her name and beauty will be long
    remembered because of the poet's verses, a favorite theme of Shakes-

peare, strikes one as a trifle presumptuous until he reflects that the lines have now lasted 400 years.

18 "Carpe Diem." The Latin title, from Horace (literally "seize the day") has become the familiar designation for this theme. Herrick's "Gather ye rosebuds while ye may" serves as a suitable English equivalent. In the mid portion of Ronsard's poem, the grim death-warnings are comparable to Marvell's

> "The grave's a fine and private place,
> But none I think do there embrace."

19 "To Remi Belleau." Belleau (1528–1577) was one of the original group forming the Pléiade. He was called "the gentle poet."

20 "Epitaph on Rabelais." Rabelais, one of the immortals of French literature, published his series of books on a family of hearty giants under the titles of *Gargantua* and *Pantagruel* (vols. 1–4) between 1532 and 1556. These books are filled with broad farce, Rabelaisian (ribald and scatalogical) language, and Gargantuan (prodigious) feats of fighting and feasting and—above all—drinking. The tales are as completely uninhibited in their vulgarity and their merriment as any ever written. They are also treasurehouses offering some of the most extraordinary learning and wise doctrine of the Renaissance.

The references in Ronsard's poem to Gargantua, Panurge, Friar John, and Episteme recall prominent characters in the works of Rabelais.

## DU BELLAY

21 "L'Olive, XIV." The early volume of his poems was entitled *L'Olive* to form an anagram on the name of Mlle de Viole. This sonnet bears a fairly close resemblance to one by Louise Labé (Sonnet IX), even to the ivy figure, though the conclusions differ.

22 "To His Friend in Elysium." This pleasant picture of the peaceful life of the dead is effectively keyed to the vocabulary and associations of the classics. Elysium and Charon are familiar. "Obolus" (l. 8) is the small coin placed in the hand of the corpse to pay Charon for the passage into Hades.

23 "A Sonnet to Heavenly Beauty." The Platonic—or Augustinian— theme, familiar through Petrarch, Michelangelo, and many others.

24 "Rome." One of a considerable series of sonnets written in Italy, mostly about Rome, mostly disillusioned and satirical. Du Bellay must have come to Rome in high hopes, his mind filled with visions of ancient glories, the product of his early classical education.

25 "Heureux Qui, Comme Ulysse." A moving expression of a man homesick in Rome.

26 "Sonnet: I Hate the Money-Lending Avarice." This poem gives the impression of being the vituperations of a dyspeptic traveler until, in the last line, we discover a clever turn, directing the worst of the sting toward a single human type.

DESPORTES

27 "Invocation." We are refreshed with an entirely unexpected turn in this address to Sleep. This time the poet sues for sleep for someone else, not for himself.

MAYNARD

28 "Armand! I Lose My Vital Heat." The illustrious king of France he expects to meet in heaven is Francis I, great soldier and patron of the arts. The reference to Pavia recalls a battle in which Francis was defeated and captured by Emperor Charles V.

SCHÉLANDRE

29 "To the Poets of Our Time." A stricture apparently directed against the doctrine of correctness of the new school principally under the rule of Malherbe.

DE LA CEPPÈDE,
*Théorèmes Spirituels*

30 The six poems included from this work are in sonnet form in the original. The translator has given them a freer form in the hope of preserving the sense and emotion as faithfully as possible.

31 "O Kingdom of Christ." This is identical in doctrine and in language with the poetry of the Spanish mystics.

> ". . . He summons you
> *To come and live in Him*, in His chapels of mystery."
> "Come then, fair one, *your groom* asks it."

Cf. Saint Teresa of Jesús and Saint John of the Cross. The violence, or extravagance, of metaphysical paradox is evident in:

> "He will keep it in His living stone;
> He will wrest it living from His own death's stone."

32 "Great Sun, Flame of Christ." With extraordinary ingenuity he has traced the parallels between the career of Christ and four signs of the Zodiac.

SPONDE

33 "Sonnets d'Amour III." This has something of the suggestive power of Henry Vaughan's "The World":

"I saw eternity the other night
Like a great ring of pure and endless light,
All calm as it was bright; . . ."

34 "Sonnets d'Amour XXVI." Here is a sonnet falling in the Petrarchan pattern, the whole poem being built around a conceit, the detailed analogy between the calming power of love and the Halcyon's ability to calm the sea.

35 "Sonnets de la Mort IV." This theme of the futility of man's struggle is to be found in occasional poems by Marino, Quevedo, and Góngora, but here in Sponde's work it is treated over and over. Throughout this group of sonnets there is the constant cry, "vanity of vanities," in a tone of almost unrelieved pessimism, though a note of trust or a prayer is introduced at times.

36 "All Swells Against Me." The dramatic use of staccato phrases and questions produces a moving effect, comparable to passages in Michelangelo or the *Holy Sonnets* of John Donne.

THÉOPHILE

37 "Ode." A remarkable example of the development of the vein of the bizarre and the grotesque which, except for the writings of Théophile and Saint-Amant, was not to be found until the romantics.

38 "To Corinna." Here we see touches of the feeling for nature for which Théophile is especially noted. Though there are occasional classical echoes of naiads, dryads, and amorous Zephyrs, the enjoyment of the woodlands and untamed nature is effectively conveyed. This is a much abbreviated version of "La Solitude." A detailed analysis of the poem as a demonstration of the rich exploitation of the rhetorical situation appears in Lowry Nelson, Jr., *Baroque Lyric Poetry*, New Haven, Yale University Press, 1961.

MALHERBE

39 "Consolation to M. du Périer." A dignified exhortation to a father to abandon his long mourning for his daughter. The father was a courtier friend of the author, the daughter was named Marguerite. The translator has rendered the first seven and the last three stanzas of the original, which has twenty-one stanzas. The middle section contains allusions to Tithonis, Priam, and Francis I.

D'URFÉ

40 "Song of the Inconstant Hylas." This song of "disdain returned" presents a theme extremely popular among the Cavalier poets: e.g.,

"Shall I, wasting in despair,
Die, because a woman's fair. . . .?"
George Wither

"Why so pale and wan, fond lover. . . .?"
Sir John Suckling

### SAINT-AMANT

41 "The Enjoyment." Here are fused the themes of sweet contentment in retirement, the enjoyment of untamed nature, and passionate amour in a poem which represents the poet's tastes and skills most effectively. The familiar mythological allusions are mixed in with touches of metaphysical imagery. The conversation in stanza 7 ("Then to my dear . . .") about the eyes as crystals reflecting miniature pictures is startlingly reminiscent of Donne's imagery. Indeed the poem suggests a kind of vague parallel to Donne's "The Ecstasy," even before we come to the final stanza:

"Awhile, our senses stol'n away,
Lost in this ecstasy we lay,
Till both together rais'd to life, . . ."

The translation quoted here gives us only half of the original, a poem of 180 lines.

42 "The Orgy." The racy, bibulous, and scatalogical vein was typical of a fair portion of St.-Amant's work. It bears close resemblance to the praise of drink in poems by Ronsard, Redi, and Quevedo, but seems even closer to the free spirit and frank speech of Rabelais.

It should be noted that in the translation of the latter section of the piece where the poet pledges Bacchus "By — —," Mrs. Richards has not adhered to the identical order of the lines in the original; but this could hardly have disturbed St.-Amant, since the line sequence is of no consequence except in a few instances, and these have been kept intact.

### CORNEILLE

43 "Stanzas to the Marquise." This theme, familiar through Ronsard and Shakespeare, among many, that the lady's beauty and fame will be immortalized through verse, is here set down with more formality than usual.

## NOTES ON SPANISH POEMS

### ANONYMOUS

1 "Galleys of Spain." One of a group of traditional songs from *Cancioneros*, a body of popular literature which has been handed down from

Medieval and Renaissance times but which did not gain much critical
acclaim until the present century.

VICENTE

2  "Ballad of Flérida." A literary ballad in the tradition of the popular
Medieval *romances*.

SAINT TERESA

3  "Let Mine Eyes See Thee." A striking example of the simplicity of this
poet—employing short lines, very few adjectives, and few figures.

4  "On the Words '*Dilectus Meus Mihi*'." This represents a formal type
of exercise piece in which a scriptural text provides a theme for poetic
elaboration. We note here, as not infrequently in the poems of the
mystics, that almost the entire piece could be read as an amorous
declaration.

5  "Vertiendo Está Sangre." A striking feature is the treatment of time-
planes. They are shedding the blood of the infant Jesus. He is tor-
mented and dying for our sins, and yet, it is remarked, he will be a
mighty shepherd. This non-logical distortion of time phases is ordinarily associated with the metaphysical poets of the seventeenth
century.

It should be noted that the translation is inaccurate at two points.
In the first stanza *inocente* is translated *child*, an interpretation which
can be justified by the use of *niño inocente* later in the poem.

The other point is perhaps more critical. "*O qué gran Zagal/Será
por mi fe!*" is translated in the present instead of future ("What a
mighty Shepherd/Have we, by my fay!"), thereby escaping the
significant tense development.

6  "En las Internas Entrañas." It is not difficult to read into this poem an
imagined experience of the stigmata.

7  "Lines Born of the Fire of Love for God." In this plea for speedy death
we are reminded of the longing for martyrdom, which led Teresa to
run away at the age of seven in quest of death among the Saracens,
and which undoubtedly visited her in later life.

GUEVARA

8  "To Christ Crucified." This poem, called by Peers "The most famous
sonnet of religious inspiration in Spanish literature," has been vari-
ously attributed to San Francisco Xavier, Fray Pedro de los Reyes,
San Ignacio de Loyola, and even to Santa Teresa. However, it has
recently been established without much doubt as the work of Miguel
de Guevara through a manuscript in Mexico.

LEÓN

9 "Ode to Filipe Ruiz." The "prison drear " in the opening line must be taken as a reference to his actual imprisonment (see biographical note), but it also surely symbolizes this world. The longing for flight is one of the familiar features of Fray Luis's mysticism. His vision of the wonders of heaven is as unusual for what it does not picture—glorious sights and sounds—as for what he dwells on—the joy of understanding, of unravelling the simple mysteries of nature. He echoes the language of Job in stanzas 3 and 4.

"Where wast thou when I laid the foundations of the earth? . . . Who has laid the measures thereof? . . . or who hath stretched the line upon it? whereupon are the foundations thereof fastened? or who laid the corner stone thereof; . . . ?" (Job 38:4–6). Then later (stanzas 8–10) he imitates a passage from Virgil's First Georgic (ll. 316–34).

10 "The Life of the Blessed." This furnishes a distinct contrast to the "Ode to Filipe Ruiz" for its treatment of heaven. The emphasis on light in this poem is noteworthy as one of the strong characteristics of the poet. The suggestion has been made by Peers that Fray Luis, writing in his prison cell, may have had in memory a painting he had seen.

ALCÁZAR

11 "Tres Cosas." Aubergine: eggplant.

HERRERA

12 "Ideal Beauty." The poet's great love was the Countess de Gelves, to whom he refers in his poetry under the poetic name of Doña Luz, Lady Light. This poem, beginning "Serena Luz," is one of a number of poems in which the symbol and identification of his lady are combined.

13 "To Don Juan de Austria." Don John, an illegitimate son of Emperor Charles V, commanded the forces of the allied Christian nations against the Turks at the Battle of Lepanto (1571). This great naval engagement in the Adriatic has been called one of the fifteen most decisive battles of the world. It was in this battle, incidentally, that Cervantes was wounded.

SAINT JOHN OF THE CROSS

14 "Dark Night of the Soul." This is one of the most famous examples of the mystical union of the lovers, Christ representing the male and the soul representing the female. In a note to the poem Peers points out that it was probably written after the author's escape from prison,

and he suggests that the intense joy expressed here is a result of his experience, noting especially the opening lines.

15 "O Flame of Living Love." The intensity of the lover's feeling is translated almost entirely through light and heat—a flame. The paradoxical concepts of the second stanza, "O burn that burns to heal," etc., represents a favorite device of the seventeenth century metaphysicals, but it can be traced to the Middle Ages as well. Cf. Chaucer, "O bussh unbrent, brennynge in Moyses sighte."

16 "Spiritual Canticle: Songs between the Soul and the Spouse." This work appears in three versions, one written in metrical, rhymed stanzas, the other two in the canticle form generally followed in printing the verses of the Scriptures. In the versified version, several more changes of speaker are indicated. The work is obviously rooted in the *Song of Songs*, employing the language of passionate love poetry and following the interpretive symbolism of the marriage of Christ and the soul or of Christ and the Church. Echoes of Biblical imagery are important to the effect of the poem.

17 "Other Stanzas with a Divine Meaning Concerning Christ and the Soul." The development is deceptively simple, treating the figure of the disconsolate shepherd without any hint of a second level of meaning up to the last stanza. There the tree image for the cross produces a highly dramatic conclusion.

CERVANTES

18 "Ye Trees and Shrubs." Almost all of the verses quoted here from *Don Quixote* are extravagant parodies of popular poetic types. This demonstrates the kinds of inanities perpetrated by bad poets in their desperate search for rhymes.

19 "Love's Mariner Am I." An exception to the above remarks, this poem is offered as a genuine lyric piece.

20 "Oh, Could My 'Was' an 'Is' Become." A burlesque on the learned type of poem involving a text and gloss. Cf. St. Teresa's "On the Words *'Dilectus Meus Mihi.'*"

21 "Oh Thou above Who in Thy Bed." This love song was addressed in mock seriousness to Don Quixote by a damsel of the court when Quixote and Sancho were being feted at the castle of the duke and duchess and, as a practical joke, being treated like royalty. Much of the rich humor arises from the ineptness of the language. You just don't say things like that in a poem. Cf. Chaucer's *Rime of Sir Thopas*.

GÓNGORA

22 "The Rosemary Spray." Góngora's reputation for the Gongoristic— for elaborate ornamentation and obscurity—tends to overshadow the

fact that he wrote a great many poems in a manner which was easy, graceful, and completely available. The first poems in our collection are of this character, and it is clear that by their freshness, their polish, their sheer lyricism, they would have won the author a place of merit in the world of poetry, though hardly the spectacular position which he now occupies.

23   "The Rose of Life." This sonnet has been discussed in the introduction to the present volume in connection with a study of variant translations. The theme, though exceedingly well worn, is handled impressively. In Fanshawe's admirable translation one deception occurs. The expression, "and many Herods lie in wait," which strikes us as peculiarly characteristic of Góngora, is not in the original.

24   "Let Me Go Warm." An unexpected side of the author's nature is revealed here. This spirited piece in praise of the simple pleasures, the scorn for court ambitions, would be hard to surpass. The English "Back and Sides Go Bare" is in much the same spirit and swings with a like joyous rhythm.

25   "Love in Reason." In revolt against the long-standing allegiance to the doctrine of constancy—the *semper fidelis* theme—this poem speaks out with entertaining spirit. At this same time, John Donne was leading a revolt in England against the theme of love single and everlasting.

26   "The Nativity of Christ." The new style is clearly manifest in this ornate piece through the number and the extravagance of the figures.

27   "Clear Honor of the Liquid Element." The conceit developed here is a good sample of strained ingenuity—a plea to the stream to flow gently lest the image of his beloved which is printed on its surface be shattered on its journey to the sea. Another Gongoristic device appears in his practice of referring to an object by some attribute rather than by its name; e.g., "the liquid element."

28   "Sonnet: Yesterday a Human Deity." Instead of writing in complimentary elegiac terms about the death of a great lady, the Duchess of Lerma, the author makes this the occasion for a gloomy reminder of mortality. The octave is as plain as anything could be; in the sestet he develops some strikingly original figures.

29   "Sonnet: The Planking of the Vessel Torn Apart." Among the eccentricities of this sonnet is the fact that it is written in several languages. The first line is Castilian, the second Latin, the third Italian, and the fourth Portuguese.

> Las tablas de el baxel despedaçadas
> (Signum naufragij pium et crudele),
> Del tempio sacro con le rotte vele,
> Ficaraon nas paredes penduradas.

In addition the poem illustrates the fondness for obscurity, which is one of the trademarks of Gongorism. For a fuller treatment of the terrors of the ocean, see *The Solitudes*. Had Góngora sailed with the Armada, one might imagine this poem to have been written on his return home.

30 "Sonnet: Dear Geese." In the controversy waged between the cultists of Góngora's school and the traditionalists, Góngora satirizes his opponents, particularly Lope de Vega, and lauds his own work with unqualified assurance.

31 "When Don Luis was in Cuenca." The charming and wholly unsophisticated description of girls in the country serves as a radical contrast to scenes in *The Solitudes*, which represent the quintessence of the baroque style.

*The Solitudes*

32 "Europa's perjured robber": taurus, sign of the zodiac representing a bull.

33 "Remora": a sucking fish that attaches itself to the side of a larger fish or ship, supposed to slow down the progress of the ship; hence a drag or hindrance.

34     "What fiercest tiger or most wild wild boar . . .
    Was foster-parent to that ploughman dark,
    The first to furrow in an evil hour
    The spumy country in ill-destined bark . . .?"

Freely, this asks: Who was the brave man that first sailed a ship on the ocean? This passage is clearly reminiscent of the *aes triplex* passage in Horace:

    "Sure he, who first the passage tried,
    In harden'd oak his heart did hide,
    As ribs of iron arm'd his side!"
               (Dryden trans.)

35 "Clytie." The water nymph who, having fallen in love with Apollo, was transformed into a sunflower and always turned her face in the direction of the sun. In this passage, the primitive sailboat veers in the direction of the wind as Clytie's direction is governed by the sun.

36 "Nautical industry that mineral found" refers to the development of the compass with its consequent effects upon navigation.

37 "Three fir trees late . . ." refers to the three ships of Columbus.

38 "The flying vipers from the Carib bow": poisoned arrows of the Indians. The passage describes skirmishes with Indians in Panama.

39 "The kingdoms of the Dawn": the East Indies.

40   "A glorious pine": the ship of Magellan.
41   "The elusive hinge of silver fine": the Straits of Magellan.
42   "That fixed armada in the eastern sea": the East Indies.
43   "The wood of islets in their foam": the Moluccas Islands.

VEGA

44   "If Her Forehead Was Not Snow." Although Lope was generally
     ranked in the school opposed to Gongorism, as we have noted in
     connection with Góngora's satirical sonnet "Dear Geese," it is evi-
     dent from these verses that Lope adopted the vein on occasion and
     that he could handle the new style with as much dash as the master.

QUEVEDO

45   "The Fly." A delightful diversion from the elegance of style and con-
     ventionality of thought of the main stream of poetry in the period,
     this sparkles with the fresh gaiety of Redi's "Bacchus in Tuscany" or
     St.-Amant's "The Orgy."
46   "To a Nose." This fantastic satire on a nose reminds us of nothing so
     much as Rostand's Cyrano de Bergerac. The real Cyrano was a
     contemporary of Quevedo. In his *Voyage to the Moon* Cyrano pro-
     vided material for a well known passage in Rostand's play, but he did
     not furnish the matter for the discourse on noses.
47   "Sonnet: Death Warnings." Here the author further shows his versa-
     tility and his power. The modern reader, knowing the course of
     Spain's history, finds a special poignancy in the premonition of the
     decay of the nation.

CALDERON

48   "Sonnet: Those Flakes of Fire." The setting of the poem in the play
     *El Príncipe Constante* is interesting. The hero presents his beloved
     with a bouquet and thereupon recites a sonnet to her comparing his
     fate to the flowers. The lady in reply "improvises" this sonnet on the
     stars, giving him a hint of hope. However, even if read out of context,
     the poem is a polished and effective piece.
49   "The Dying Eusebio's Address to the Cross." The multiplication of
     fanciful images for the cross, while it bears the metaphysical stamp,
     achieves a highly dramatic quality in this passage.

# *Acknowledgments*

For grants which have assisted me in travel and research, I wish to express my sincere gratitude to *Il Circolo Italiano* of Denver; to the Shell Companies, Inc., Foundation; and to the faculty research fund of the University of Denver.

I am much indebted for assistance in research to Captain Joseph E. Berthelot, Judith McDowell, Ida Fasel, and Wayne Rollins.

To the colleagues and associates who have reviewed portions of my manuscript and given me their advice and support in many ways, my sincere appreciation: Harvey S. Gross, Sigwald Palleske, Marcellino Penuelas, R. Russell Porter, Judith McDowell, and Captain Joseph E. Berthelot.

The translations in the anthology which have not previously been published—other than my own—were contributed by: Major John R. Galt, Clinton Larson, Chris Richards, Ida Fasel, Walter T. Pattison, Arthur L. Campa, Wayne Rollins, Rose E. Burckhardt, Shirley White Johnston, and Judith McDowell. I owe them my special gratitude. Professor Robert Nugent has kindly lent me translations of four sonnets prior to the publication of his: Jean de Sponde, *Sonnets on Love and Death*, with a translation and commentary by Robert Nugent, Lake Erie College Studies, 1962.

Authors to whom I am indebted for personally granting me permission to reproduce their translations are: Professor Edward Meryon Wilson, of Emmanuel College, Cambridge, for extensive selections from his translation of *The Solitudes of Don Luis de Gongora*; Professor Morris Bishop, of Cornell University, for three sonnets from *Love Rimes of Petrarch*; Mr. Wilfrid Thorley, for three French poems from *Fleur-de-Lys*; Professor Frank J. Warnke, of Yale University, for two sonnets of Marino; and Mr. Frederic Prokosch, for four poems from *The Love Sonnets of Louise Labé*.

I am happy to acknowledge my appreciation to the following publishers for texts reproduced with their permission.

David McKay Company, Inc., for four poems from *The Sonnets of Petrarch* translated by Joseph Auslander, published by Longmans, Green and Company.

The Renaissance Society of America, for two sonnets of Marino first published in *Studies in the Renaissance*, vol. II, and later in Professor Warnke's *European Metaphysical Poetry*, Yale University Press, 1961.

Pantheon Books, Inc., for two sonnets from *Petrarch's Sonnets and Songs*, translated by Anna Maria Armi.

Yale University Press, for Thomas Bergin's translation of one sonnet of Petrarch from *Lyric Poetry of the Italian Renaissance*, collected by L. R. Lind.

William Heinemann, Ltd., for British rights, and Alfred A. Knopf, Inc., for American rights to reproduce eleven poems from Lorna de' Lucchi's *An Anthology of Italian Poems*.

Farrar, Straus and Cudahy, Inc., for eight poems from *The Complete Poems of Michelangelo*, translated by Joseph Tusiani.

Charles Scribner's Sons, for two translations of poems by Michelangelo from George Santayana's *Poems*.

The Bodley Head, Ltd. for five poems from *An Anthology of Italian Lyrics*, translated by Romilda Rendel.

Penguin Books, Ltd., for two poems from *The Penguin Book of Italian Verse*; two poems from *The Penguin Book of French Verse*, vol. II; and one poem from *The Penguin Book of Spanish Verse*.

Alan Swallow, Publisher, for twelve poems from Wallace Fowlie's *Sixty Poems of Scève*, copyright 1949 by Wallace Fowlie; and the translation of one sonnet by Du Bellay from *Collected Poems* by Yvor Winters, copyright 1952, 1960, by Yvor Winters.

Macmillan Company, Ltd., London, for six French poems from *Ronsard and la Pléiade* by George Wyndham.

Cassell and Company, Ltd., for British rights for three poems from the *Treasury of French Poetry*, translated by Alan Conder. For the American rights I am indebted to Mrs. Doris Conder Cohen of Birmingham, England.

Oxford University Press, London, for four French poems from R. N. Currey's *Formal Spring*.

New Directions, Publisher, for the United States and Canadian rights to reproduce four poems from *The Love Sonnets of Louise Labé*, translated by Frederic Prokosch, copyright 1947 by Frederic Prokosch. British Commonwealth rights were granted by Mr. Prokosch.

University of Wisconsin Press, for five poems from William Frederic Giese's *French Lyrics in English Verse*.

The Macmillan Company, New York, for American rights and Miss Ann Wolfe for world rights for two poems from *Sonnets pour Hélène*, translated by Humbert Wolfe.

The Hispanic Society of America, for eight poems from *Translations from the Hispanic Poets*.

The Johns Hopkins Press, for a sonnet of Calderon from *Ten Centuries of Spanish Poetry*, edited by Eleanor L. Turnbull.

Exposition Press, Inc., for two poems from Mildred E. Johnson's *Spanish Poems of Love*.

The Viking Press, for six poems from *Don Quixote* translated by Samuel Putnam, copyright 1949 by The Viking Press and reprinted by their permission.

The Newman Press, for American rights, and Burns and Oates, Ltd., for British rights, to reproduce four poems from E. Allison Peers' *The Complete Works of St. John of the Cross.*

The University of North Carolina Press, for three poems from Elisha K. Kane's *Gongorism in the Golden Age.*

Sheed and Ward, Ltd., London, for British rights, and Sheed and Ward, Inc., New York, for American rights to "Vertiendo Está Sangre" from *The Complete Works of Saint Teresa*, translated and edited by E. Allison Peers from the critical edition of P. Silverio de Santa Teresa, C.D., published in three volumes by Sheed and Ward, Inc., New York.

The Clarendon Press, Oxford, for "Ode to Filipe Ruiz" from Aubrey F. G. Bell's *Lyrics of Luis de León.*

# Bibliography

## COLLECTIONS OF TRANSLATIONS

*An Anthology of World Poetry*, ed. Mark Van Doren. New York, Albert and Charles Boni, 1928.

### ITALIAN

*Lyric Poetry of the Italian Renaissance*, ed. L. R. Lind. New Haven, Yale University Press, 1954. Italian poems with verse translations.

*An Anthology of Italian Poems*, selected and translated by Lorna de' Lucchi. New York, Alfred Knopf, 1924. Italian poems and verse translations.

*Penguin Book of Italian Verse*. Introduced and edited by George Kay. Penguin Books, 1958. Italian poems and prose translations.

*An Anthology of Italian Lyrics*, translation by Romilda Rendel. New York, Frank-Maurice, 1926. Italian poems and verse translations.

*The Sonnets of Petrarch*, trans. by Joseph Auslander. New York, Longmans, Green and Company, 1931.

*Sonnets, Triumphs, and Other Poems of Petrarch*. New York, Hurst and Company, London, Bohn Library, 1909.

*Songs and Sonnets of Petrarch*, trans. by Anna Maria Armi. New York, Pantheon Books, 1946.

*The Sonnets of Michelangelo*, trans. by John Addington Symonds. London, Vision Press, 1950. Italian text with verse translations.

*Complete Poems of Michelangelo*, trans. by J. Tusiani. New York, Noonday Press, 1960.

*Sonnets and Madrigals of Michelangelo*, trans. by William Wells Newell. Boston, Houghton Mifflin and Company, 1900.

### FRENCH

*Penguin Book of French Verse*, 3 vols. Introduced and edited by Geoffrey Brereton. Penguin Books, 1958. French poems with prose translations.

*Anthology of French Poetry*, trans. by Henry Carrington. London, Henry Frowde, 1900. Verse translations.

*Fleurs-de-Lys*, A Book of French Poetry freely translated by Wilfrid Thorley. Boston, Houghton Mifflin, 1920.

*French Lyrics in English Verse*, W. F. Giese. Madison, University of Wisconsin Press, 1946.

*Treasury of French Poetry*, trans. by A. Conder. London, Cassell, 1950.

*Ronsard and La Pléiade*, Selections and translations by George Wyndham. New York, Macmillan Company, 1906. French poems and verse translations.

*Ronsard, Sonnets pour Hélène*, trans. by Humbert Wolfe. New York, Macmillan Company, 1934. French poems with verse translations.

*Sixty Poems of Scève*, trans. by Wallace Fowlie. New York, The Swallow Press and William Morrow, 1949. French poems with prose translations.

*Love Sonnets of Louise Labé*, trans. by Frederic Prokosch. Norfolk, Conn., New Directions, 1947. French poems and verse translations.

### SPANISH

*Penguin Book of Spanish Poetry*, Introduced and edited by J. M. Cohen. Penguin Books, 1956. Spanish poems with prose translations.

*Ten Centuries of Spanish Poetry*, ed. by Eleanor L. Turnbull. New York, The Grove Press, 1955. Spanish poems with verse translations by various translators.

*Hispanic Anthology*, ed. by Thomas Walsh. New York, G. P. Putnam's Sons, 1920.

*Spanish Poems of Love*, trans. by M. E. Johnson. New York, Exposition Press, 1955.

*Translations from Hispanic Poets*. New York, Hispanic Society of America, 1938.

*An Anthology of Spanish Poetry from Garcilaso to García Lorca*, ed. by Angel Flores, Garden City, N.Y., Anchor Books, 1961. Spanish poems with verse translations.

*Gongora*, trans. by Edward Churton, 2 vols., London, John Murray, 1862. Verse translations.

*The Solitudes of Don Luis de Gongora*, trans. into English verse by Edward Meryon Wilson. Cambridge, Eng., Gordon Fraser, The Minority Press, 1931.

*The Complete Poems of Saint Teresa of Jesus*, translated and edited by E. Allison Peers from the critical edition of P. Silverio de Santa Teresa, C.D.; Vol. III. London: Sheed and Ward, 1950.

*Minor Works of Saint Teresa: Conceptions of the Love of God, Exclamations, Maxims, and Poems of Saint Teresa of Jesus*, translated by the Benedictines of Stanbrook. Revised with notes and an introduction by the Reverend Father Benedict Zimmerman, O.C.D. of Wincanton Friary. London, Thomas Baker, 1913.

*The Complete Works of St. John of the Cross*, translated and edited by E. Allison Peers. London, Burns, Oates and Washbourne, 1947.

*The Poems of St. John of the Cross*, translated by John Frederick Nims. New York, Grove Press, 1959. Spanish poems with verse translations.

## SECONDARY SOURCES

Hiram Haydn. *The Counter-Renaissance.* New York, Charles Scribner's Sons, 1950.

Odette de Mourgues. *Metaphysical, Baroque and Précieux Poetry.* Oxford, The Clarendon Press, 1953.

Lowry Nelson, Jr. *Baroque Lyric Poetry.* New Haven and London, Yale University Press, 1961.

Mario Praz. *The Flaming Heart,* Studies in the Relations between Italian and English Literature. Garden City, N.Y., Anchor Books, 1958.

Wylie Sypher. *Four Stages of Renaissance Style: Transformations in Art and Literature, 1400–1700.* Garden City, New York, Anchor Books, 1955.

Frank J. Warnke. *European Metaphysical Poetry.* New Haven and London, Yale University Press, 1961.